Publishers
PAUL ENS and SCOTT CHITWOOD

Book Design
JEFF POWELL

ATOMIC ROBO PRESENTS REAL SCIENCE ADVENTURES VOLUME 2

Copyright © 2013. All rights reserved. Atomic Robo, the Atomic Robo logo, and all characters, likeness and situations featured herein are trademarks and/or registered trademarks of Brian Clevinger and Scott Wegener. Except for review purposes, no portion of this publication may be reproduced or transmitted, in any form or by any means, without the express written permission of Red 5 Comics, Ltd. All names, characters, locations and events in this publication are fictional. Any resemblance to actual persons (living or dead), events, institutions, or locales, without satiric intent, is coincidental.

This volume collects ATOMIC ROBO PRESENTS REAL SCIENCE ADVENTURES #7 through #12 of the comic book series originally printed by Red 5 Comics.

Published by
RED 5 COMICS
298 Tuscany Vista Rd NW, Calgary, Alberta, Canada, T3L 3B4

www.red5comics.com

To find a comics shop in your area, call the Comic Shop Locator Service toll-free at 1-888-266-4226

First edition:
ISBN: 978-0-9868985-5-6

Printed in Canada.

ATOMIC ROBO PRESENTS

REAL SCIENCE ADVENTURES

VOLUME 2

WORDS
BRIAN CLEVINGER

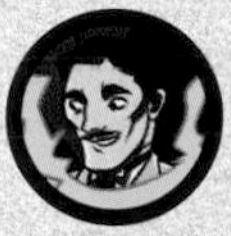
CHAPTER 1
ART BY **ERICA HENDERSON**

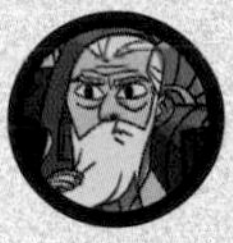
CHAPTER 4
ART BY **ERICH OWEN**

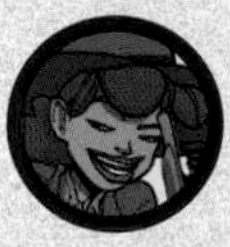
CHAPTER 2
ART BY **CAANNAN GRALL**

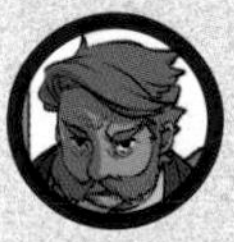
CHAPTER 5
ART BY **ENDURO**

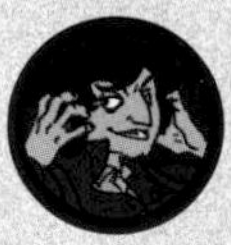
CHAPTER 3
ART BY **RYAN CODY** & **LEELA WAGNER**

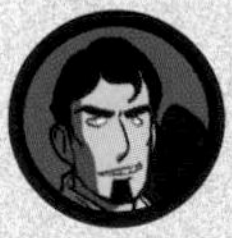
CHAPTER 6
ART BY **M.D. PENMAN**

COLORS
ERICA HENDERSON

LETTERS
JEFF POWELL

EDITS
LEE BLACK

SERIES COVER ART
SCOTT WEGENER & **NICK FILARDI**

COLLECTION COVER ART
SCOTT WEGENER & **ANTHONY CLARK**

THERE ARE SO MANY, MANY THINGS TO LOVE ABOUT *ATOMIC ROBO: REAL SCIENCE ADVENTURES.*

Even without the presence of Atomic Robo himself in this volume, there is so much to love.

I'm not really qualified to talk about the art or the coloring, so I won't, except to say that the former is glorious and clean and tight, and the latter subtly wonderful. What I can talk about is the scripts.

Oh, those scripts.

I could talk about how eminently quotable they are. About the great characters, and their great characterization, and the great dialogue. About how these stories are some of the best modern action/adventure comics out there, but entirely lacking the abiding sins of modern comics: self-seriousness, affected angst, ignoble protagonists, and a complete lack of sense of humor. If anything, *Real Science Adventures* is the opposite: Clevinger takes his art seriously but not himself, the angst within the stories is earned, not affected, the heroes are suitably and genuinely heroic, and a real good humor shines through every page.

I could talk about how these stories are pulp in the best of senses: a story of good heroes defeating dastardly villains, featuring high adventure and "action science"—what a glorious phrase—but also containing an essential innocence and, best of all, an abiding sense of fun. These are fun stories—wonderfully so. About how the many references complement the stories and add to them, rather than being the point of the stories.

I could talk about any of those. But instead, I'm going to talk about adventurous expectancy. "Adventurous expectancy" is a phrase H.P. Lovecraft coined, to express the sense of "marvel and liberation" he associated with "rare...vistas" and "obscure dimensions." For me, and I suspect for many of Clevinger's readers, the adventurous expectancy aroused by *Real Science Adventures* comes from the careful, and clever, deployment of real history, real people, and fictional characters, so that the cumulative effect is to widen Clevinger's fictional universe in pleasing, fun ways. Put simply, the universe of Atomic Robo is cool; thanks to *Real Science Adventures*, we see that Atomic Robo's universe is larger and cooler than we previously knew. Like the Wold Newton Universe and Kim Newman's *Anno Dracula* and Moore and O'Neill's *League of Extraordinary Gentlemen*, the universe of *Real Science Adventures* is full of notable people and potential-laden characters interacting in intriguing and entertaining ways.

I love this book. I could talk all day about it. Did I mention the action sequences? Or the lettering? Or the....

Jess Nevins
October, 2013
Tomball, Texas

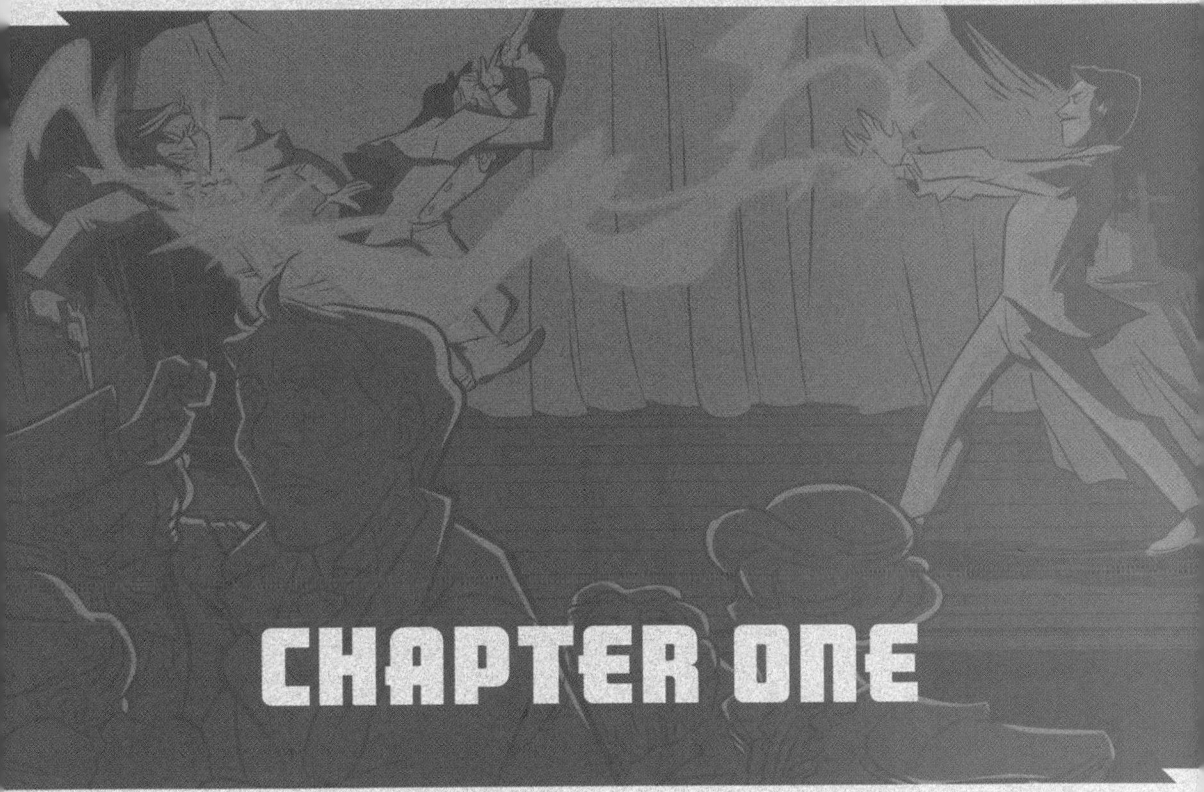

CHAPTER ONE

CLEVINGER
HENDERSON
POWELL

ATOMIC ROBO

PRESENTS

REAL SCIENCE ADVENTURES

STILL ONL
$2.75

No. 7

APRI

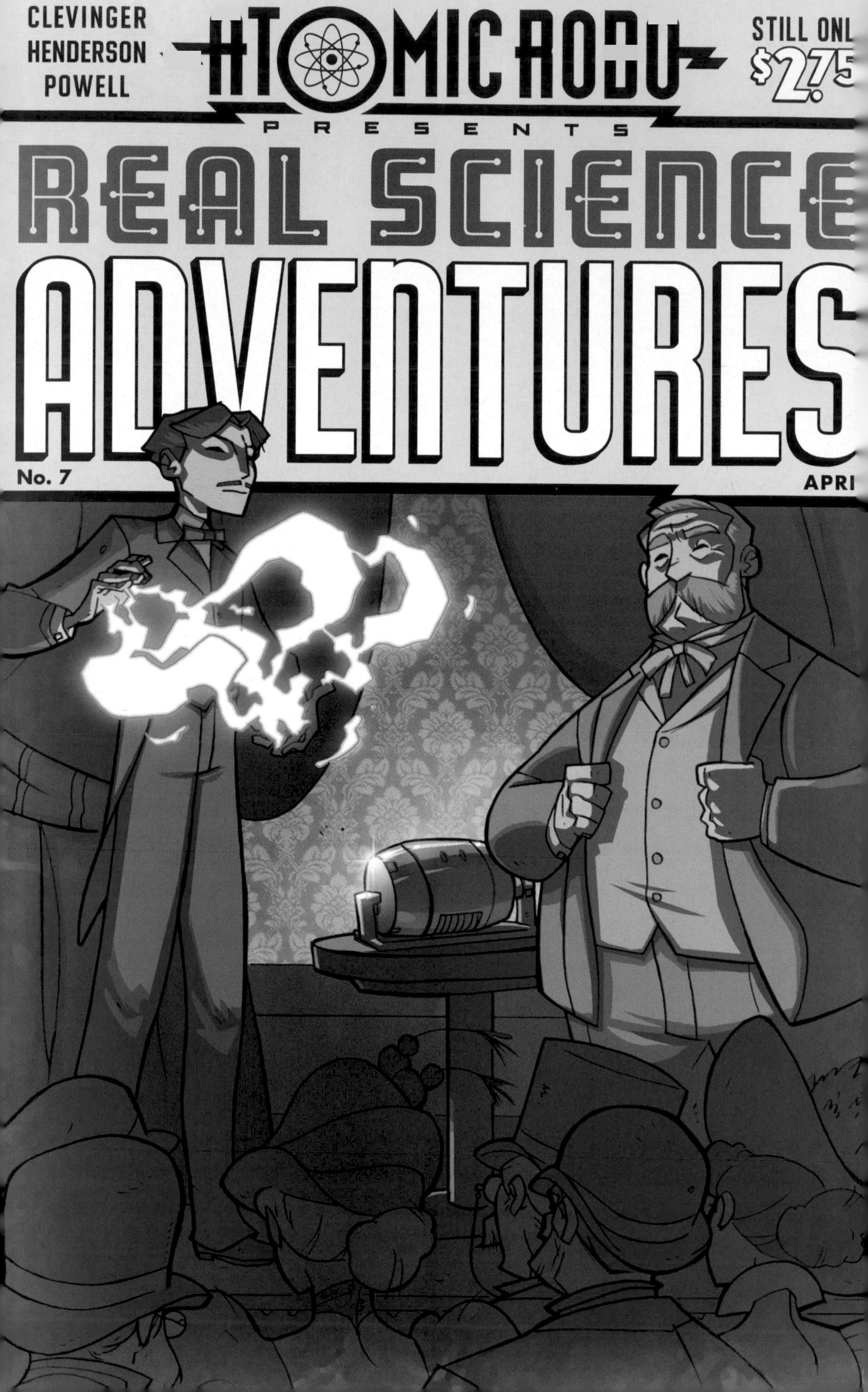

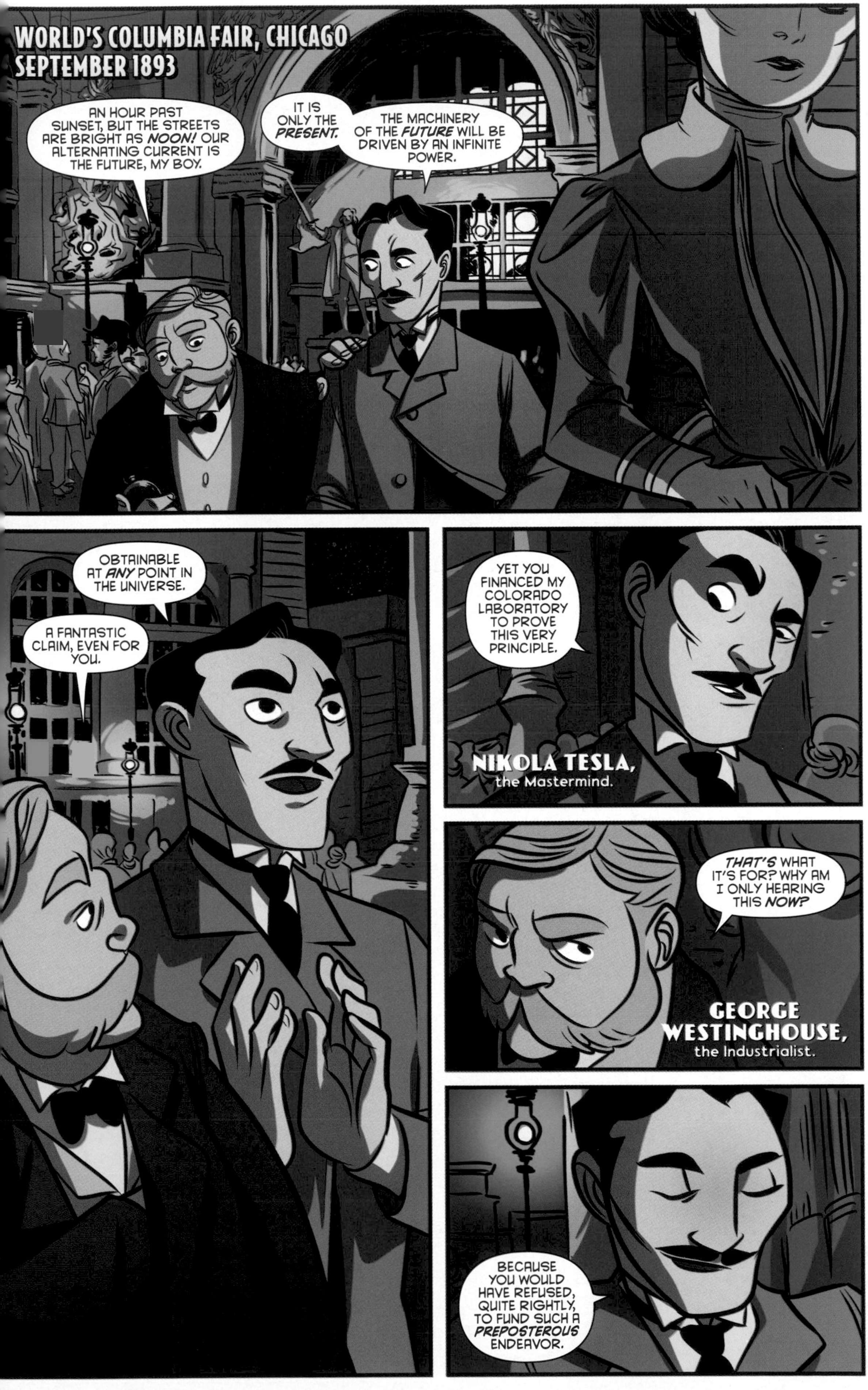
WORLD'S COLUMBIA FAIR, CHICAGO
SEPTEMBER 1893
AN HOUR PAST SUNSET, BUT THE STREETS ARE BRIGHT AS *NOON!* OUR ALTERNATING CURRENT IS THE FUTURE, MY BOY.
IT IS ONLY THE *PRESENT.*
THE MACHINERY OF THE *FUTURE* WILL BE DRIVEN BY AN INFINITE POWER.
OBTAINABLE AT *ANY* POINT IN THE UNIVERSE.
A FANTASTIC CLAIM, EVEN FOR YOU.
YET YOU FINANCED MY COLORADO LABORATORY TO PROVE THIS VERY PRINCIPLE.
NIKOLA TESLA,
the Mastermind.
THAT'S WHAT IT'S FOR? WHY AM I ONLY HEARING THIS *NOW?*
GEORGE WESTINGHOUSE,
the Industrialist.
BECAUSE YOU WOULD HAVE REFUSED, QUITE RIGHTLY, TO FUND SUCH A *PREPOSTEROUS* ENDEAVOR.

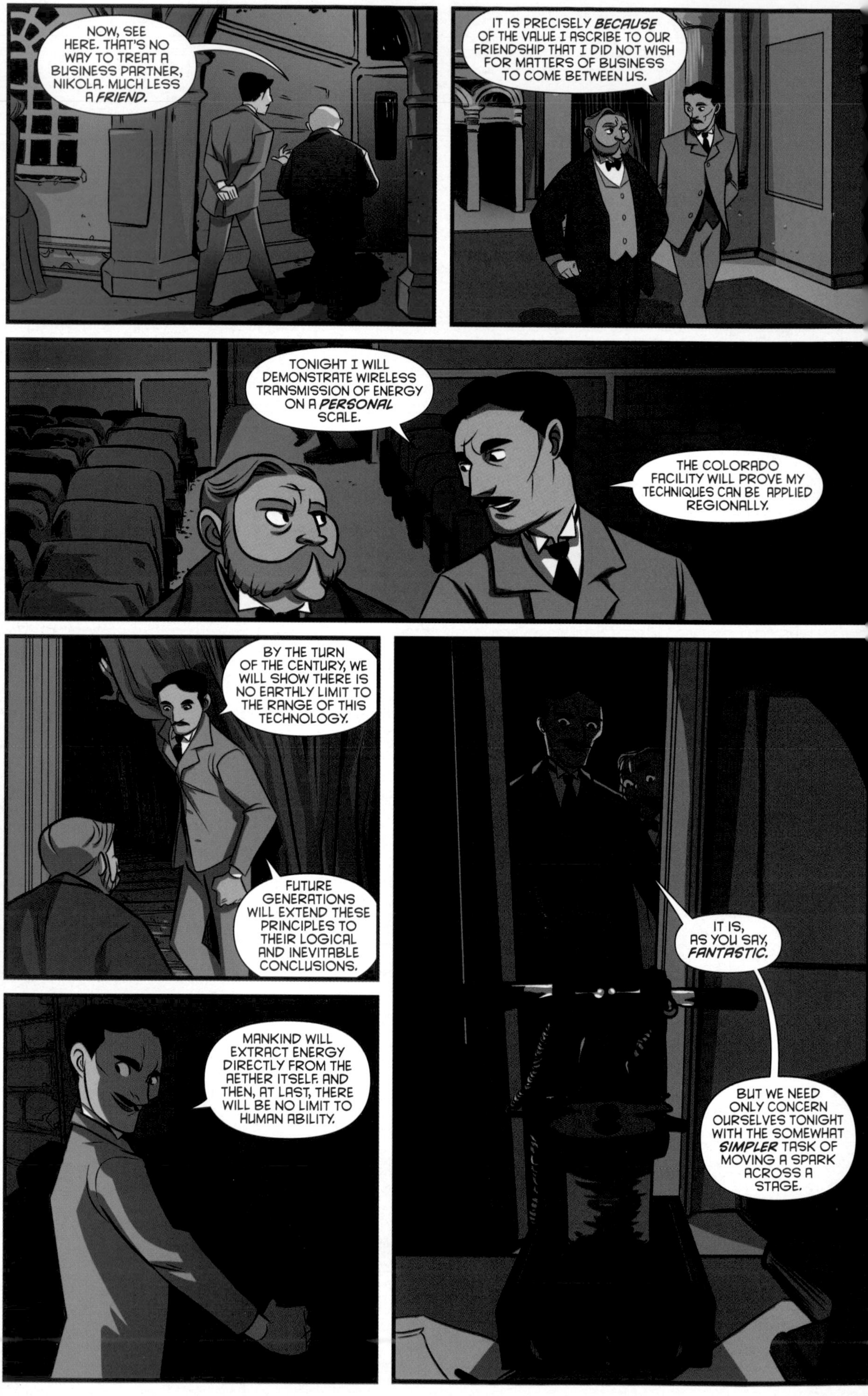
NOW, SEE HERE. THAT'S NO WAY TO TREAT A BUSINESS PARTNER, NIKOLA. MUCH LESS A FRIEND.
IT IS PRECISELY BECAUSE OF THE VALUE I ASCRIBE TO OUR FRIENDSHIP THAT I DID NOT WISH FOR MATTERS OF BUSINESS TO COME BETWEEN US.
TONIGHT I WILL DEMONSTRATE WIRELESS TRANSMISSION OF ENERGY ON A PERSONAL SCALE.
THE COLORADO FACILITY WILL PROVE MY TECHNIQUES CAN BE APPLIED REGIONALLY.
BY THE TURN OF THE CENTURY, WE WILL SHOW THERE IS NO EARTHLY LIMIT TO THE RANGE OF THIS TECHNOLOGY.
FUTURE GENERATIONS WILL EXTEND THESE PRINCIPLES TO THEIR LOGICAL AND INEVITABLE CONCLUSIONS.
MANKIND WILL EXTRACT ENERGY DIRECTLY FROM THE AETHER ITSELF. AND THEN, AT LAST, THERE WILL BE NO LIMIT TO HUMAN ABILITY.
IT IS, AS YOU SAY, FANTASTIC.
BUT WE NEED ONLY CONCERN OURSELVES TONIGHT WITH THE SOMEWHAT SIMPLER TASK OF MOVING A SPARK ACROSS A STAGE.

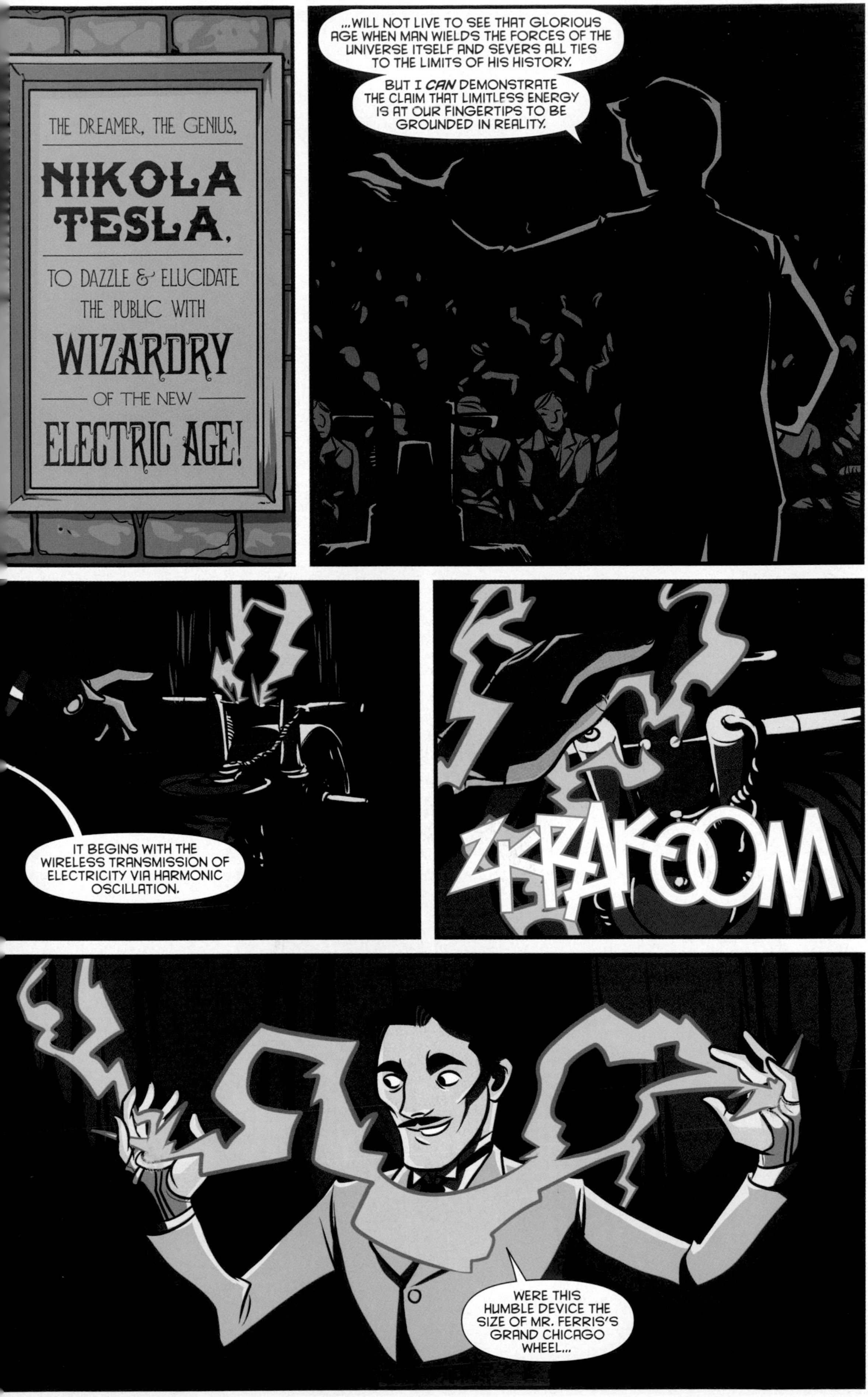
THE DREAMER, THE GENIUS,
NIKOLA TESLA,
TO DAZZLE & ELUCIDATE THE PUBLIC WITH
WIZARDRY
OF THE NEW
ELECTRIC AGE!
...WILL NOT LIVE TO SEE THAT GLORIOUS AGE WHEN MAN WIELDS THE FORCES OF THE UNIVERSE ITSELF AND SEVERS ALL TIES TO THE LIMITS OF HIS HISTORY.
BUT I CAN DEMONSTRATE THE CLAIM THAT LIMITLESS ENERGY IS AT OUR FINGERTIPS TO BE GROUNDED IN REALITY.
IT BEGINS WITH THE WIRELESS TRANSMISSION OF ELECTRICITY VIA HARMONIC OSCILLATION.
ZKRAKOOM
WERE THIS HUMBLE DEVICE THE SIZE OF MR. FERRIS'S GRAND CHICAGO WHEEL...

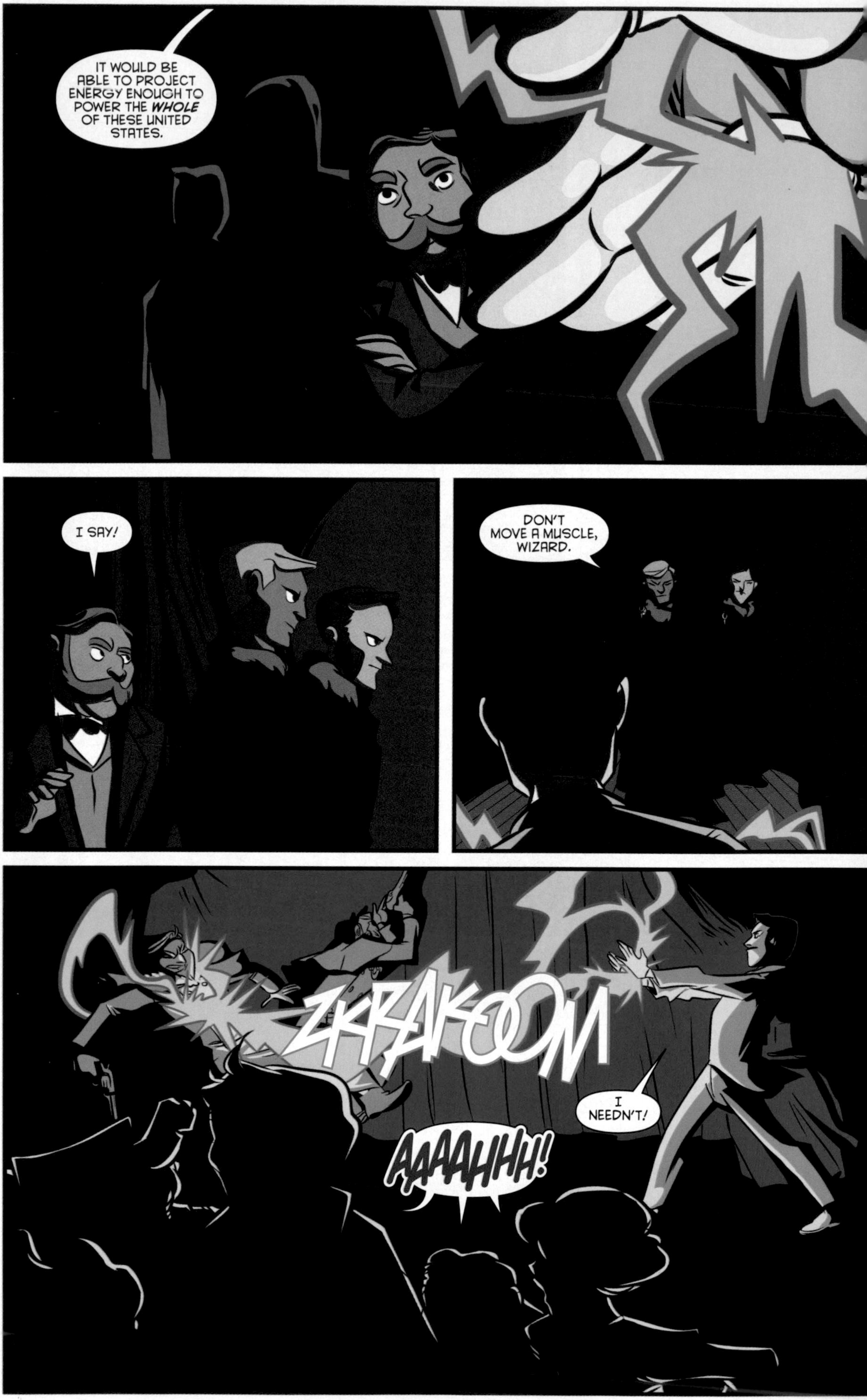
IT WOULD BE ABLE TO PROJECT ENERGY ENOUGH TO POWER THE *WHOLE* OF THESE UNITED STATES.
I SAY!
DON'T MOVE A MUSCLE, WIZARD.
ZKRAKOOM
I NEEDN'T!
AAAAHHH!

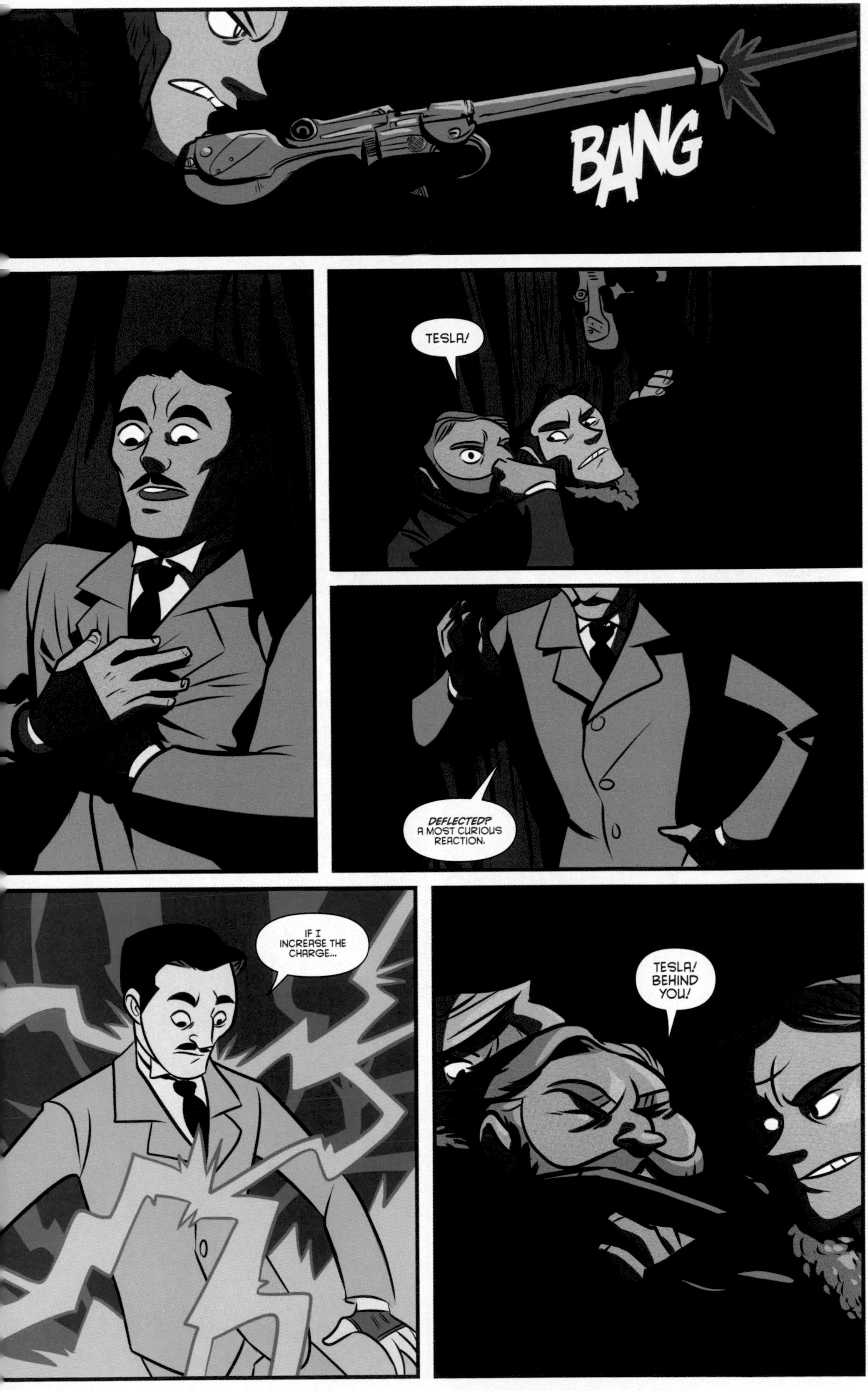
BANG
TESLA!
DEFLECTED? A MOST CURIOUS REACTION.
IF I INCREASE THE CHARGE...
TESLA! BEHIND YOU!

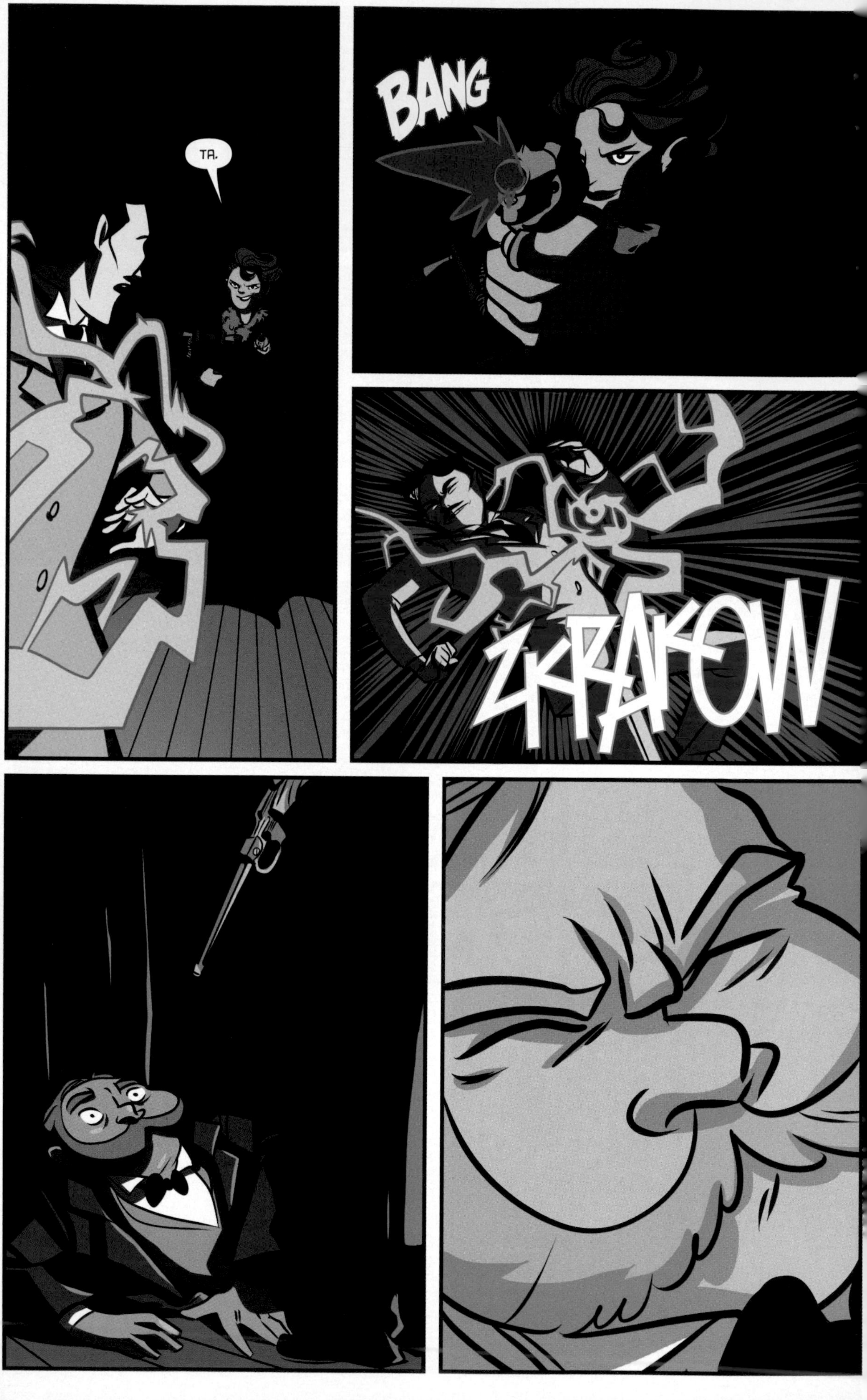
TA.
BANG
ZKRAKOW

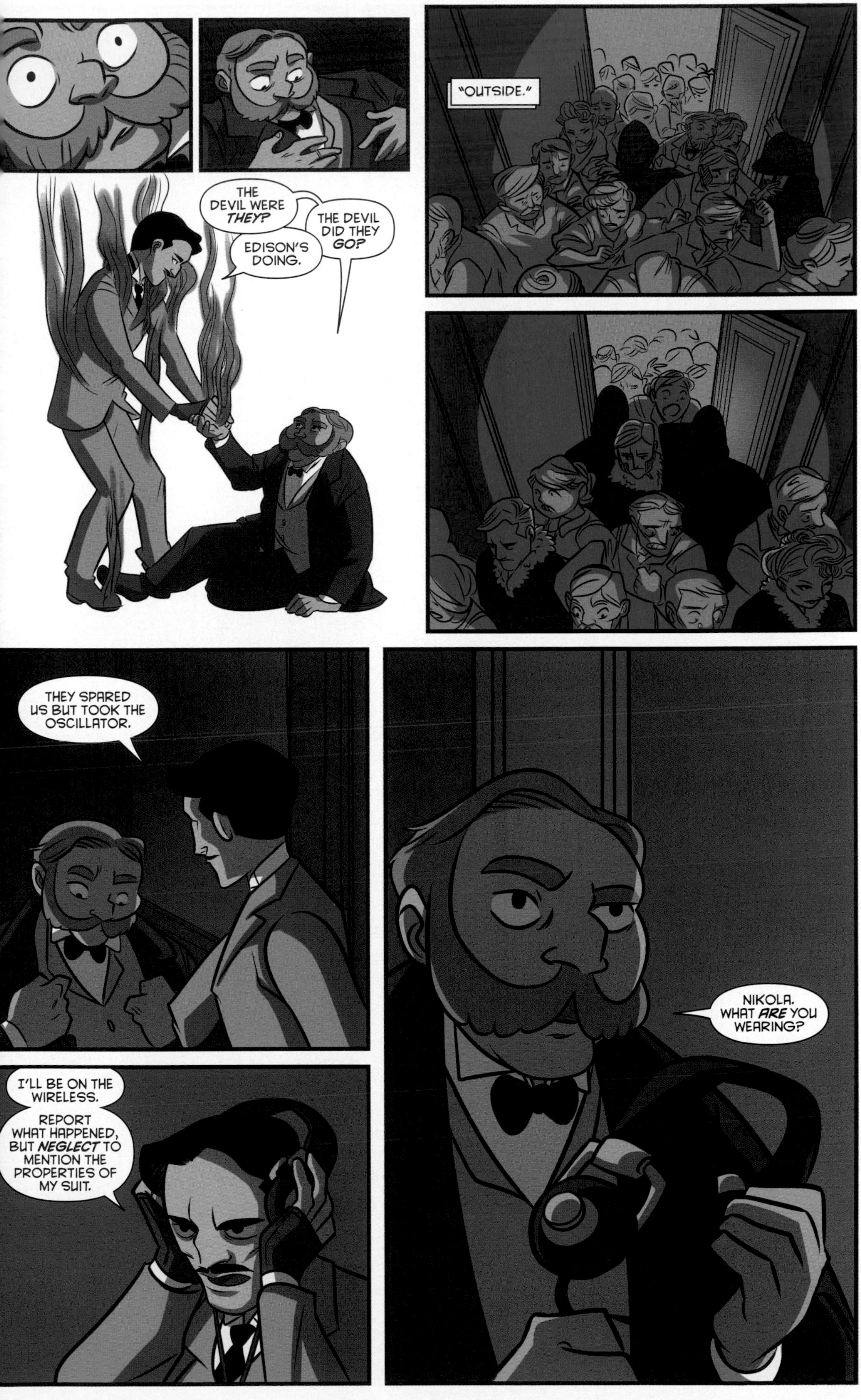
THE DEVIL WERE *THEY?*
EDISON'S DOING.
THE DEVIL DID THEY *GO?*
"OUTSIDE."
THEY SPARED US BUT TOOK THE OSCILLATOR.
I'LL BE ON THE WIRELESS.
REPORT WHAT HAPPENED, BUT *NEGLECT* TO MENTION THE PROPERTIES OF MY SUIT.
NIKOLA. WHAT *ARE* YOU WEARING?

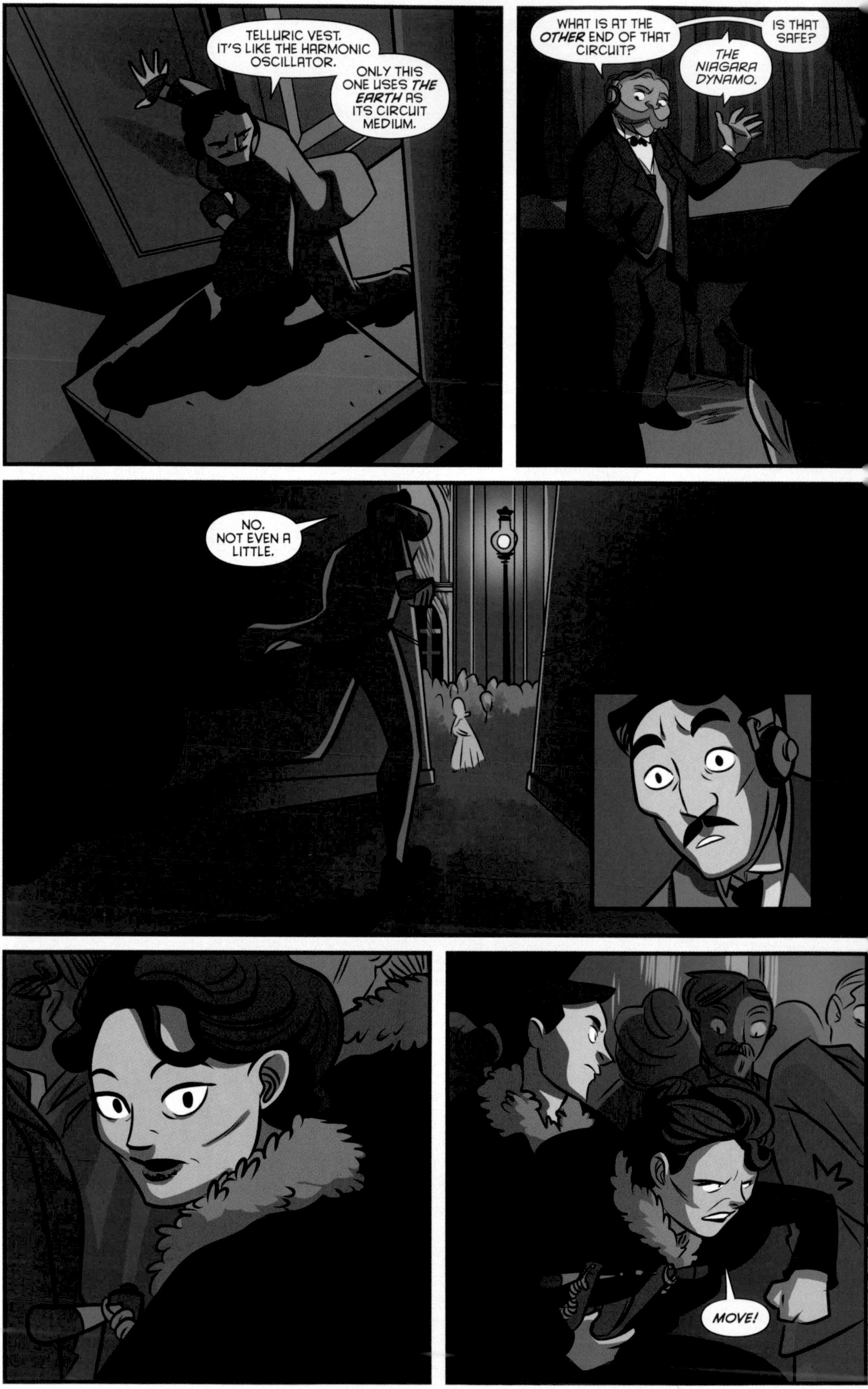
TELLURIC VEST. IT'S LIKE THE HARMONIC OSCILLATOR.
ONLY THIS ONE USES *THE EARTH* AS ITS CIRCUIT MEDIUM.
WHAT IS AT THE *OTHER* END OF THAT CIRCUIT?
THE NIAGARA DYNAMO.
IS THAT SAFE?
NO. NOT EVEN A LITTLE.
MOVE!

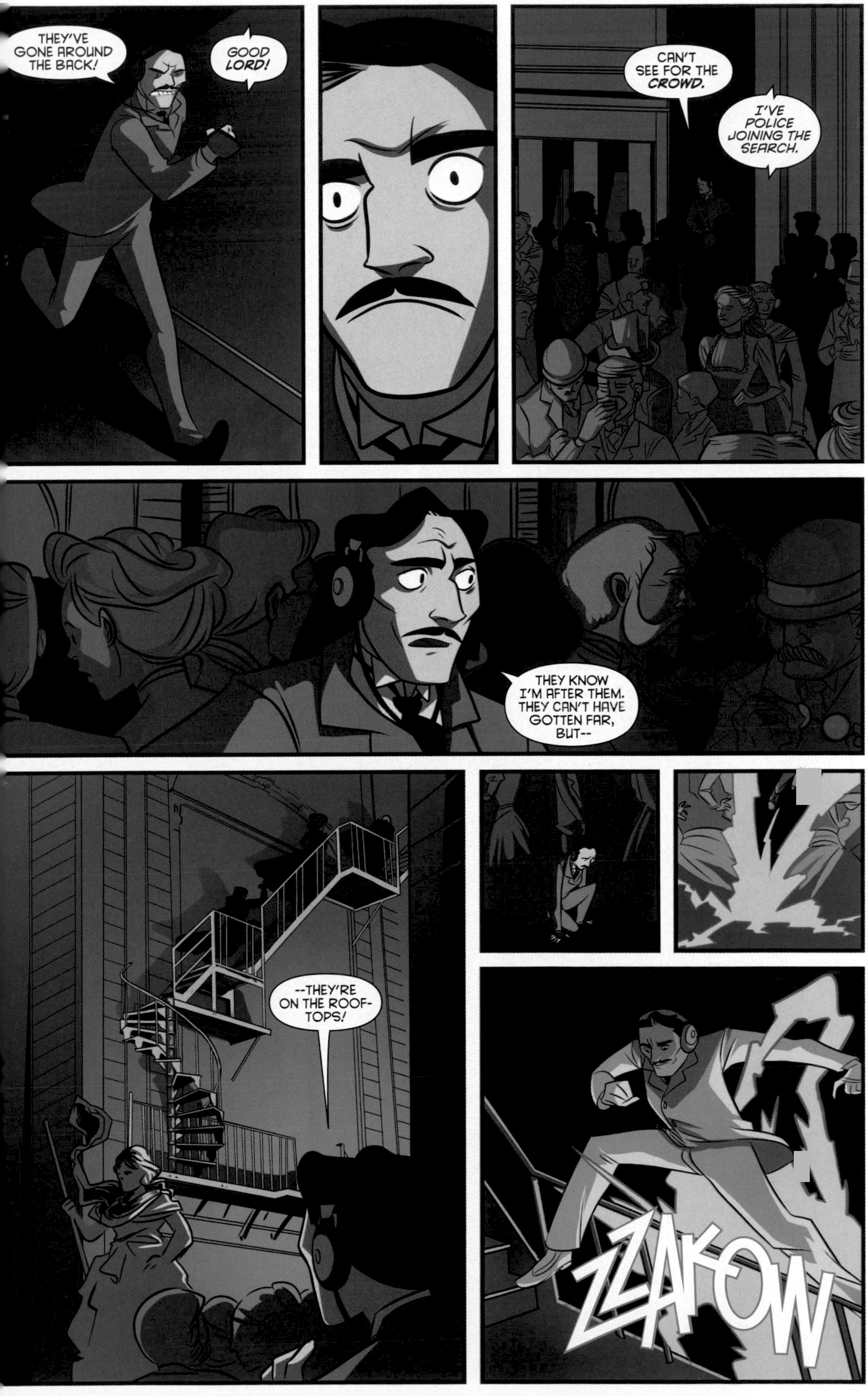
THEY'VE GONE AROUND THE BACK!
GOOD LORD!
CAN'T SEE FOR THE CROWD.
I'VE POLICE JOINING THE SEARCH.
THEY KNOW I'M AFTER THEM. THEY CAN'T HAVE GOTTEN FAR, BUT--
--THEY'RE ON THE ROOF-TOPS!
ZZAKOW

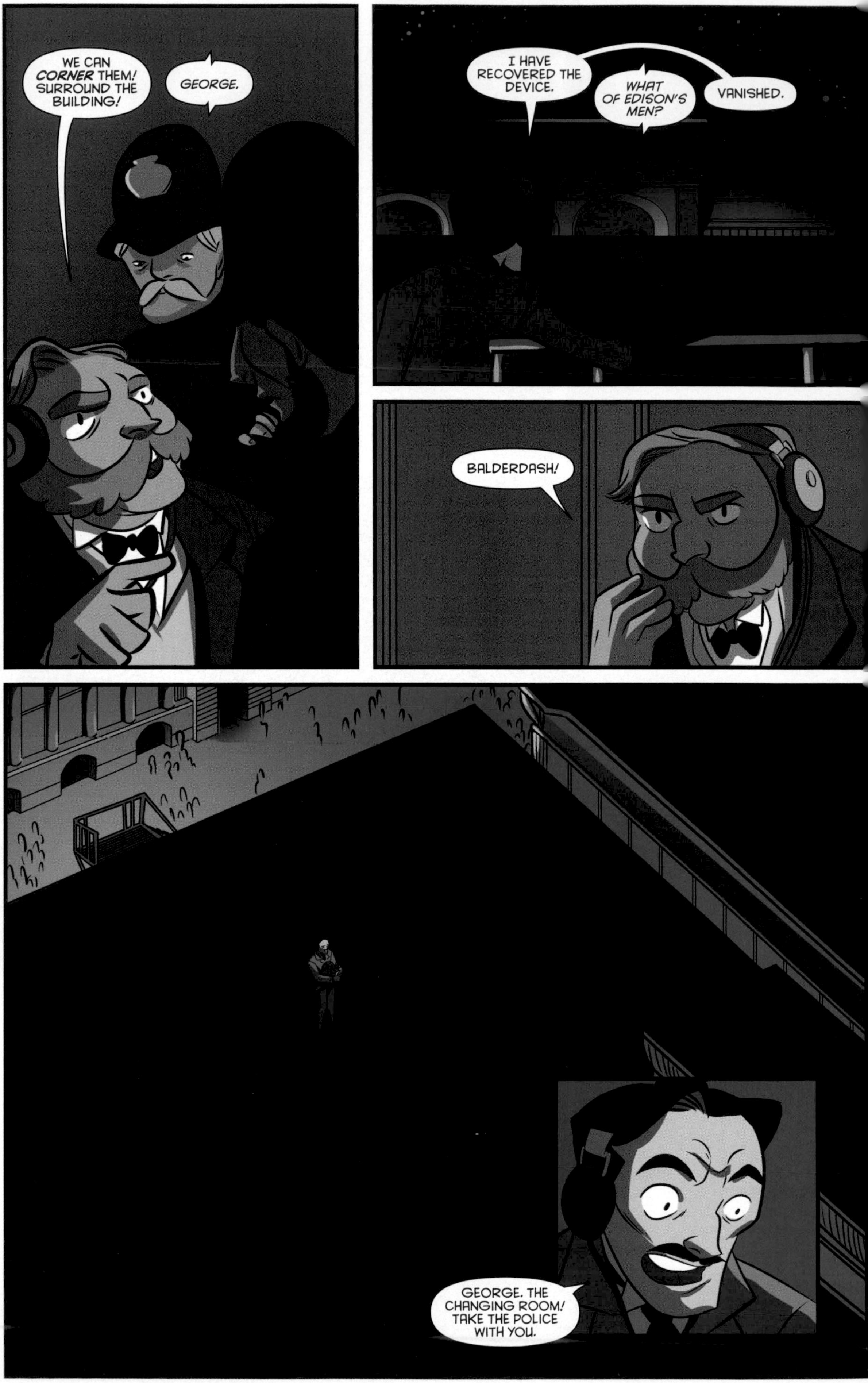
WE CAN CORNER THEM! SURROUND THE BUILDING!
GEORGE.
I HAVE RECOVERED THE DEVICE.
WHAT OF EDISON'S MEN?
VANISHED.
BALDERDASH!
GEORGE. THE CHANGING ROOM! TAKE THE POLICE WITH YOU.

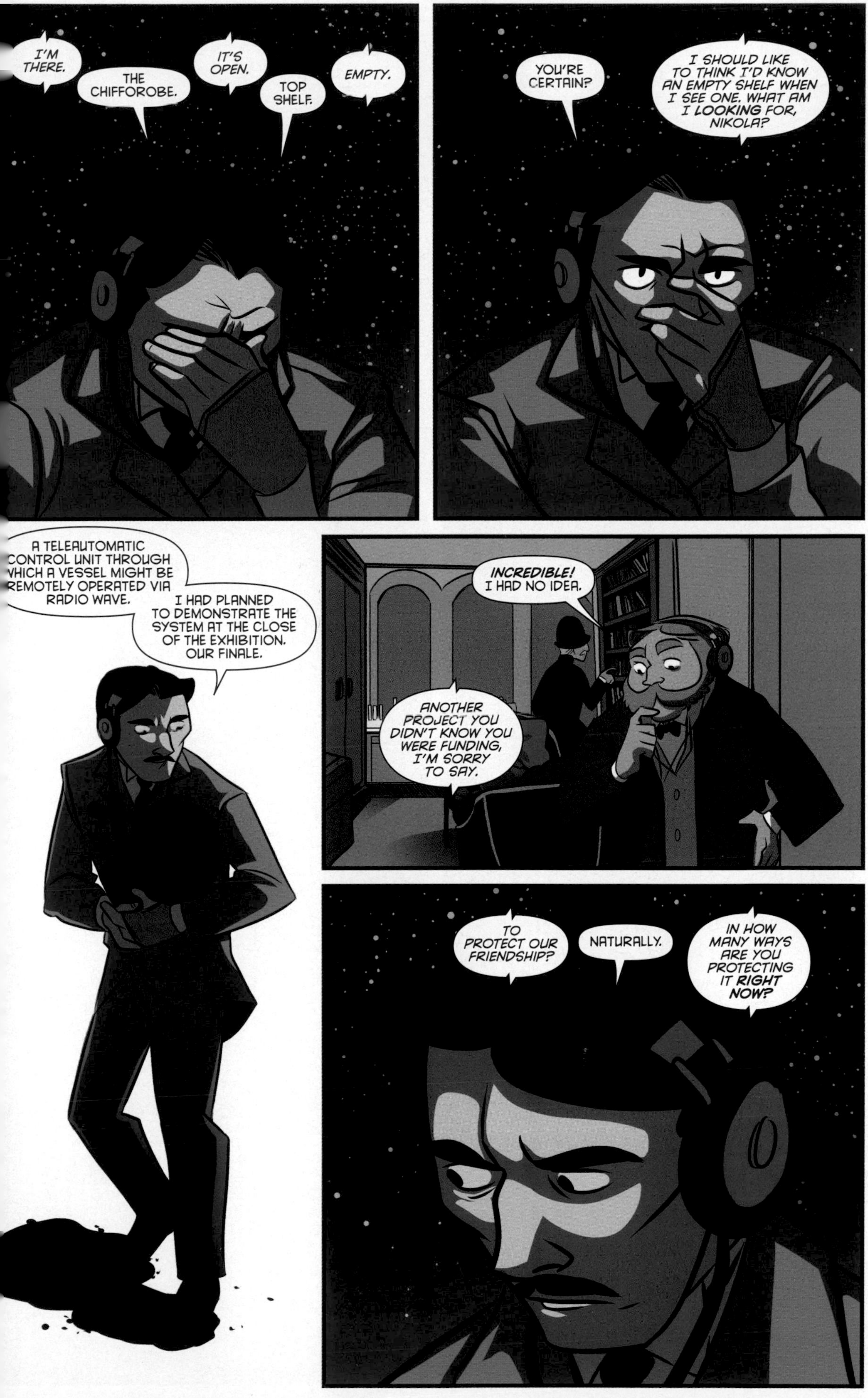
I'M THERE.
THE CHIFFOROBE.
IT'S OPEN.
TOP SHELF.
EMPTY.
YOU'RE CERTAIN?
I SHOULD LIKE TO THINK I'D KNOW AN EMPTY SHELF WHEN I SEE ONE. WHAT AM I LOOKING FOR, NIKOLA?
A TELEAUTOMATIC CONTROL UNIT THROUGH WHICH A VESSEL MIGHT BE REMOTELY OPERATED VIA RADIO WAVE.
I HAD PLANNED TO DEMONSTRATE THE SYSTEM AT THE CLOSE OF THE EXHIBITION. OUR FINALE.
INCREDIBLE! I HAD NO IDEA.
ANOTHER PROJECT YOU DIDN'T KNOW YOU WERE FUNDING, I'M SORRY TO SAY.
TO PROTECT OUR FRIENDSHIP?
NATURALLY.
IN HOW MANY WAYS ARE YOU PROTECTING IT RIGHT NOW?

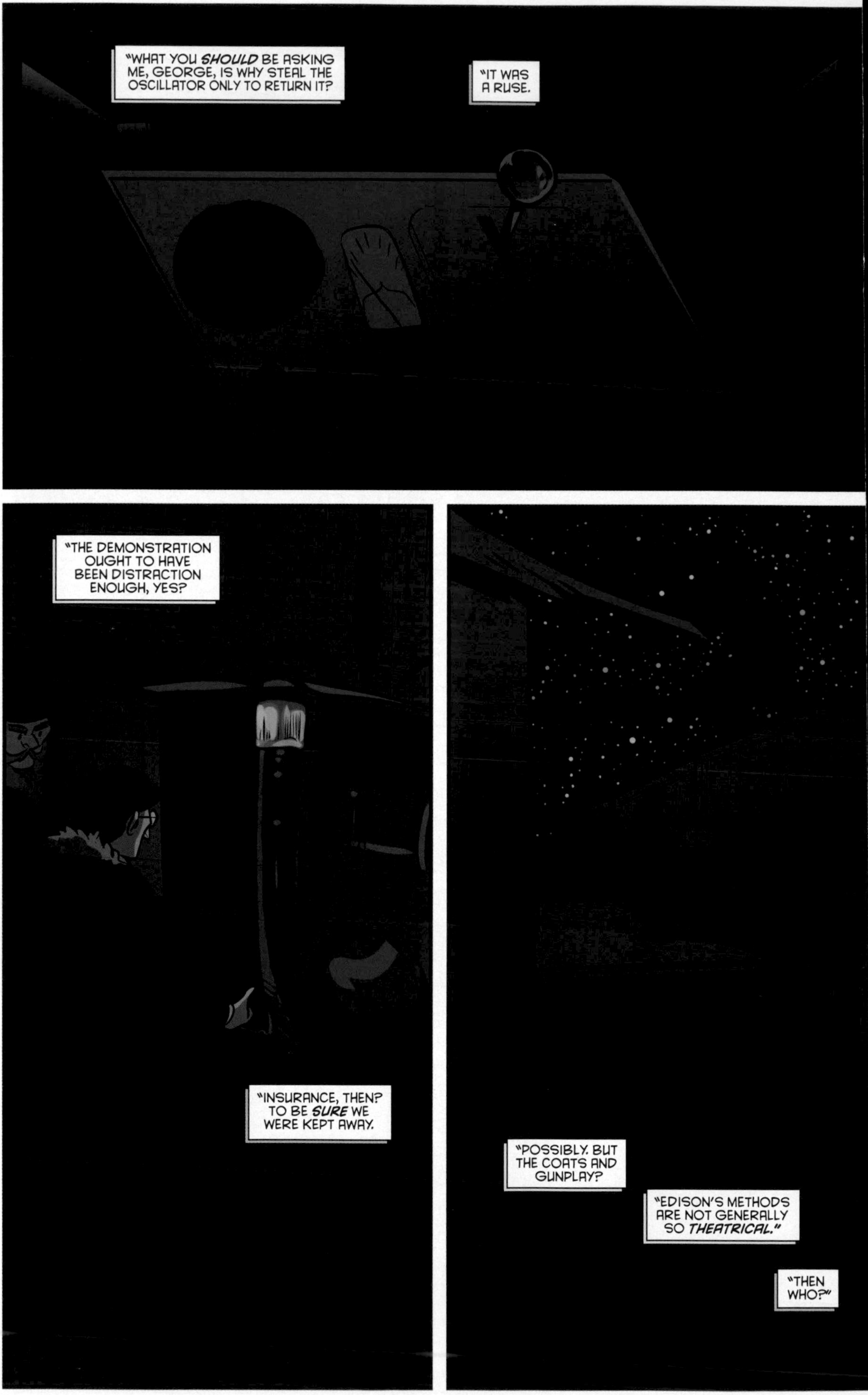
"WHAT YOU *SHOULD* BE ASKING ME, GEORGE, IS WHY STEAL THE OSCILLATOR ONLY TO RETURN IT?
"IT WAS A RUSE.
"THE DEMONSTRATION OUGHT TO HAVE BEEN DISTRACTION ENOUGH, YES?
"INSURANCE, THEN? TO BE *SURE* WE WERE KEPT AWAY.
"POSSIBLY. BUT THE COATS AND GUNPLAY?
"EDISON'S METHODS ARE NOT GENERALLY SO *THEATRICAL.*"
"THEN WHO?"

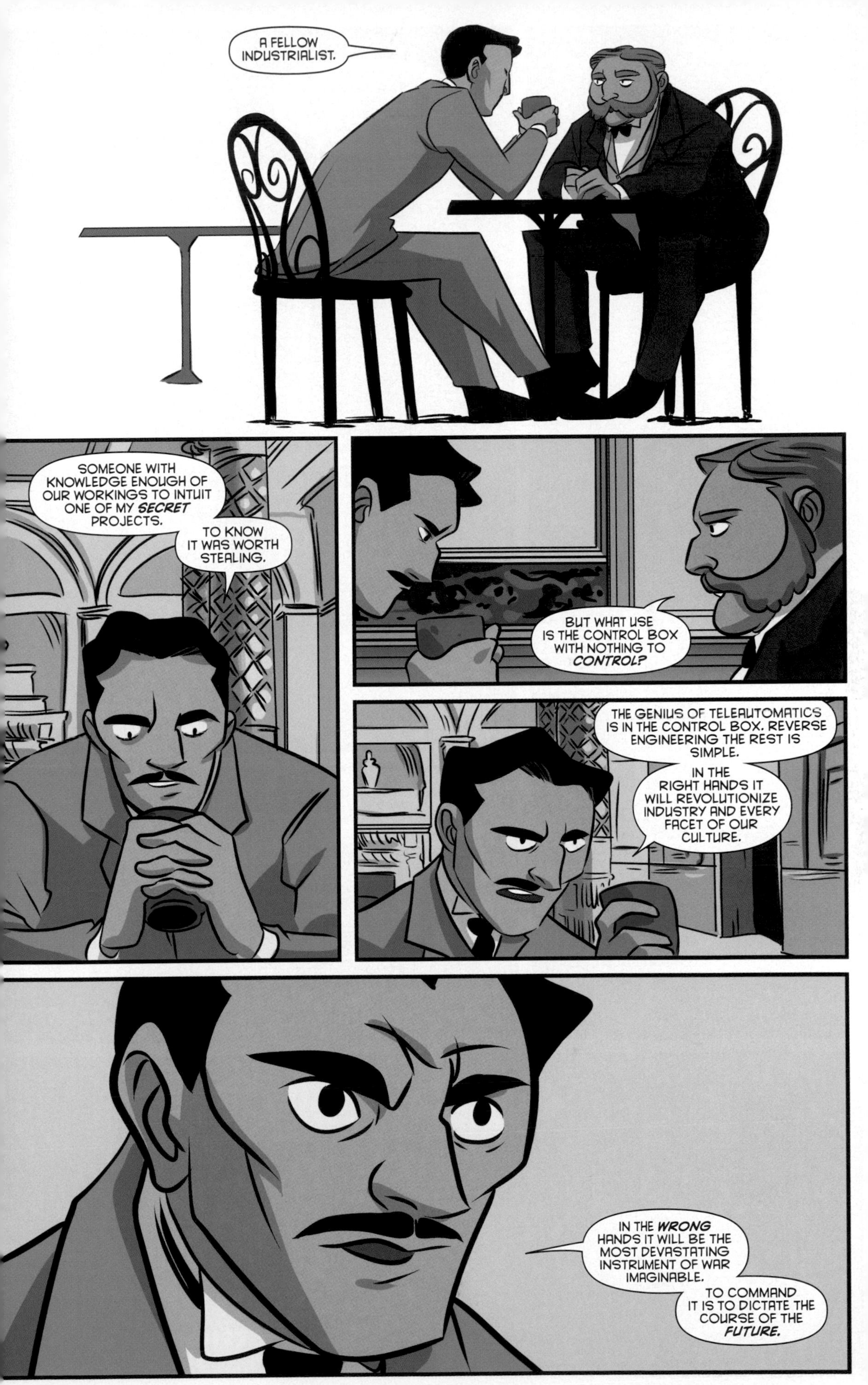

A FELLOW INDUSTRIALIST.
SOMEONE WITH KNOWLEDGE ENOUGH OF OUR WORKINGS TO INTUIT ONE OF MY *SECRET* PROJECTS.
TO KNOW IT WAS WORTH STEALING.
BUT WHAT USE IS THE CONTROL BOX WITH NOTHING TO *CONTROL?*
THE GENIUS OF TELEAUTOMATICS IS IN THE CONTROL BOX. REVERSE ENGINEERING THE REST IS SIMPLE.
IN THE RIGHT HANDS IT WILL REVOLUTIONIZE INDUSTRY AND EVERY FACET OF OUR CULTURE.
IN THE *WRONG* HANDS IT WILL BE THE MOST DEVASTATING INSTRUMENT OF WAR IMAGINABLE.
TO COMMAND IT IS TO DICTATE THE COURSE OF THE *FUTURE.*

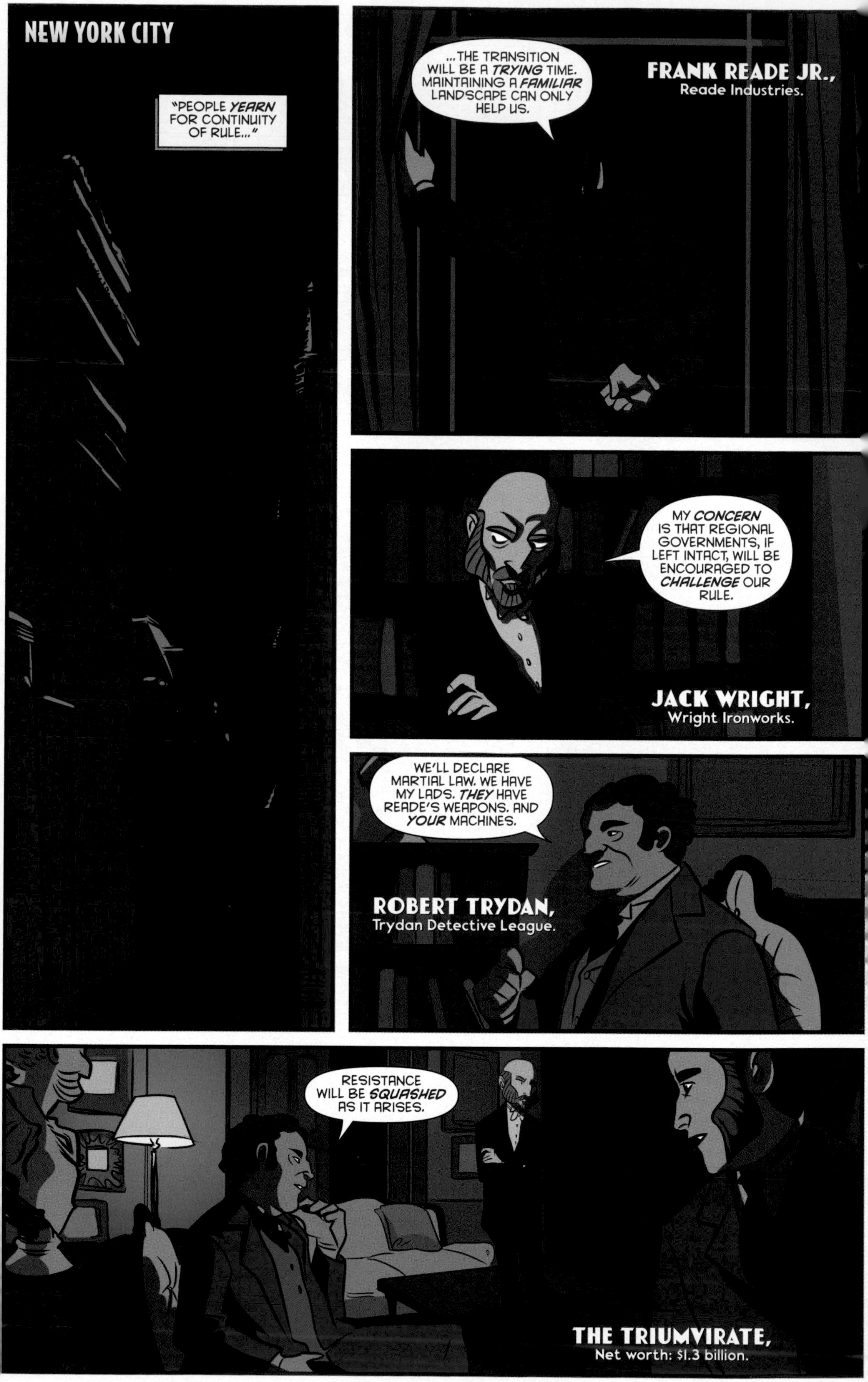
NEW YORK CITY
"PEOPLE YEARN FOR CONTINUITY OF RULE..."
...THE TRANSITION WILL BE A TRYING TIME. MAINTAINING A FAMILIAR LANDSCAPE CAN ONLY HELP US.
FRANK READE JR., Reade Industries.
MY CONCERN IS THAT REGIONAL GOVERNMENTS, IF LEFT INTACT, WILL BE ENCOURAGED TO CHALLENGE OUR RULE.
JACK WRIGHT, Wright Ironworks.
WE'LL DECLARE MARTIAL LAW. WE HAVE MY LADS. THEY HAVE READE'S WEAPONS. AND YOUR MACHINES.
ROBERT TRYDAN, Trydan Detective League.
RESISTANCE WILL BE SQUASHED AS IT ARISES.
THE TRIUMVIRATE, Net worth: $1.3 billion.

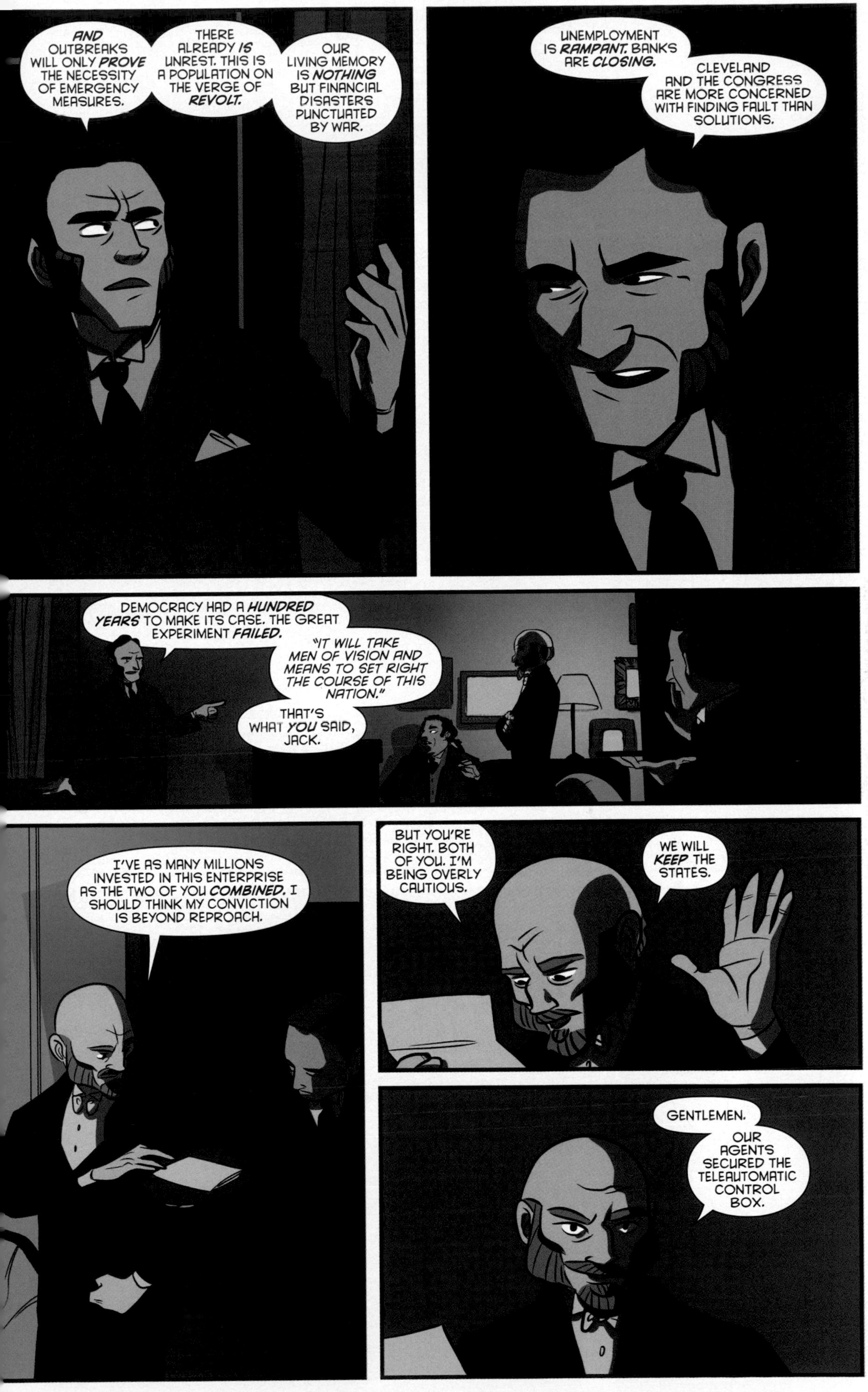
AND OUTBREAKS WILL ONLY PROVE THE NECESSITY OF EMERGENCY MEASURES.
THERE ALREADY IS UNREST. THIS IS A POPULATION ON THE VERGE OF REVOLT.
OUR LIVING MEMORY IS NOTHING BUT FINANCIAL DISASTERS PUNCTUATED BY WAR.
UNEMPLOYMENT IS RAMPANT. BANKS ARE CLOSING.
CLEVELAND AND THE CONGRESS ARE MORE CONCERNED WITH FINDING FAULT THAN SOLUTIONS.
DEMOCRACY HAD A HUNDRED YEARS TO MAKE ITS CASE. THE GREAT EXPERIMENT FAILED.
"IT WILL TAKE MEN OF VISION AND MEANS TO SET RIGHT THE COURSE OF THIS NATION."
THAT'S WHAT YOU SAID, JACK.
I'VE AS MANY MILLIONS INVESTED IN THIS ENTERPRISE AS THE TWO OF YOU COMBINED. I SHOULD THINK MY CONVICTION IS BEYOND REPROACH.
BUT YOU'RE RIGHT. BOTH OF YOU. I'M BEING OVERLY CAUTIOUS.
WE WILL KEEP THE STATES.
GENTLEMEN.
OUR AGENTS SECURED THE TELEAUTOMATIC CONTROL BOX.

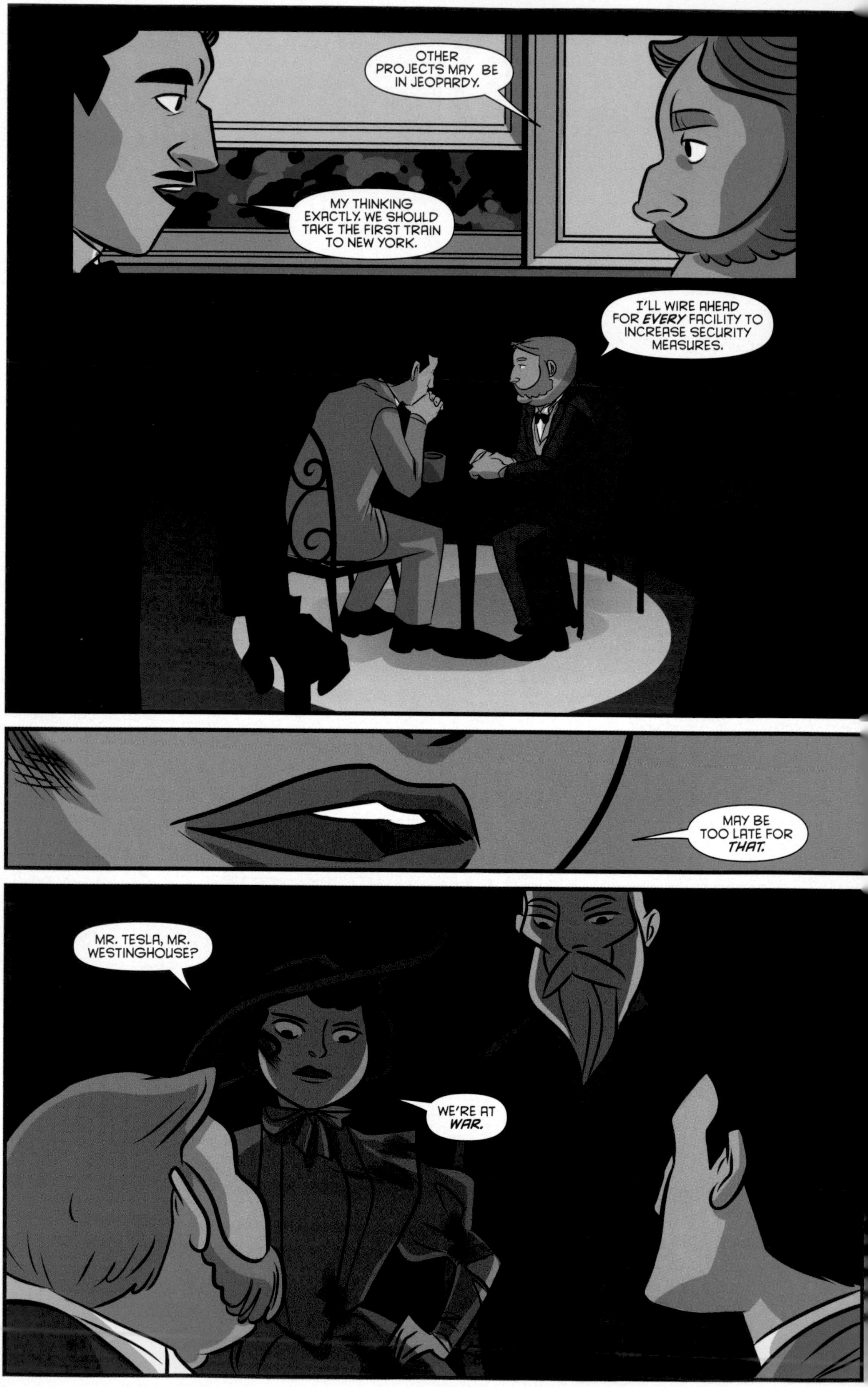

OTHER PROJECTS MAY BE IN JEOPARDY.
MY THINKING EXACTLY. WE SHOULD TAKE THE FIRST TRAIN TO NEW YORK.
I'LL WIRE AHEAD FOR *EVERY* FACILITY TO INCREASE SECURITY MEASURES.
MAY BE TOO LATE FOR *THAT.*
MR. TESLA, MR. WESTINGHOUSE?
WE'RE AT *WAR.*

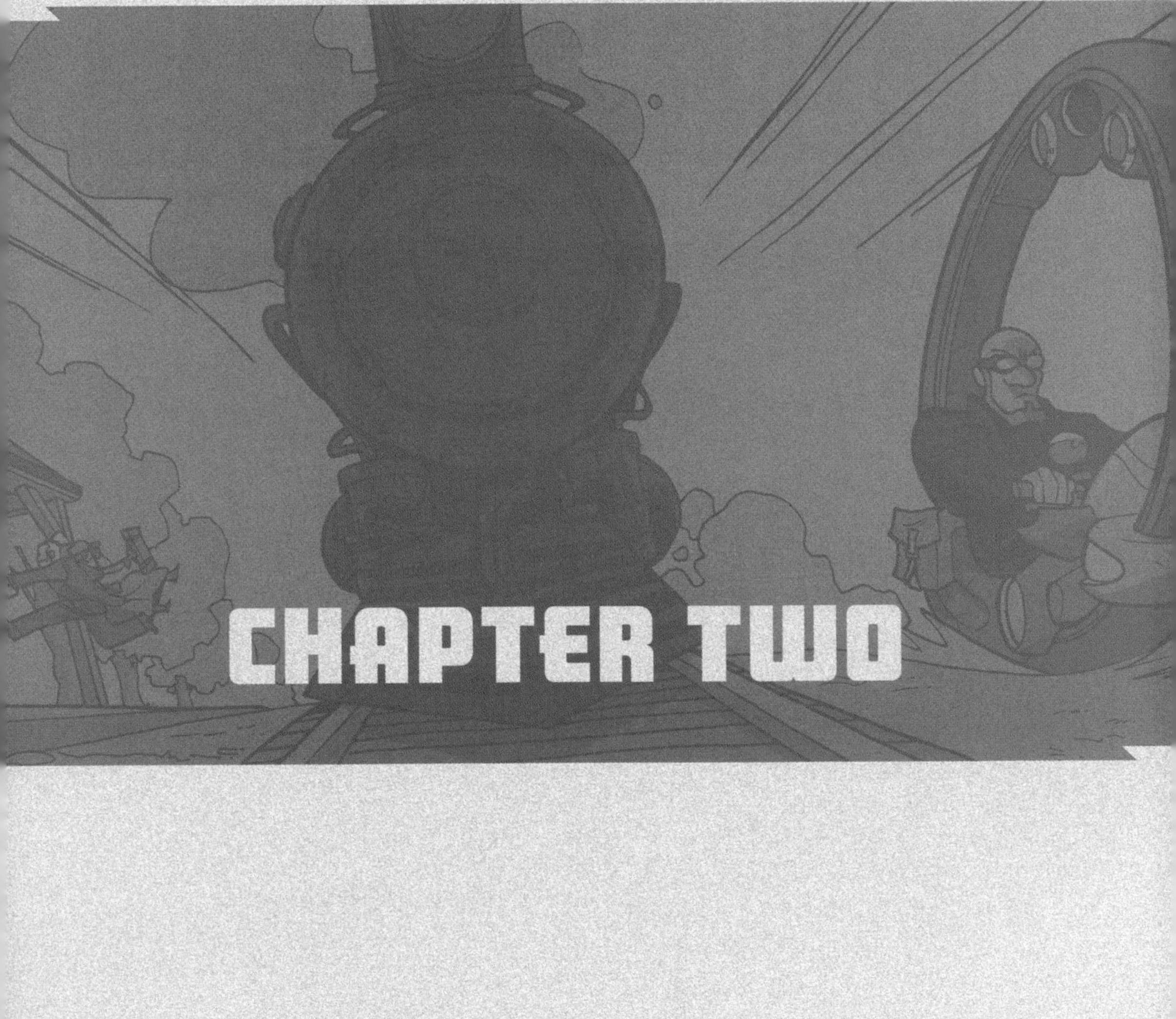

CHAPTER TWO

CLEVINGER
GRALL

ATOMIC ROBO

PRESENTS

REAL SCIENCE ADVENTURES

HENDERSO
POWELL

No. 8 $2.75 U.S.

MA

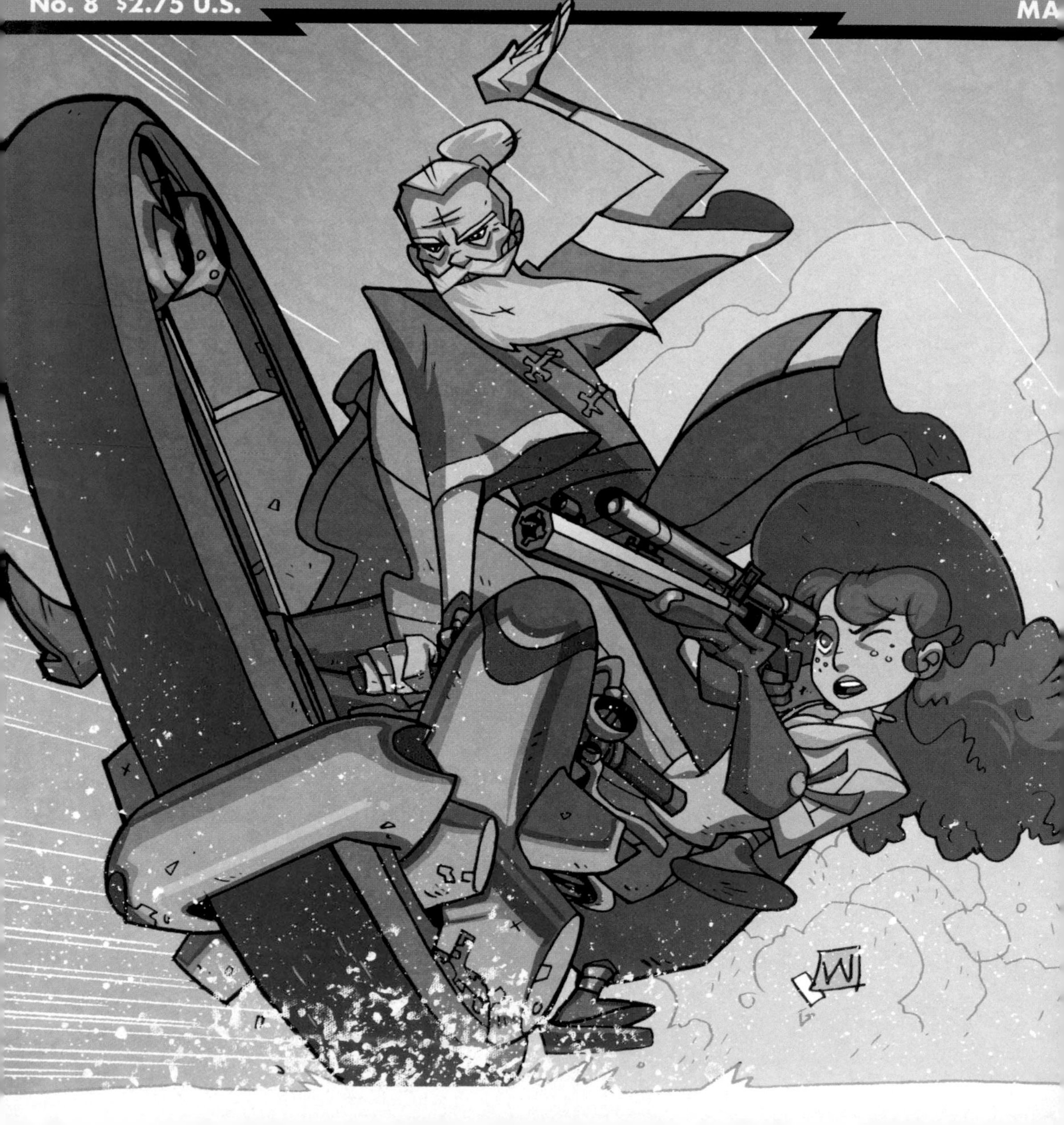

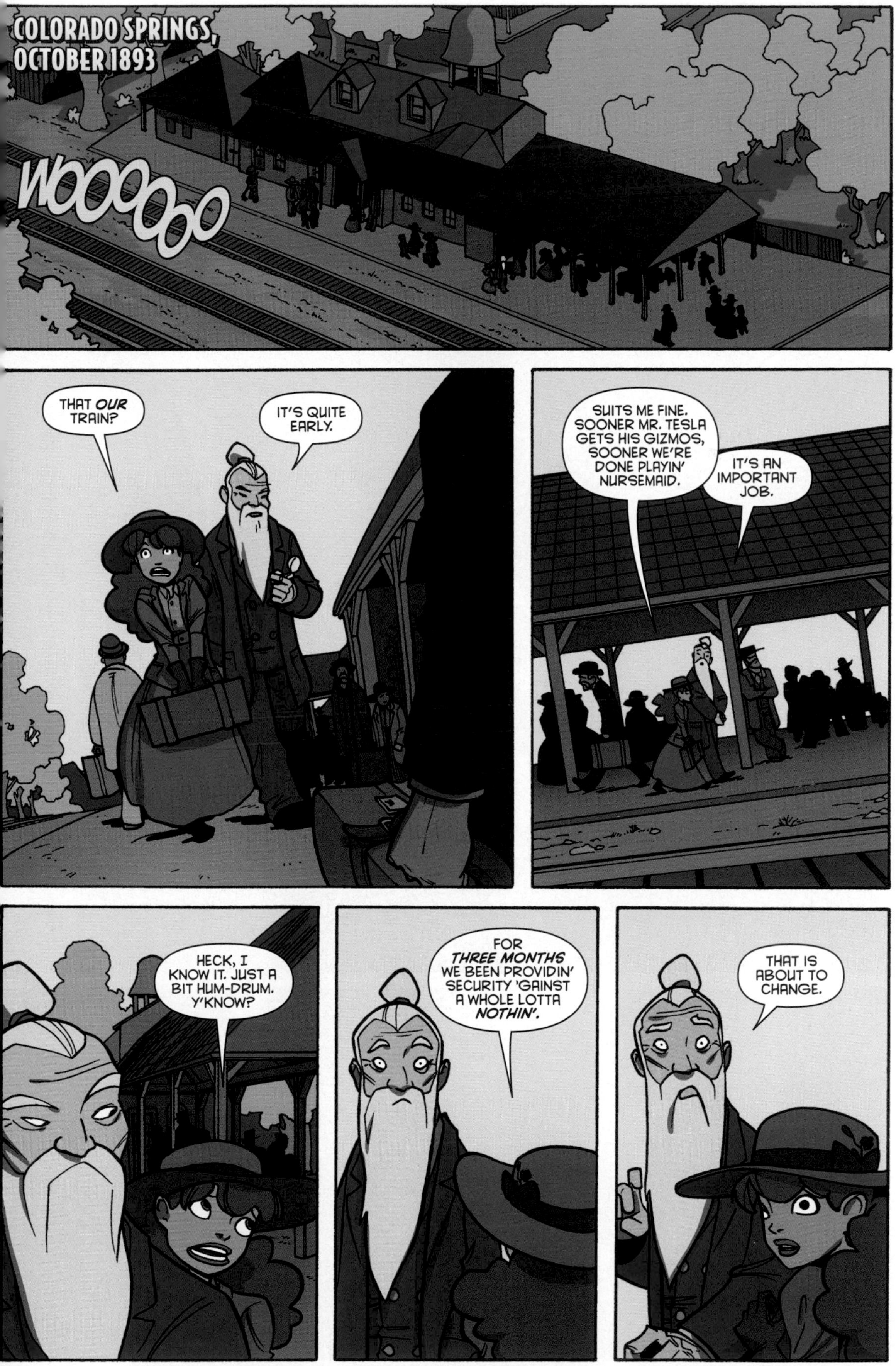
COLORADO SPRINGS, OCTOBER 1893
WOOOOOO
THAT *OUR* TRAIN?
IT'S QUITE EARLY.
SUITS ME FINE. SOONER MR. TESLA GETS HIS GIZMOS, SOONER WE'RE DONE PLAYIN' NURSEMAID.
IT'S AN IMPORTANT JOB.
HECK, I KNOW IT. JUST A BIT HUM-DRUM. Y'KNOW?
FOR *THREE MONTHS* WE BEEN PROVIDIN' SECURITY 'GAINST A WHOLE LOTTA *NOTHIN'*.
THAT IS ABOUT TO CHANGE.

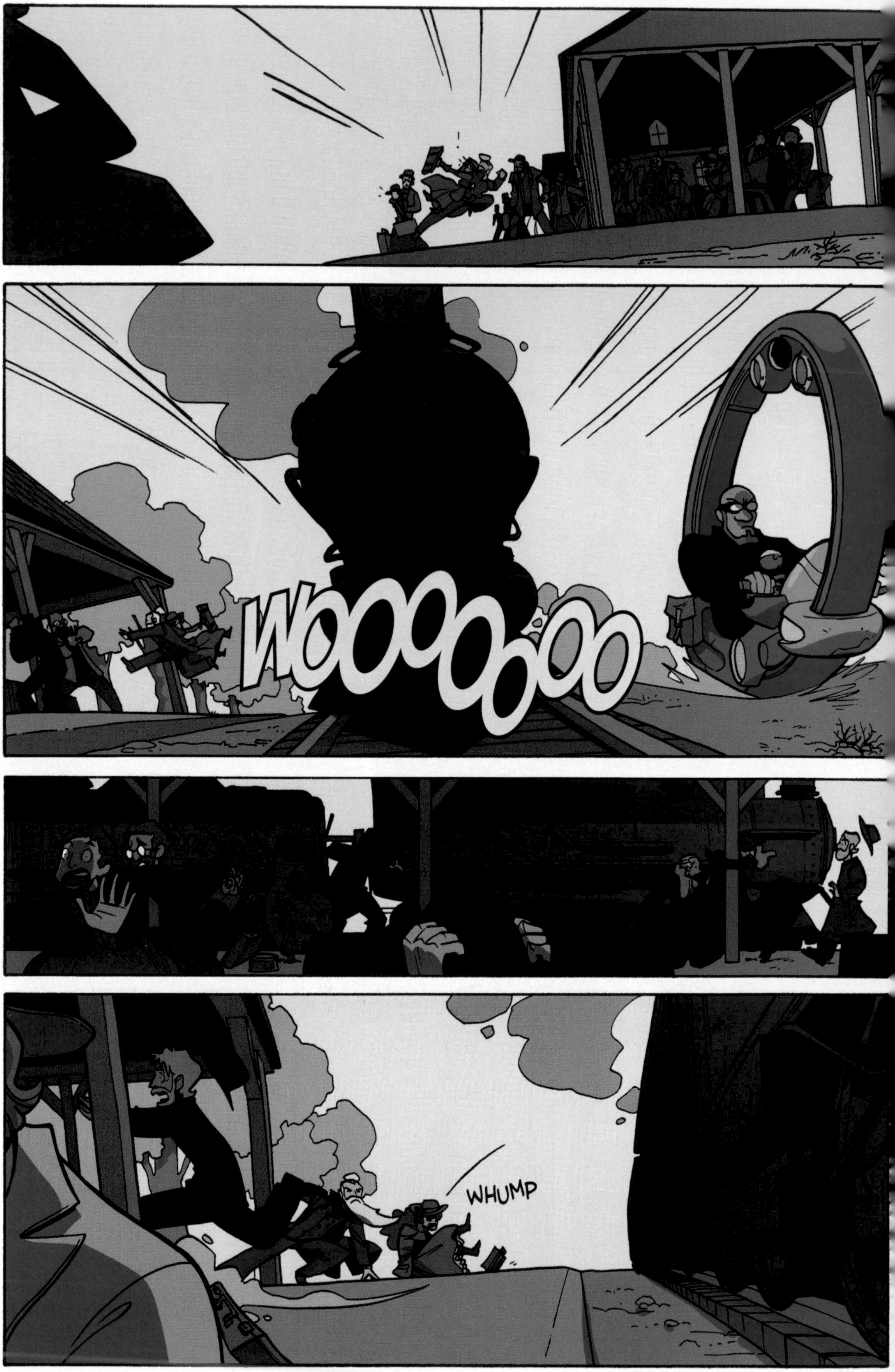
WOOOOOOO
WHUMP

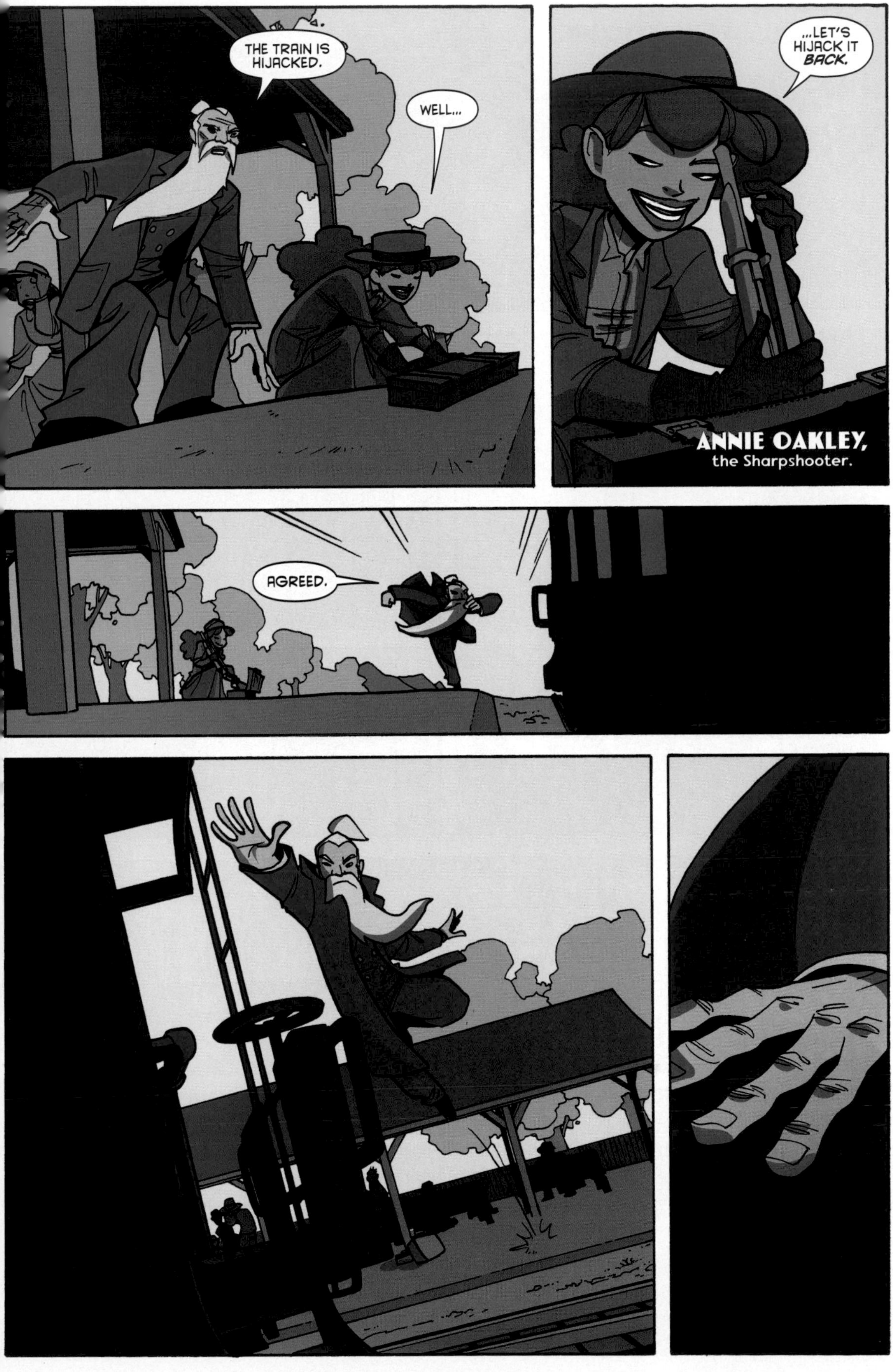
THE TRAIN IS HIJACKED.
WELL...
...LET'S HIJACK IT BACK.
ANNIE OAKLEY,
the Sharpshooter.
AGREED.

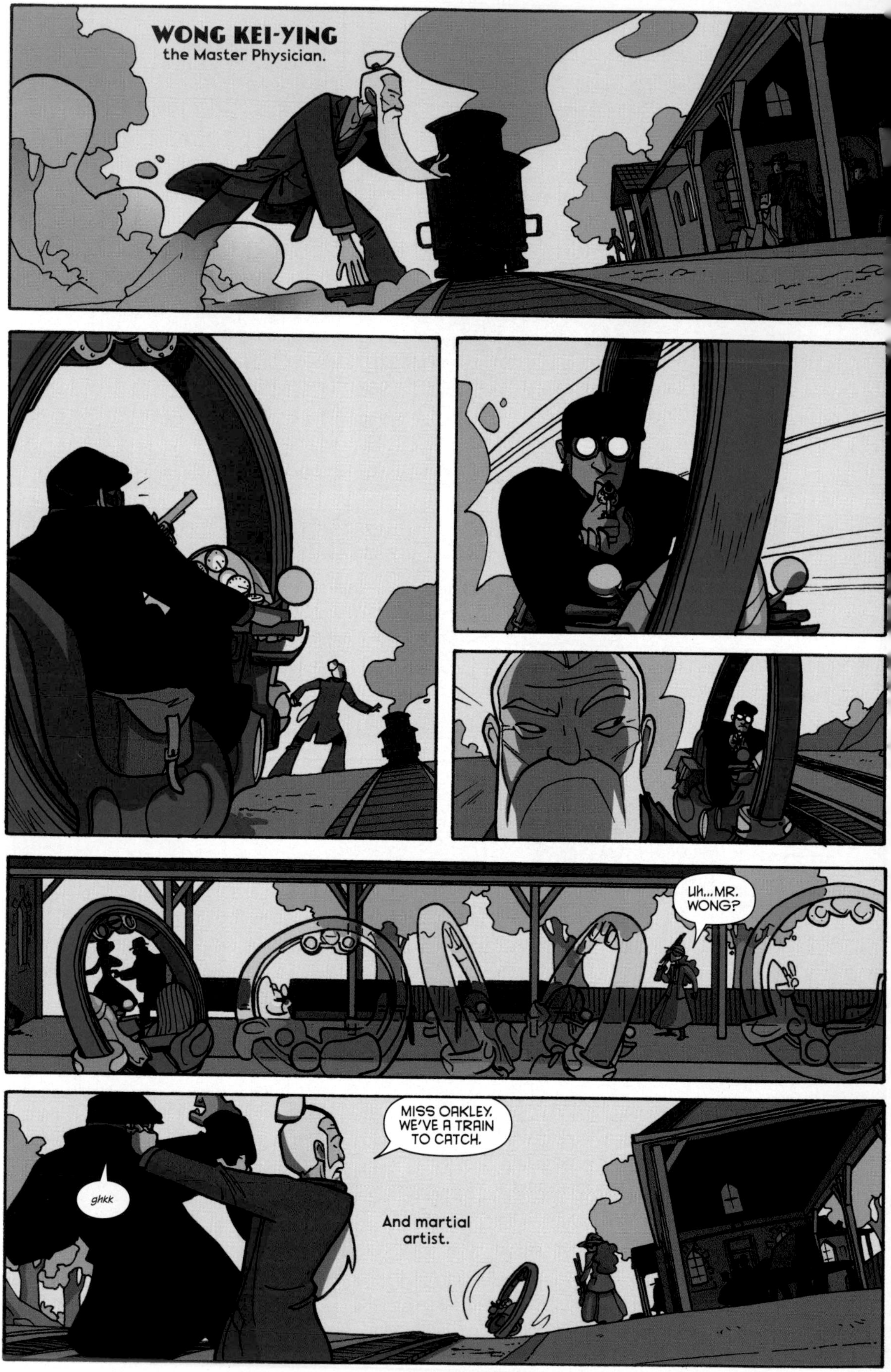
WONG KEI-YING
the Master Physician.
UH...MR. WONG?
MISS OAKLEY. WE'VE A TRAIN TO CATCH.
ghkk
And martial artist.

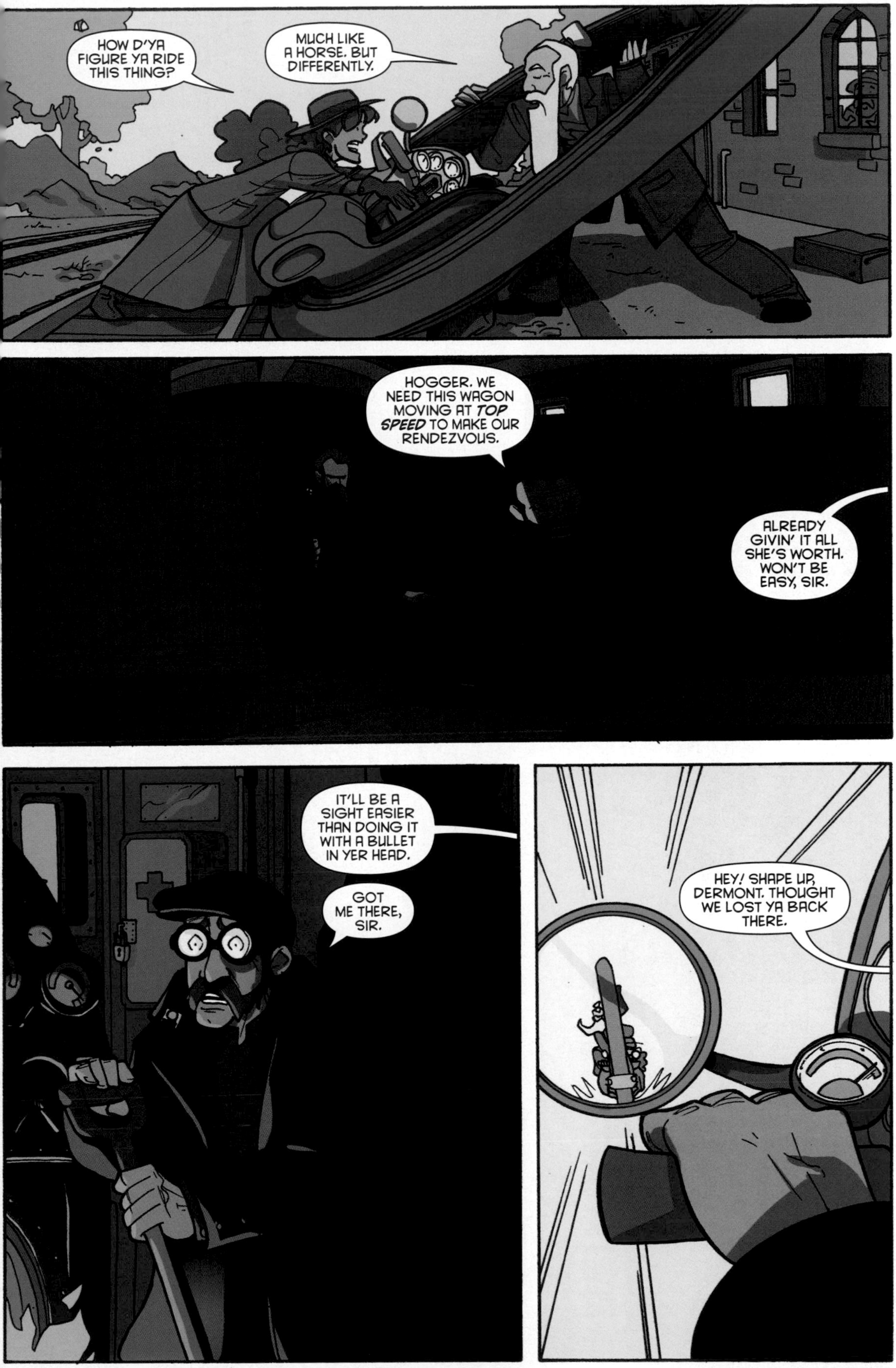
HOW D'YA FIGURE YA RIDE THIS THING?
MUCH LIKE A HORSE. BUT DIFFERENTLY.
HOGGER. WE NEED THIS WAGON MOVING AT *TOP SPEED* TO MAKE OUR RENDEZVOUS.
ALREADY GIVIN' IT ALL SHE'S WORTH. WON'T BE EASY, SIR.
IT'LL BE A SIGHT EASIER THAN DOING IT WITH A BULLET IN YER HEAD.
GOT ME THERE, SIR.
HEY! SHAPE UP, DERMONT. THOUGHT WE LOST YA BACK THERE.

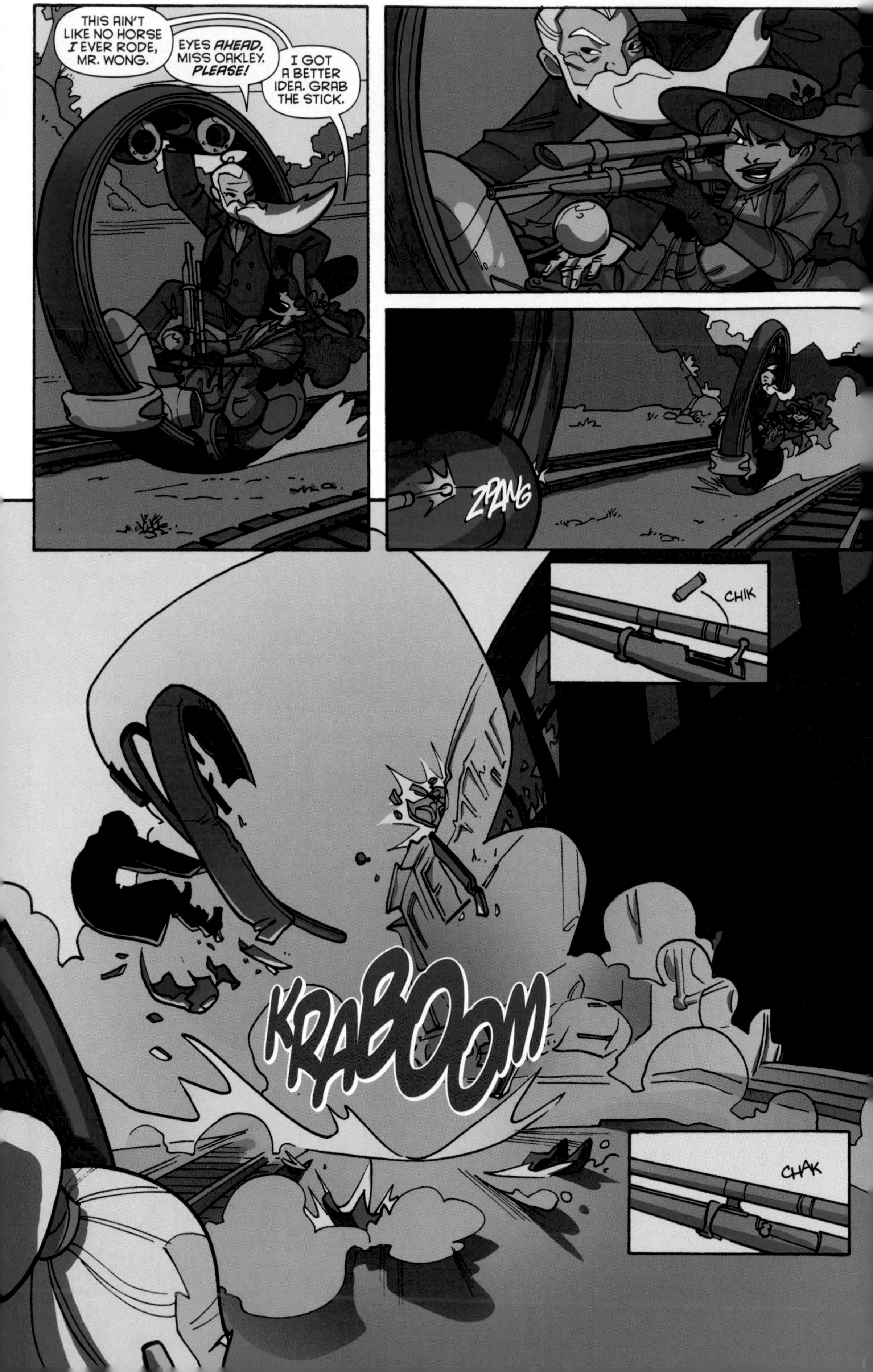
THIS AIN'T LIKE NO HORSE I EVER RODE, MR. WONG.
EYES AHEAD, MISS OAKLEY. PLEASE!
I GOT A BETTER IDEA. GRAB THE STICK.
ZPANG
CHIK
KRABOOM
CHAK

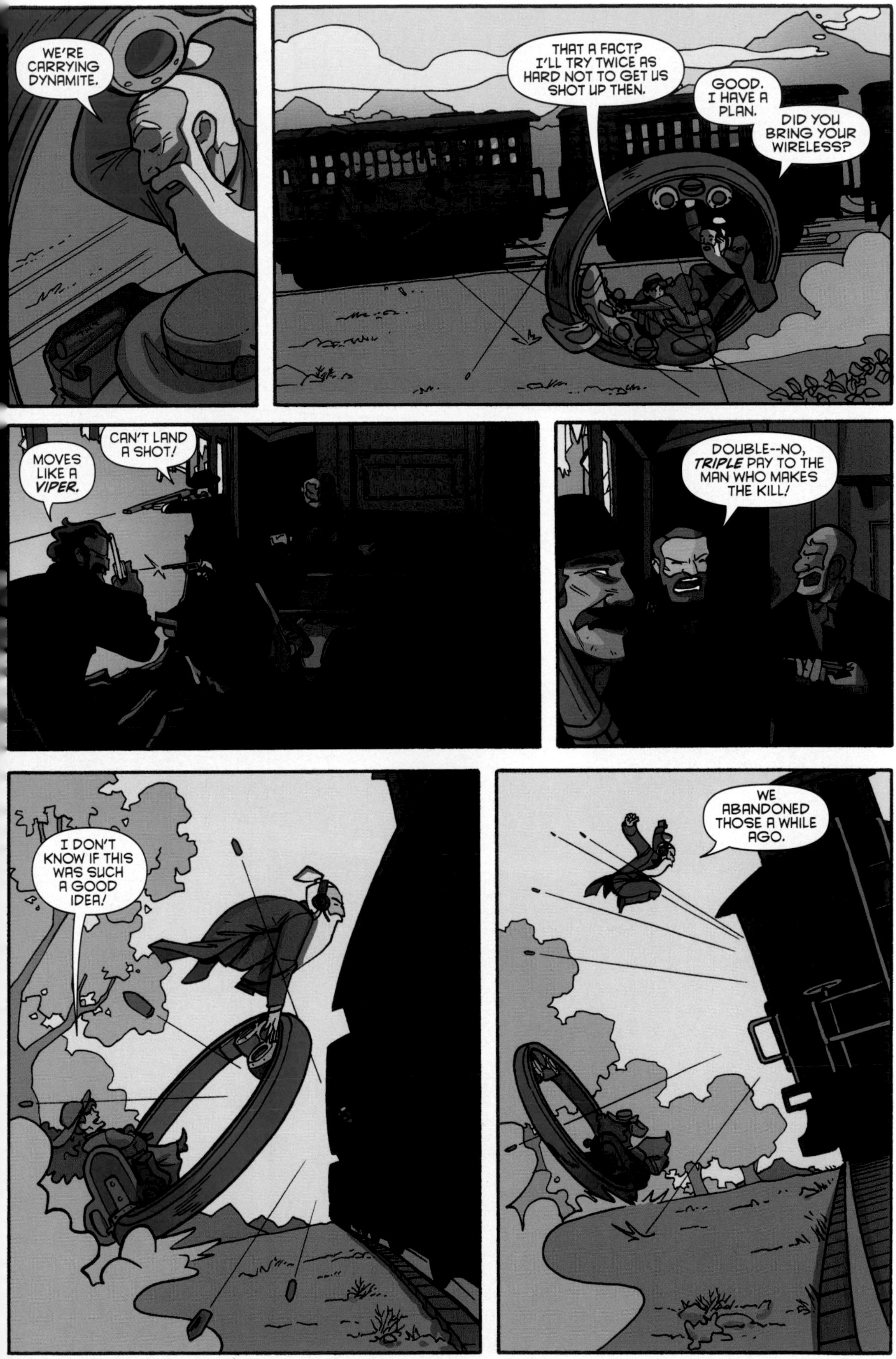
WE'RE CARRYING DYNAMITE.
THAT A FACT? I'LL TRY TWICE AS HARD NOT TO GET US SHOT UP THEN.
GOOD. I HAVE A PLAN.
DID YOU BRING YOUR WIRELESS?
MOVES LIKE A *VIPER.*
CAN'T LAND A SHOT!
DOUBLE--NO, *TRIPLE* PAY TO THE MAN WHO MAKES THE KILL!
I DON'T KNOW IF THIS WAS SUCH A GOOD IDEA!
WE ABANDONED THOSE A WHILE AGO.

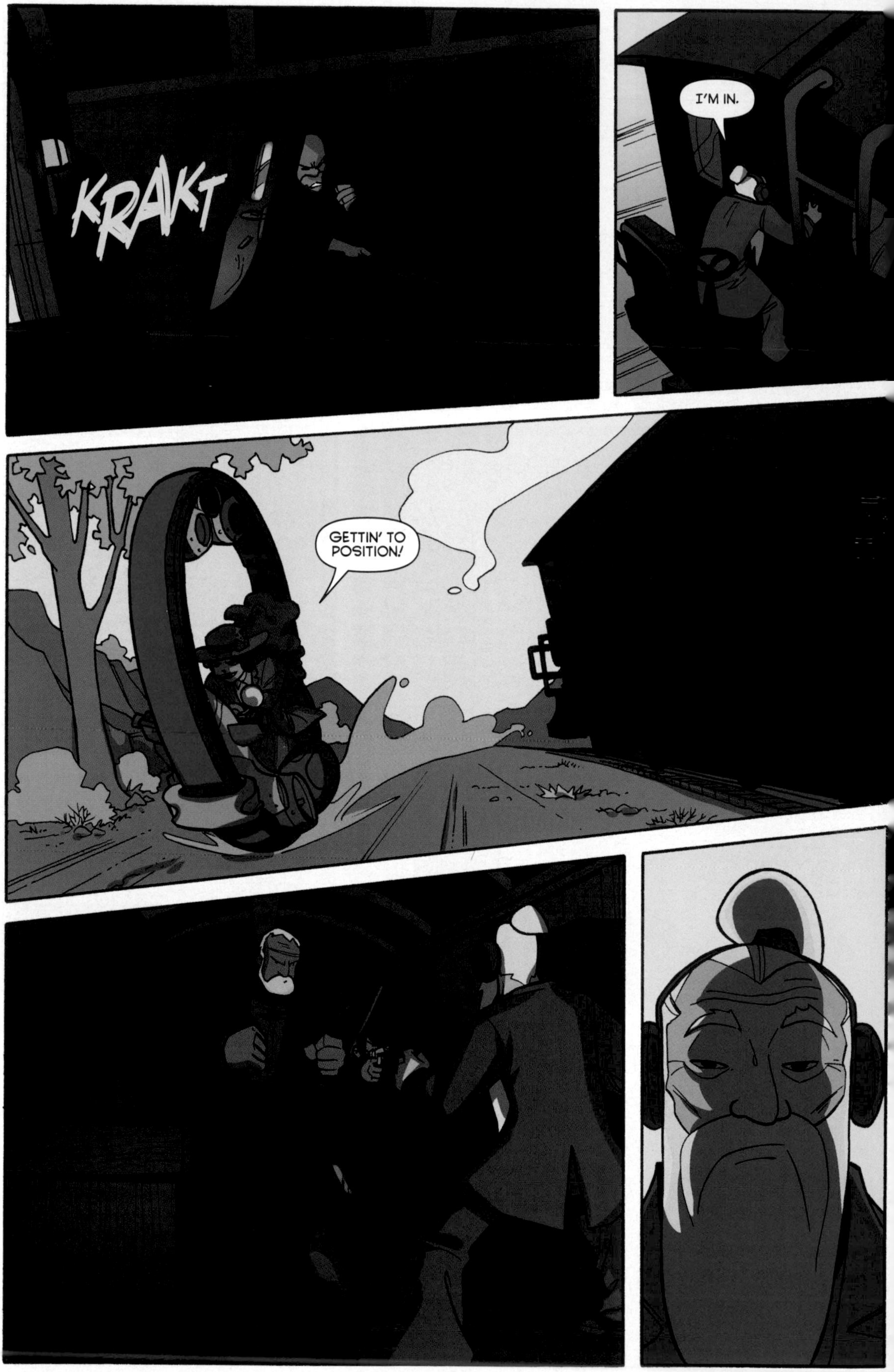
KRAKT
I'M IN.
GETTIN' TO POSITION!

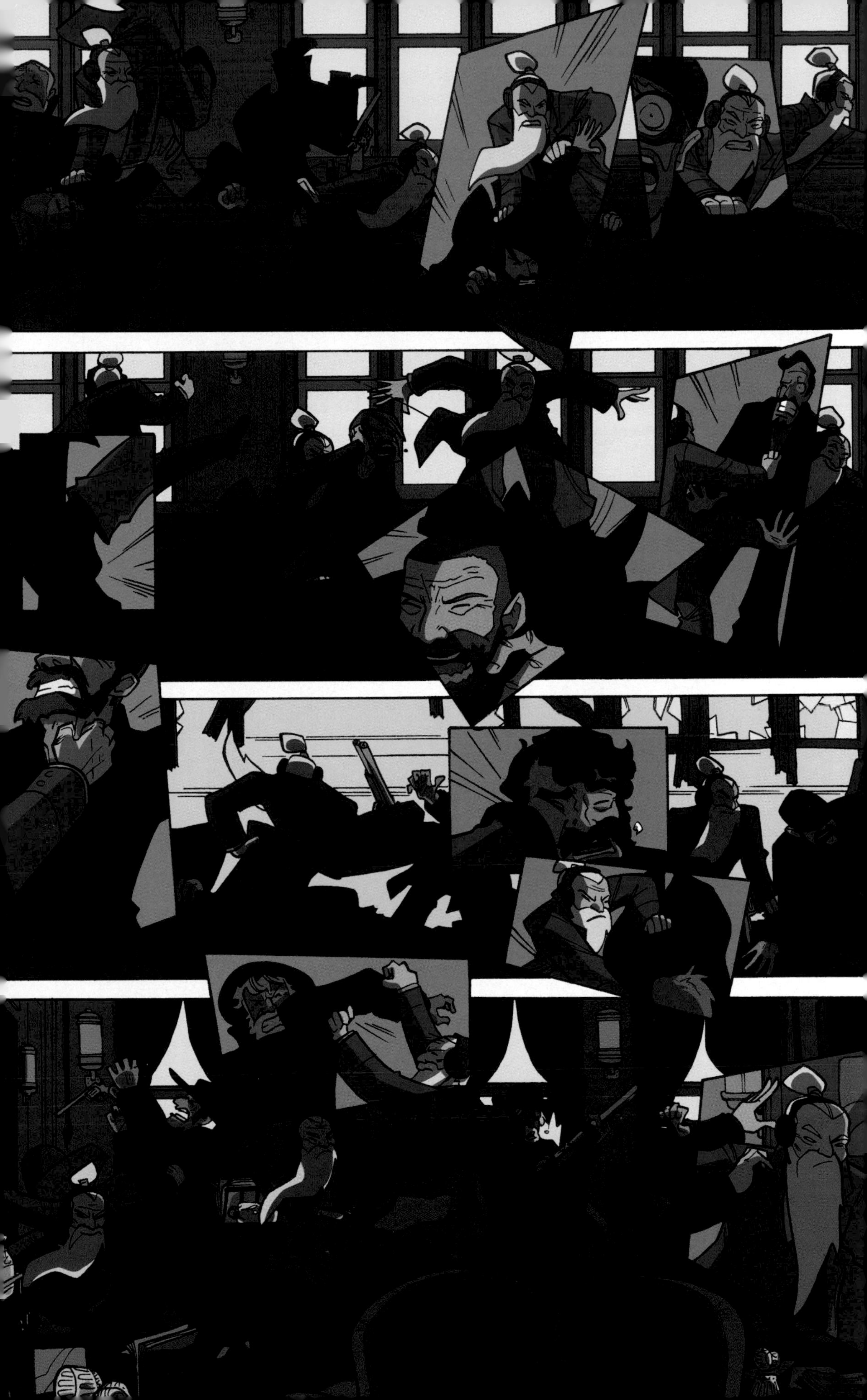

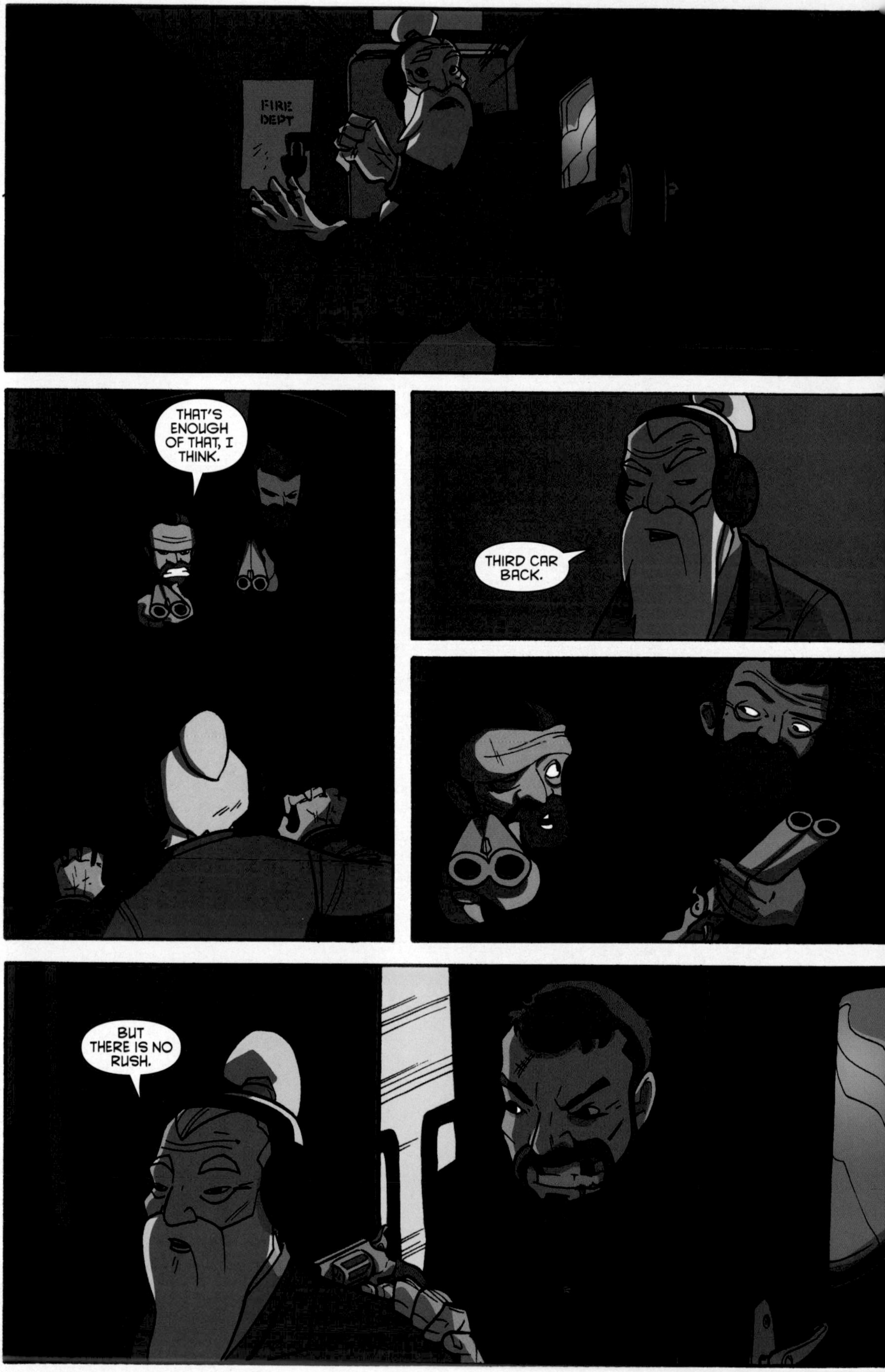
THAT'S ENOUGH OF THAT, I THINK.
THIRD CAR BACK.
BUT THERE IS NO RUSH.

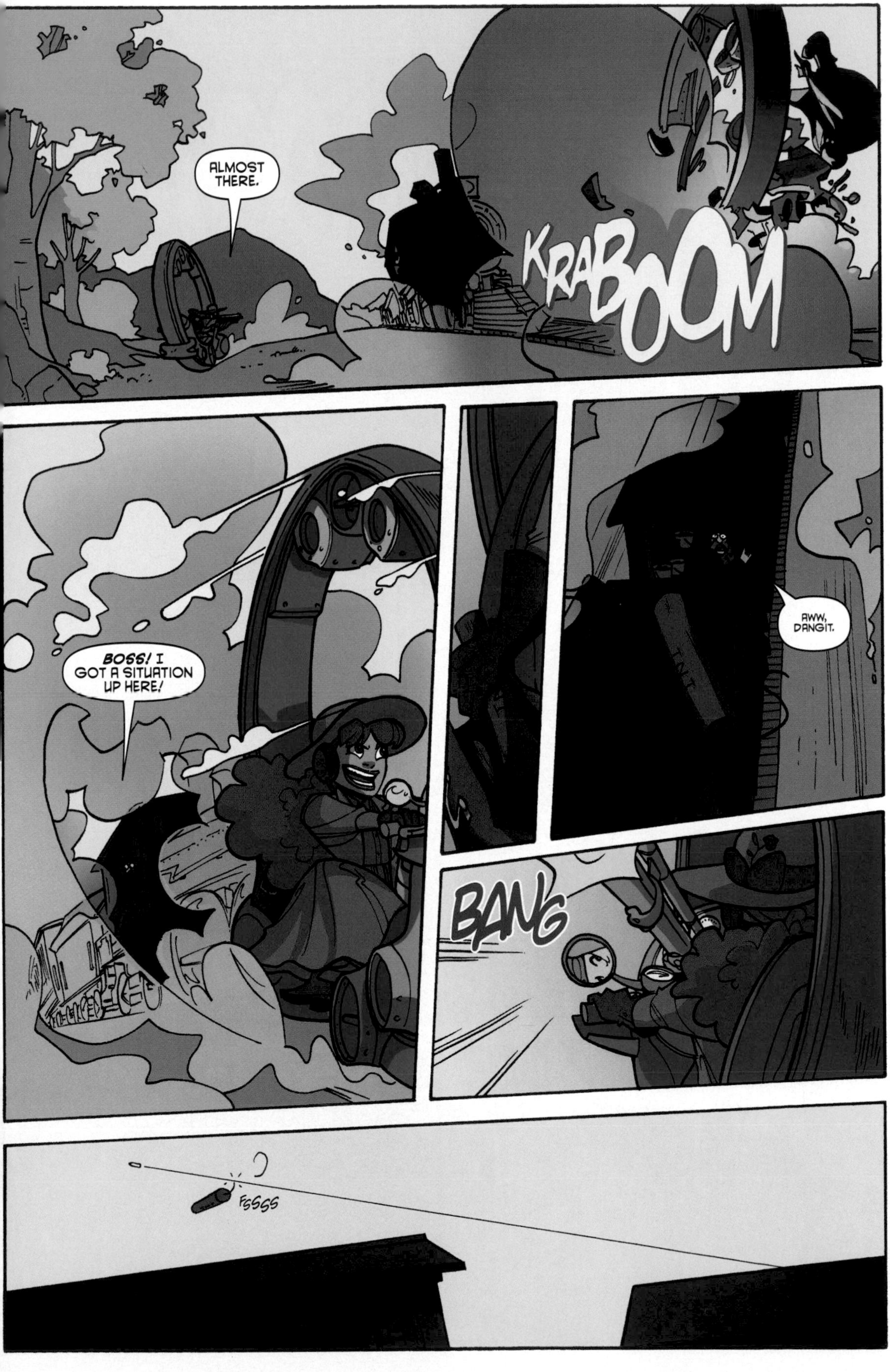
ALMOST THERE.
KRABOOM
BOSS! I GOT A SITUATION UP HERE!
AWW, DANGIT.
BANG
FSSSS

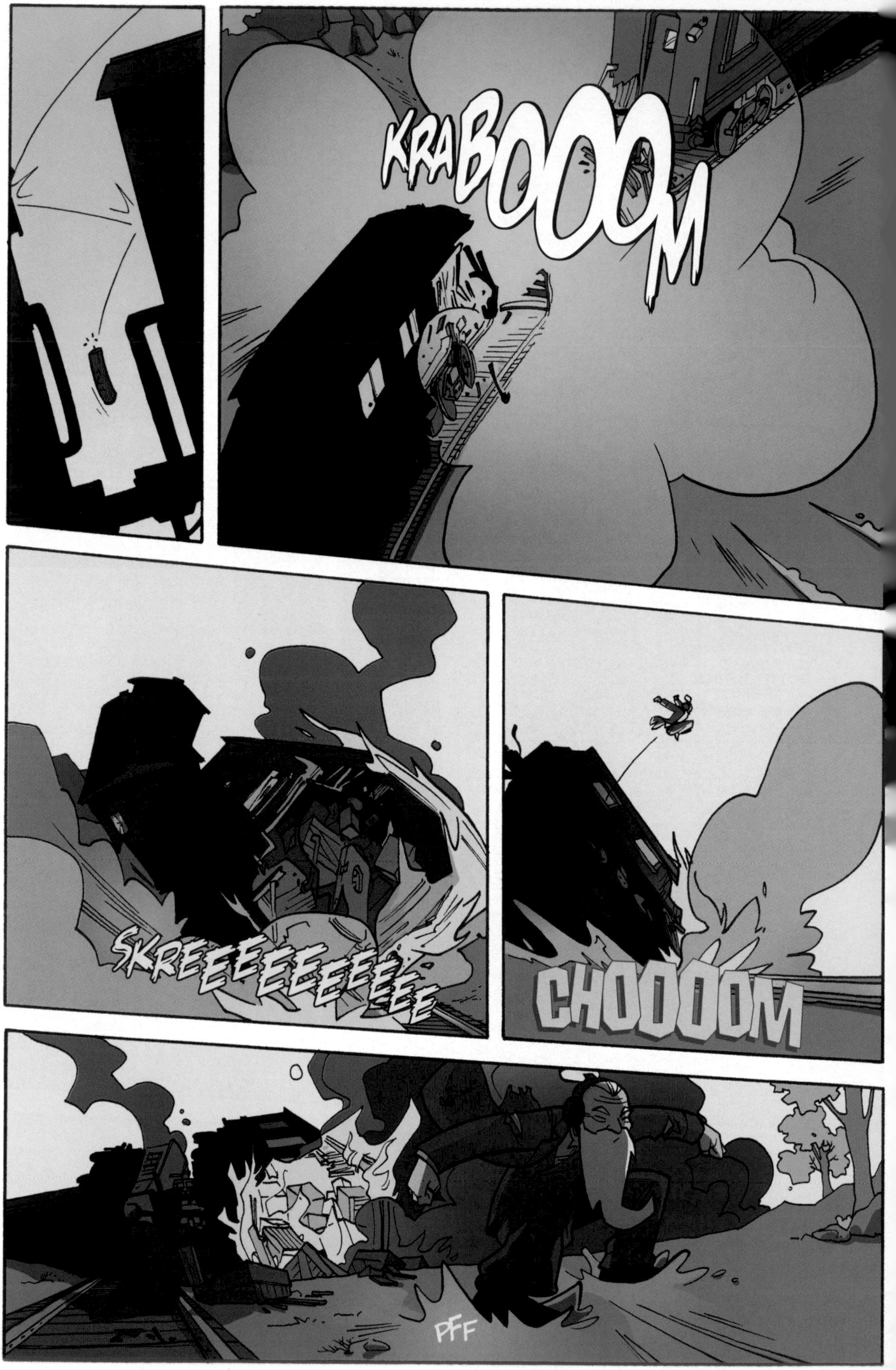
KRABOOOM
SKREEEEEEEEEEEE
CHOOOOM
PFF

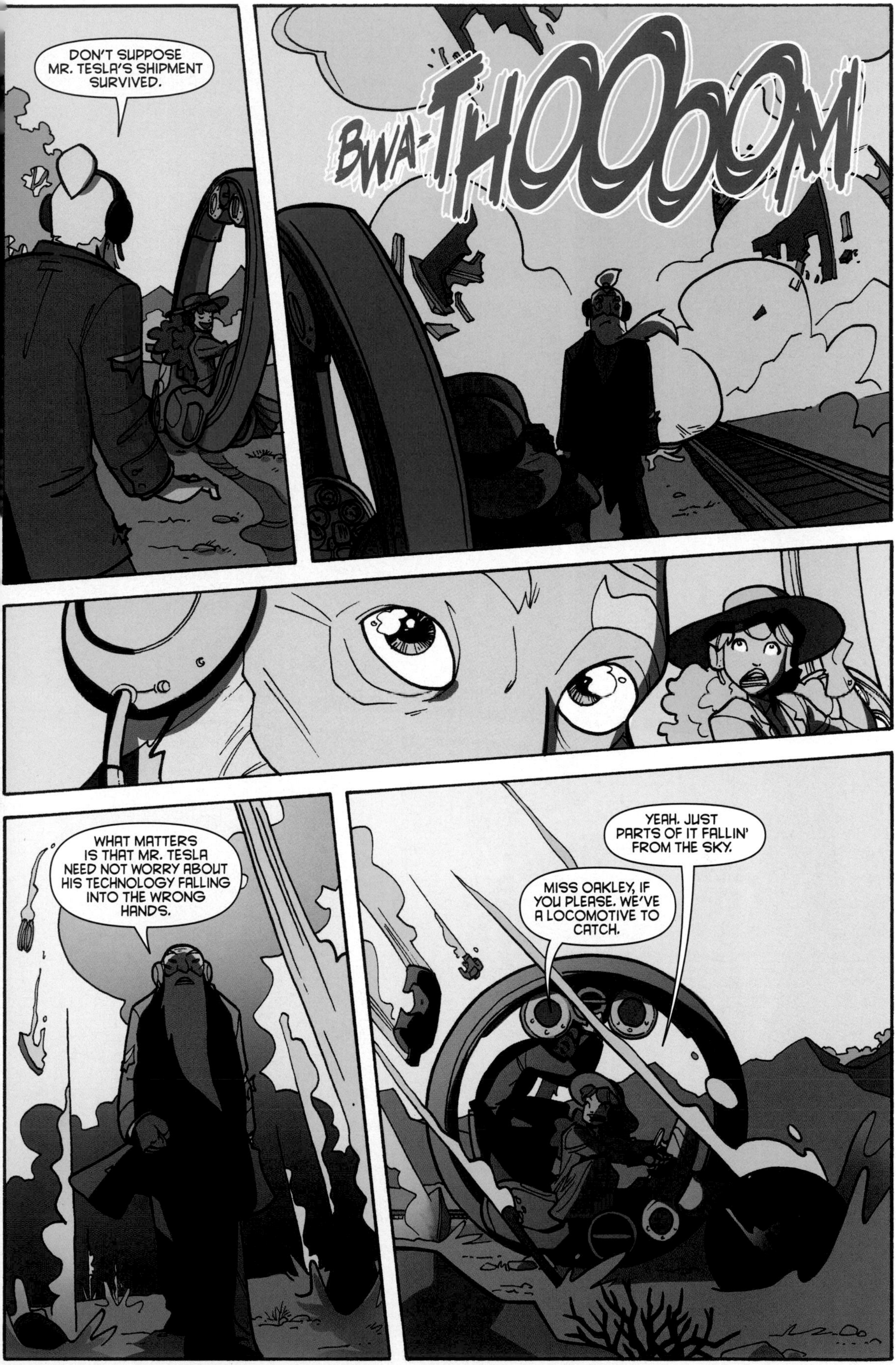
DON'T SUPPOSE MR. TESLA'S SHIPMENT SURVIVED.
BWA-THOOOOOM
WHAT MATTERS IS THAT MR. TESLA NEED NOT WORRY ABOUT HIS TECHNOLOGY FALLING INTO THE WRONG HANDS.
YEAH. JUST PARTS OF IT FALLIN' FROM THE SKY.
MISS OAKLEY, IF YOU PLEASE. WE'VE A LOCOMOTIVE TO CATCH.

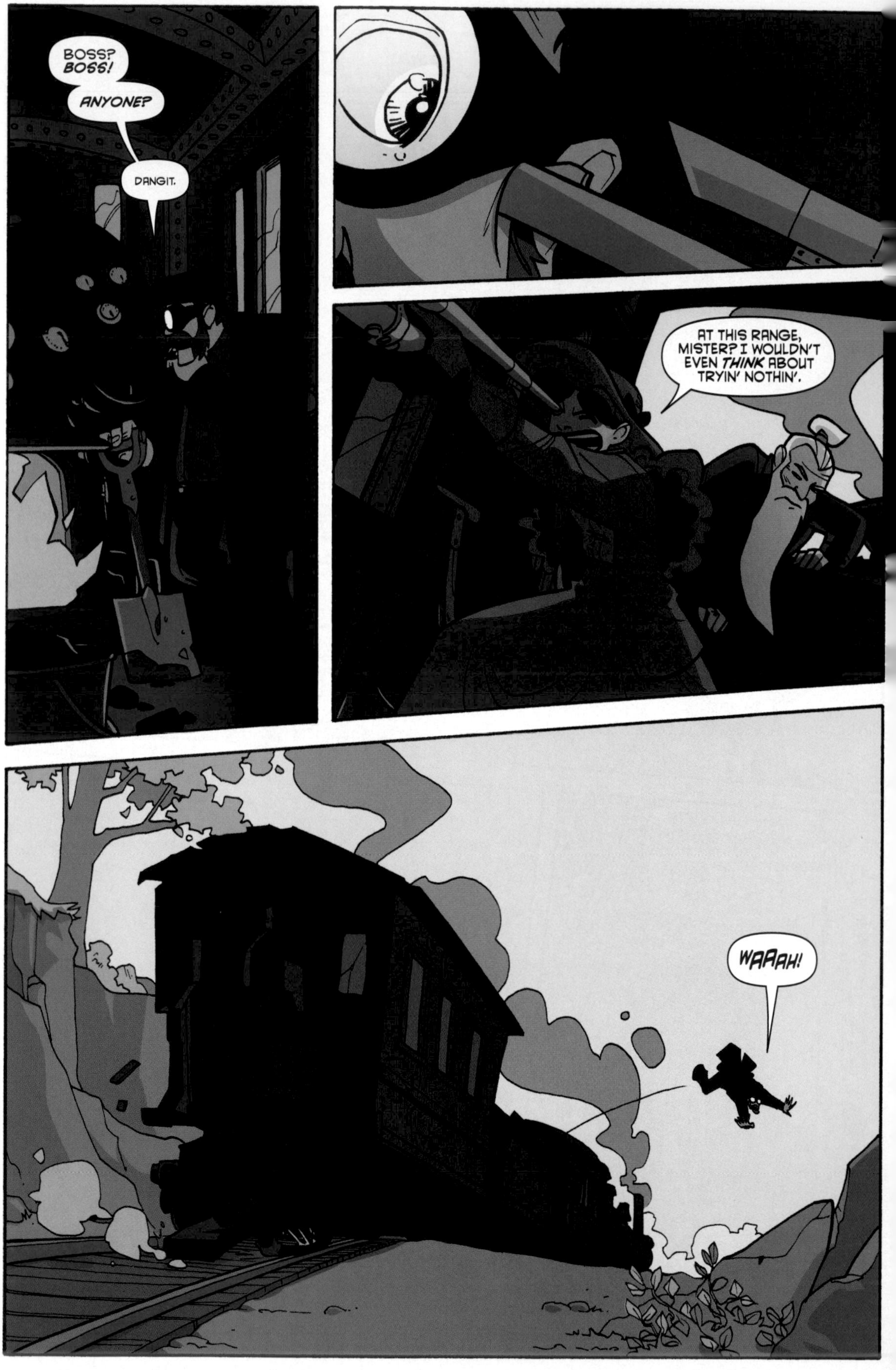
BOSS? BOSS!
ANYONE?
DANGIT.
AT THIS RANGE, MISTER? I WOULDN'T EVEN THINK ABOUT TRYIN' NOTHIN'.
WAAAH!

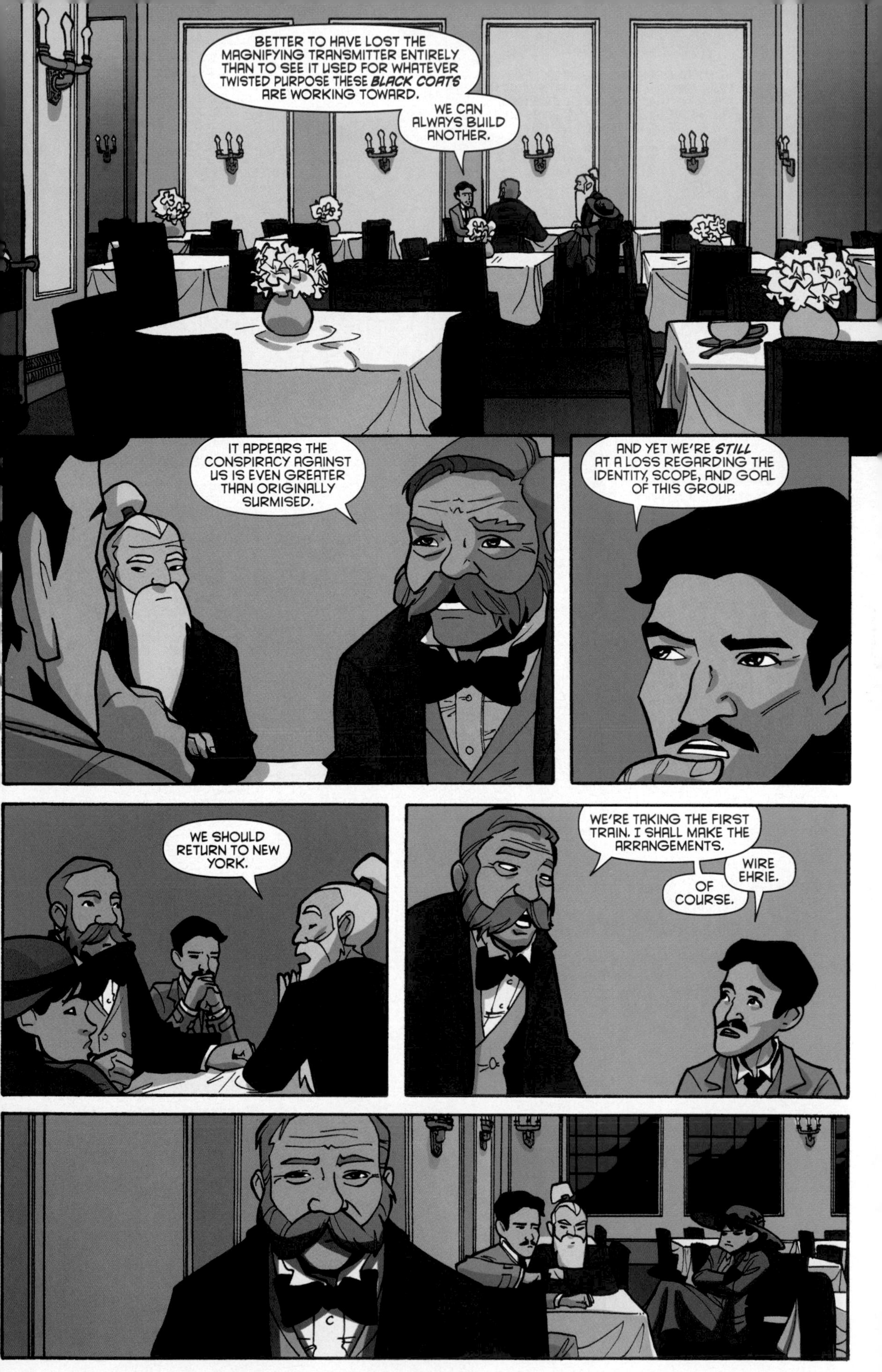
BETTER TO HAVE LOST THE MAGNIFYING TRANSMITTER ENTIRELY THAN TO SEE IT USED FOR WHATEVER TWISTED PURPOSE THESE *BLACK COATS* ARE WORKING TOWARD.
WE CAN ALWAYS BUILD ANOTHER.
IT APPEARS THE CONSPIRACY AGAINST US IS EVEN GREATER THAN ORIGINALLY SURMISED.
AND YET WE'RE *STILL* AT A LOSS REGARDING THE IDENTITY, SCOPE, AND GOAL OF THIS GROUP.
WE SHOULD RETURN TO NEW YORK.
WE'RE TAKING THE FIRST TRAIN. I SHALL MAKE THE ARRANGEMENTS.
OF COURSE.
WIRE EHRIE.

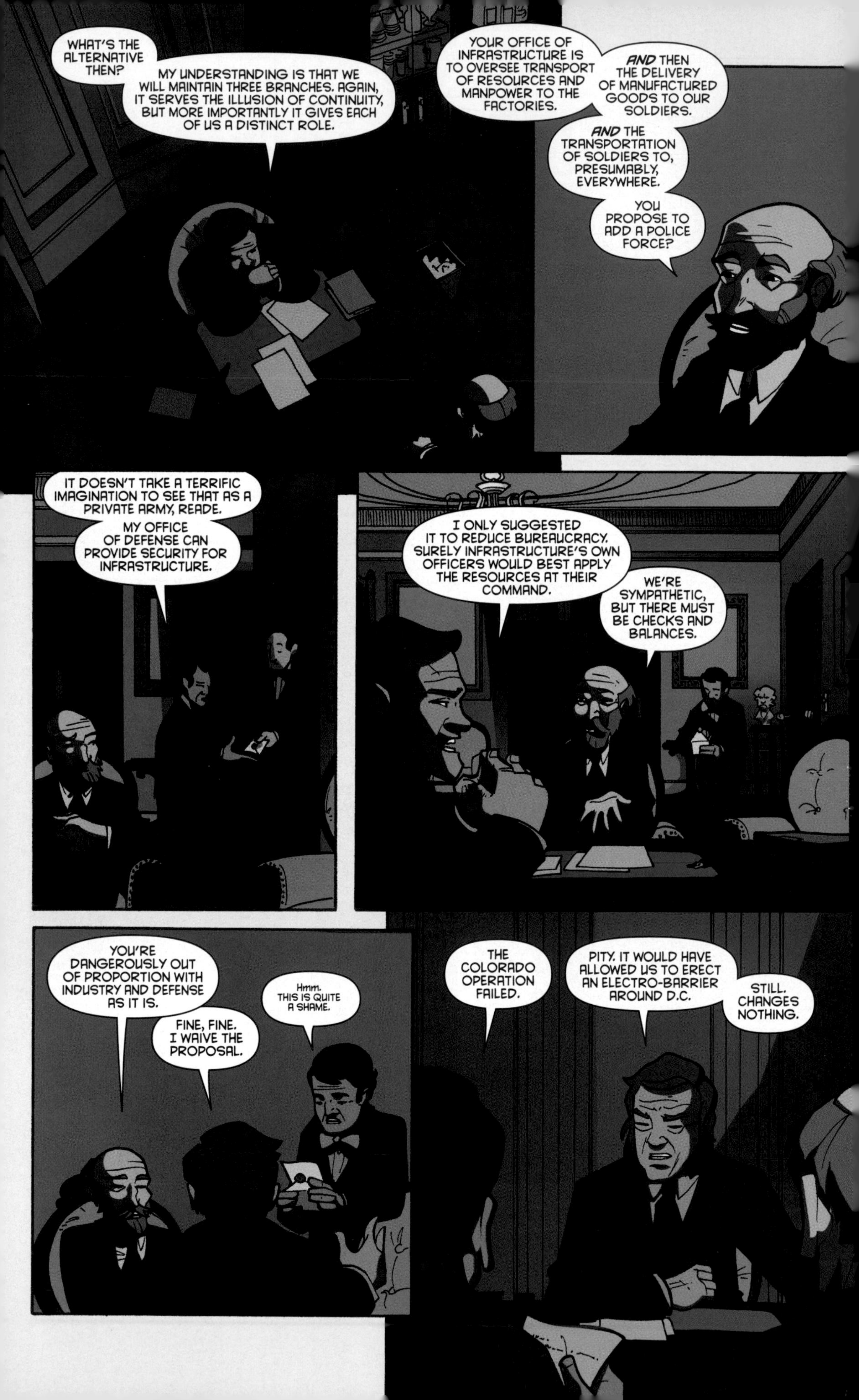
WHAT'S THE ALTERNATIVE THEN?
MY UNDERSTANDING IS THAT WE WILL MAINTAIN THREE BRANCHES. AGAIN, IT SERVES THE ILLUSION OF CONTINUITY, BUT MORE IMPORTANTLY IT GIVES EACH OF US A DISTINCT ROLE.
YOUR OFFICE OF INFRASTRUCTURE IS TO OVERSEE TRANSPORT OF RESOURCES AND MANPOWER TO THE FACTORIES.
AND THEN THE DELIVERY OF MANUFACTURED GOODS TO OUR SOLDIERS.
AND THE TRANSPORTATION OF SOLDIERS TO, PRESUMABLY, EVERYWHERE.
YOU PROPOSE TO ADD A POLICE FORCE?
IT DOESN'T TAKE A TERRIFIC IMAGINATION TO SEE THAT AS A PRIVATE ARMY, READE.
MY OFFICE OF DEFENSE CAN PROVIDE SECURITY FOR INFRASTRUCTURE.
I ONLY SUGGESTED IT TO REDUCE BUREAUCRACY. SURELY INFRASTRUCTURE'S OWN OFFICERS WOULD BEST APPLY THE RESOURCES AT THEIR COMMAND.
WE'RE SYMPATHETIC, BUT THERE MUST BE CHECKS AND BALANCES.
YOU'RE DANGEROUSLY OUT OF PROPORTION WITH INDUSTRY AND DEFENSE AS IT IS.
FINE, FINE. I WAIVE THE PROPOSAL.
Hmm. THIS IS QUITE A SHAME.
THE COLORADO OPERATION FAILED.
PITY. IT WOULD HAVE ALLOWED US TO ERECT AN ELECTRO-BARRIER AROUND D.C.
STILL. CHANGES NOTHING.

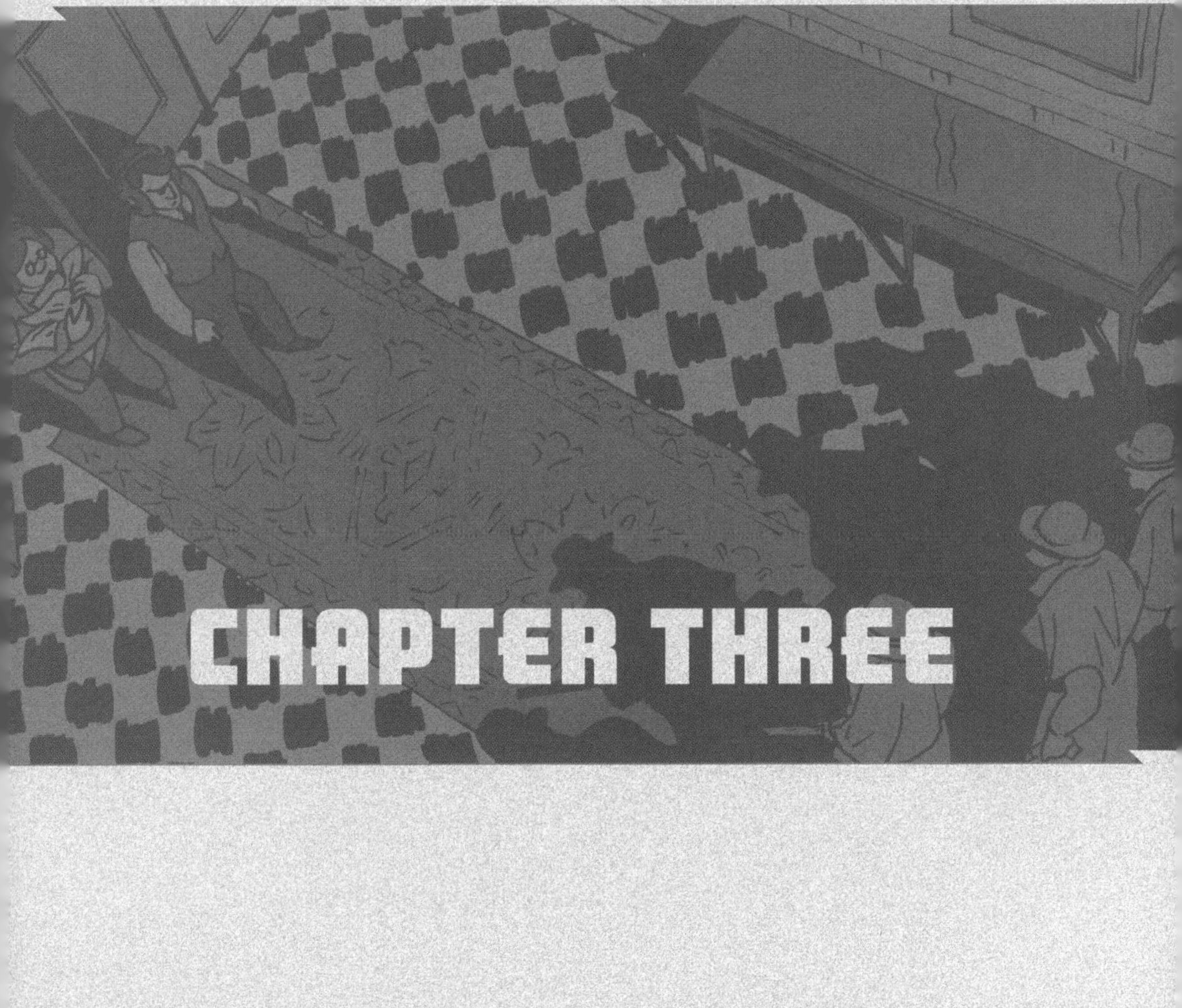

CHAPTER THREE

CLEVINGER
CODY
WAGNER

ATOMIC ROBO

HENDERSO
POWELL

PRESENTS

REAL SCIENCE ADVENTURES

No. 9 $2.75 U.S.

JUN

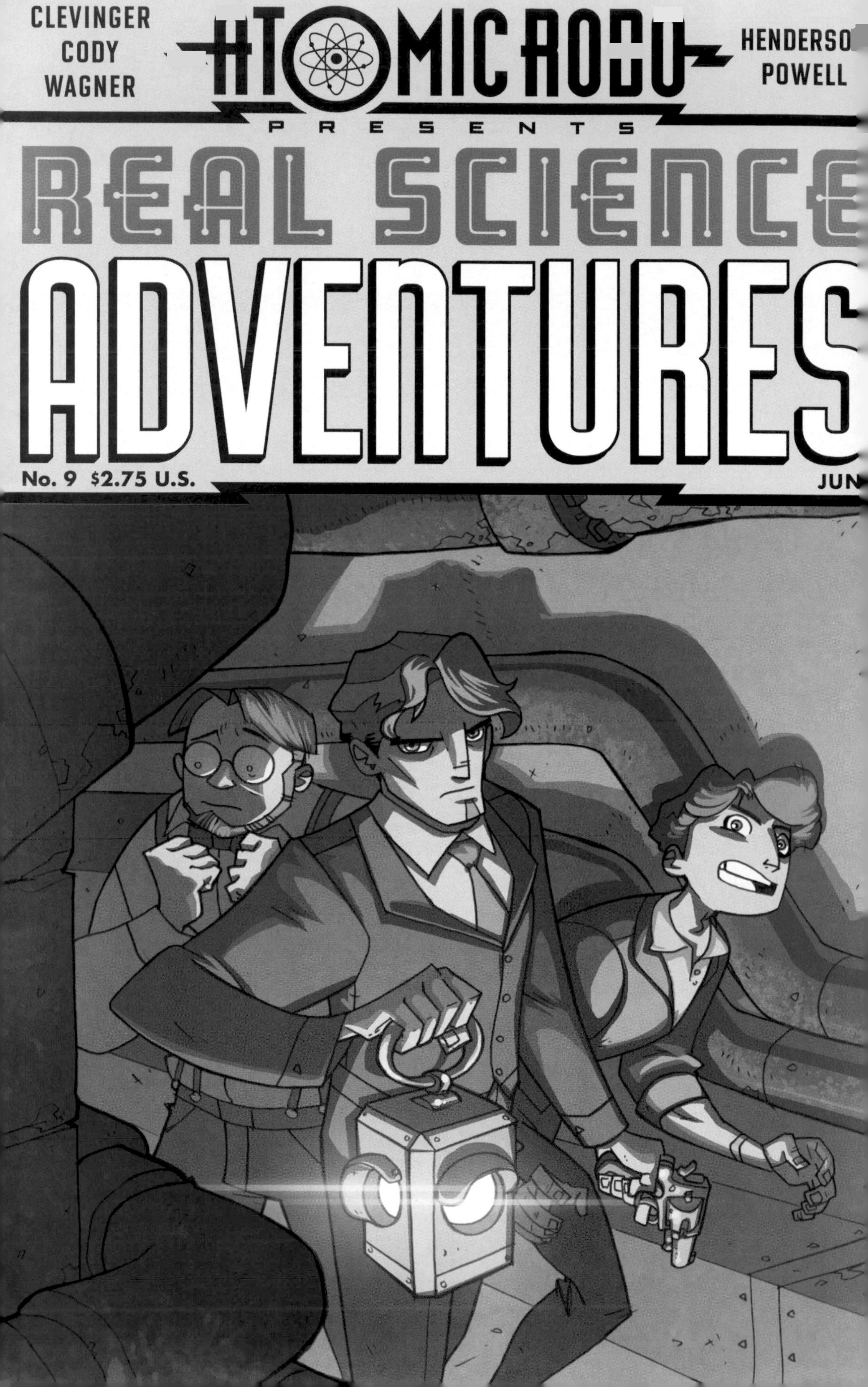

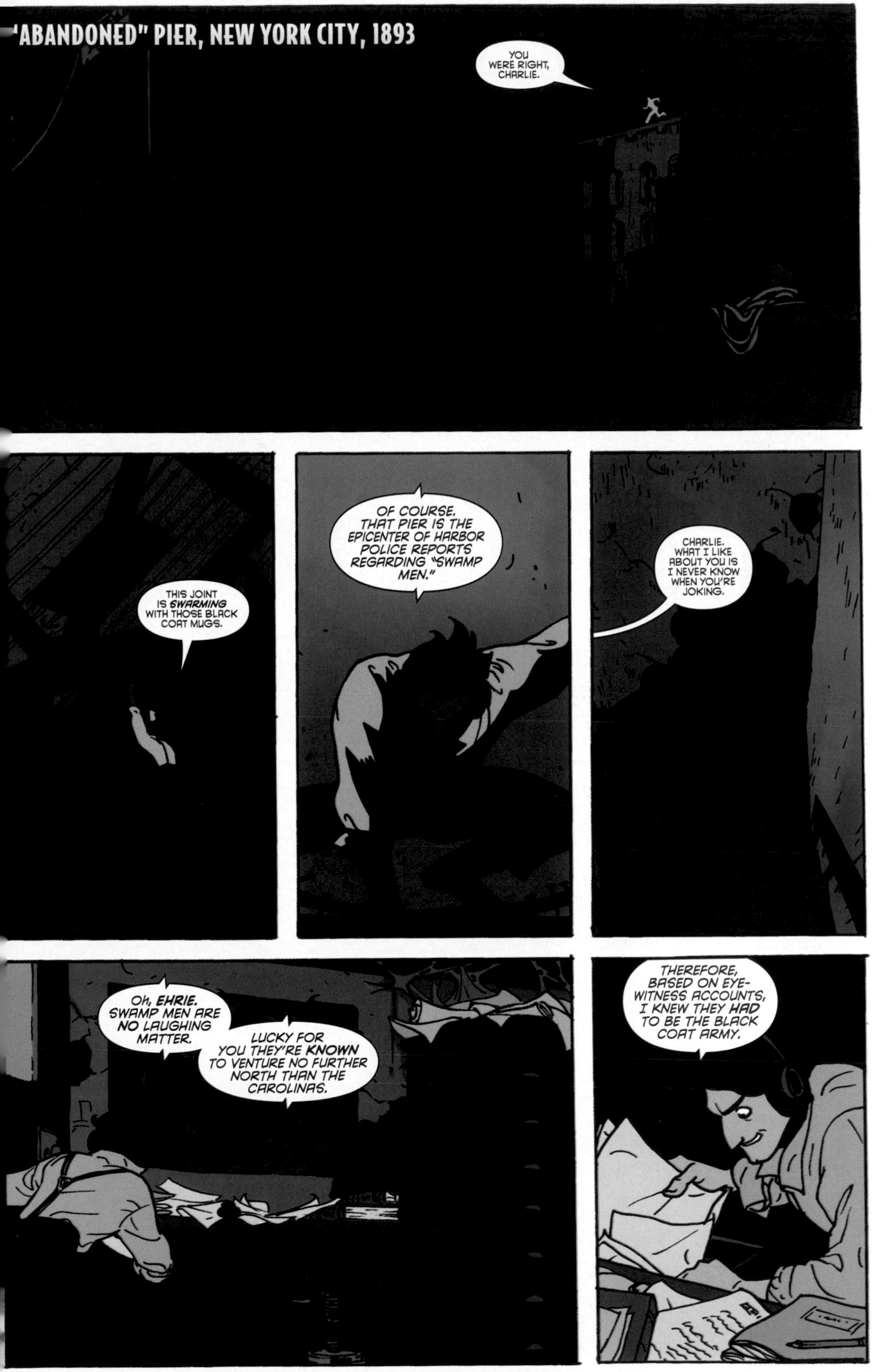
"ABANDONED" PIER, NEW YORK CITY, 1893
YOU WERE RIGHT, CHARLIE.
THIS JOINT IS SWARMING WITH THOSE BLACK COAT MUGS.
OF COURSE. THAT PIER IS THE EPICENTER OF HARBOR POLICE REPORTS REGARDING "SWAMP MEN."
CHARLIE. WHAT I LIKE ABOUT YOU IS I NEVER KNOW WHEN YOU'RE JOKING.
Oh, EHRIE. SWAMP MEN ARE NO LAUGHING MATTER.
LUCKY FOR YOU THEY'RE KNOWN TO VENTURE NO FURTHER NORTH THAN THE CAROLINAS.
THEREFORE, BASED ON EYE-WITNESS ACCOUNTS, I KNEW THEY HAD TO BE THE BLACK COAT ARMY.

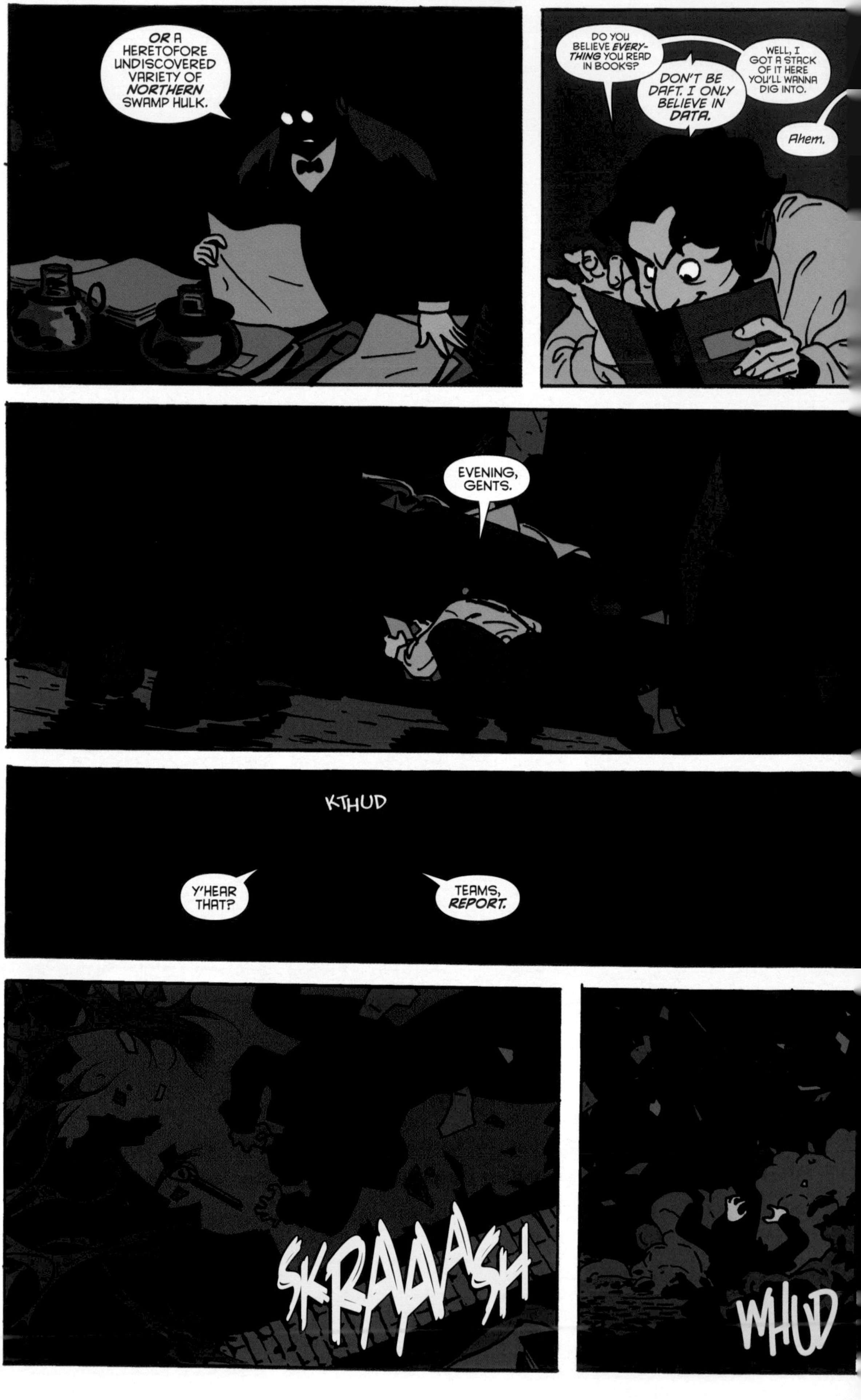
OR A HERETOFORE UNDISCOVERED VARIETY OF NORTHERN SWAMP HULK.
DO YOU BELIEVE EVERY-THING YOU READ IN BOOKS?
DON'T BE DAFT. I ONLY BELIEVE IN DATA.
WELL, I GOT A STACK OF IT HERE YOU'LL WANNA DIG INTO.
Ahem.
EVENING, GENTS.
KTHUD
Y'HEAR THAT?
TEAMS, REPORT.
SKRAAASH
WHUD

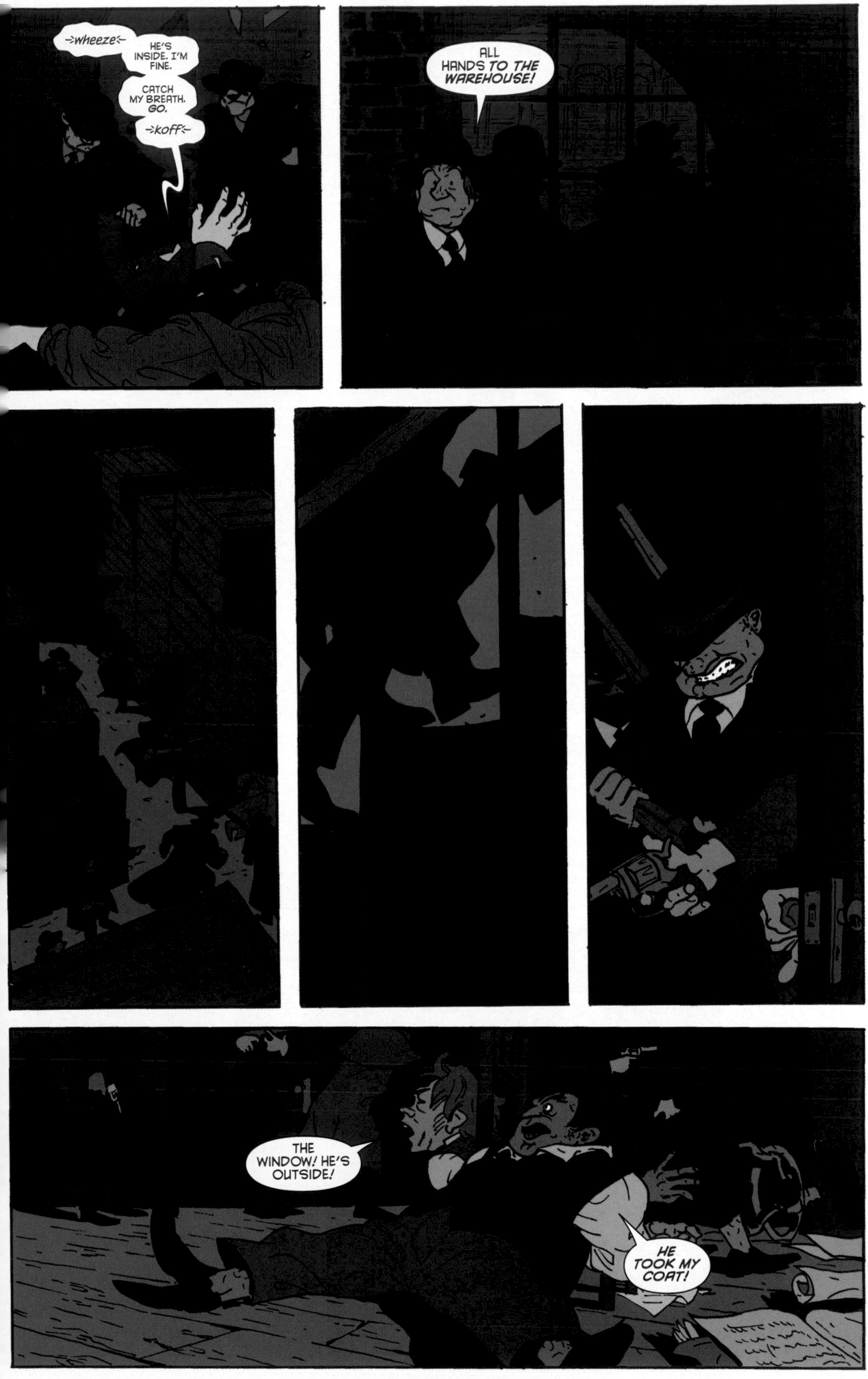

-wheeze-
HE'S INSIDE. I'M FINE.
CATCH MY BREATH. GO.
-koff-
ALL HANDS TO THE WAREHOUSE!
THE WINDOW! HE'S OUTSIDE!
HE TOOK MY COAT!

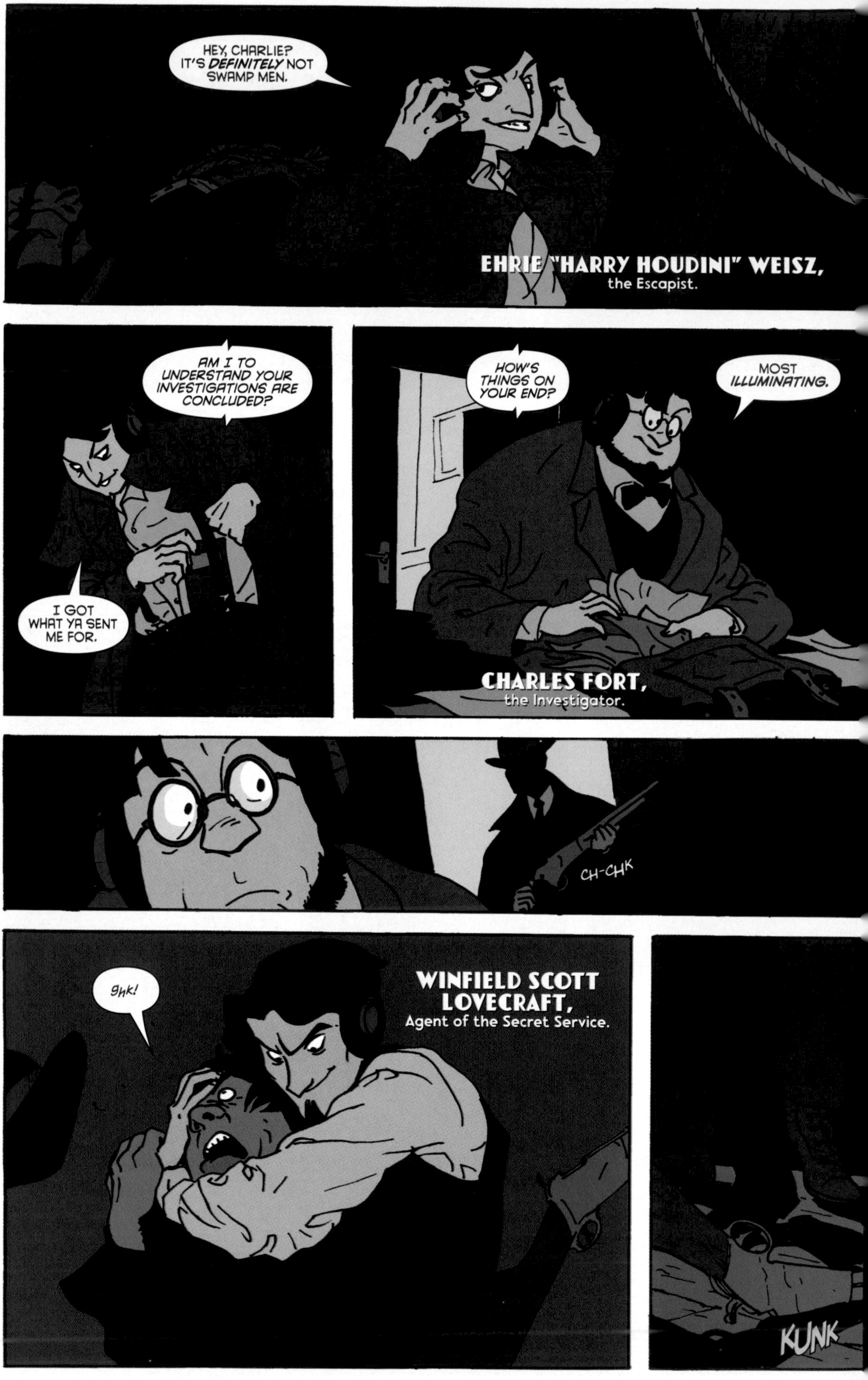
HEY, CHARLIE? IT'S DEFINITELY NOT SWAMP MEN.
EHRIE "HARRY HOUDINI" WEISZ, the Escapist.
AM I TO UNDERSTAND YOUR INVESTIGATIONS ARE CONCLUDED?
I GOT WHAT YA SENT ME FOR.
HOW'S THINGS ON YOUR END?
MOST ILLUMINATING.
CHARLES FORT, the Investigator.
CH-CHK
WINFIELD SCOTT LOVECRAFT, Agent of the Secret Service.
ghk!
KUNK

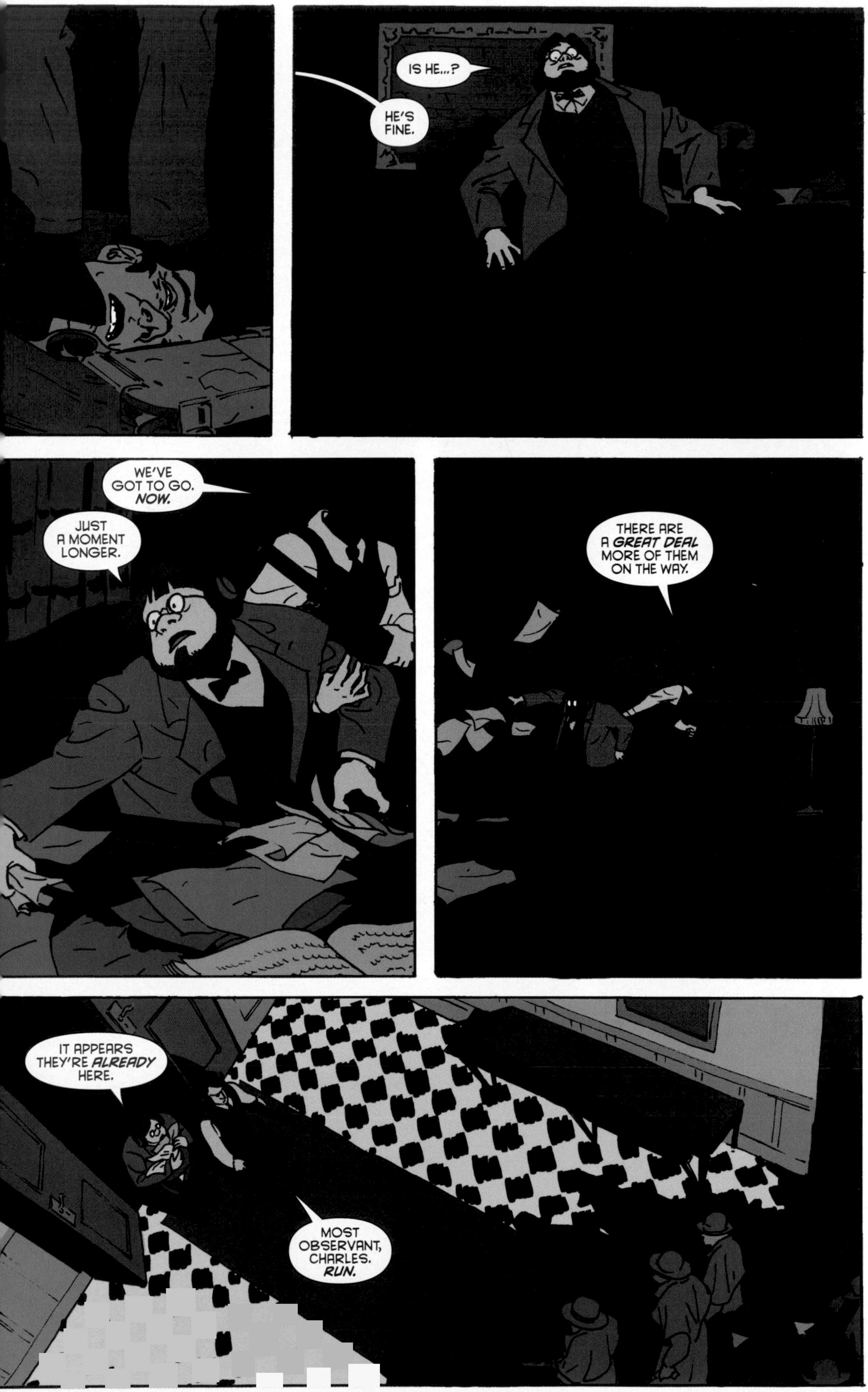
IS HE...?
HE'S FINE.
WE'VE GOT TO GO. *NOW.*
JUST A MOMENT LONGER.
THERE ARE A *GREAT DEAL* MORE OF THEM ON THE WAY.
IT APPEARS THEY'RE *ALREADY* HERE.
MOST OBSERVANT, CHARLES. *RUN.*

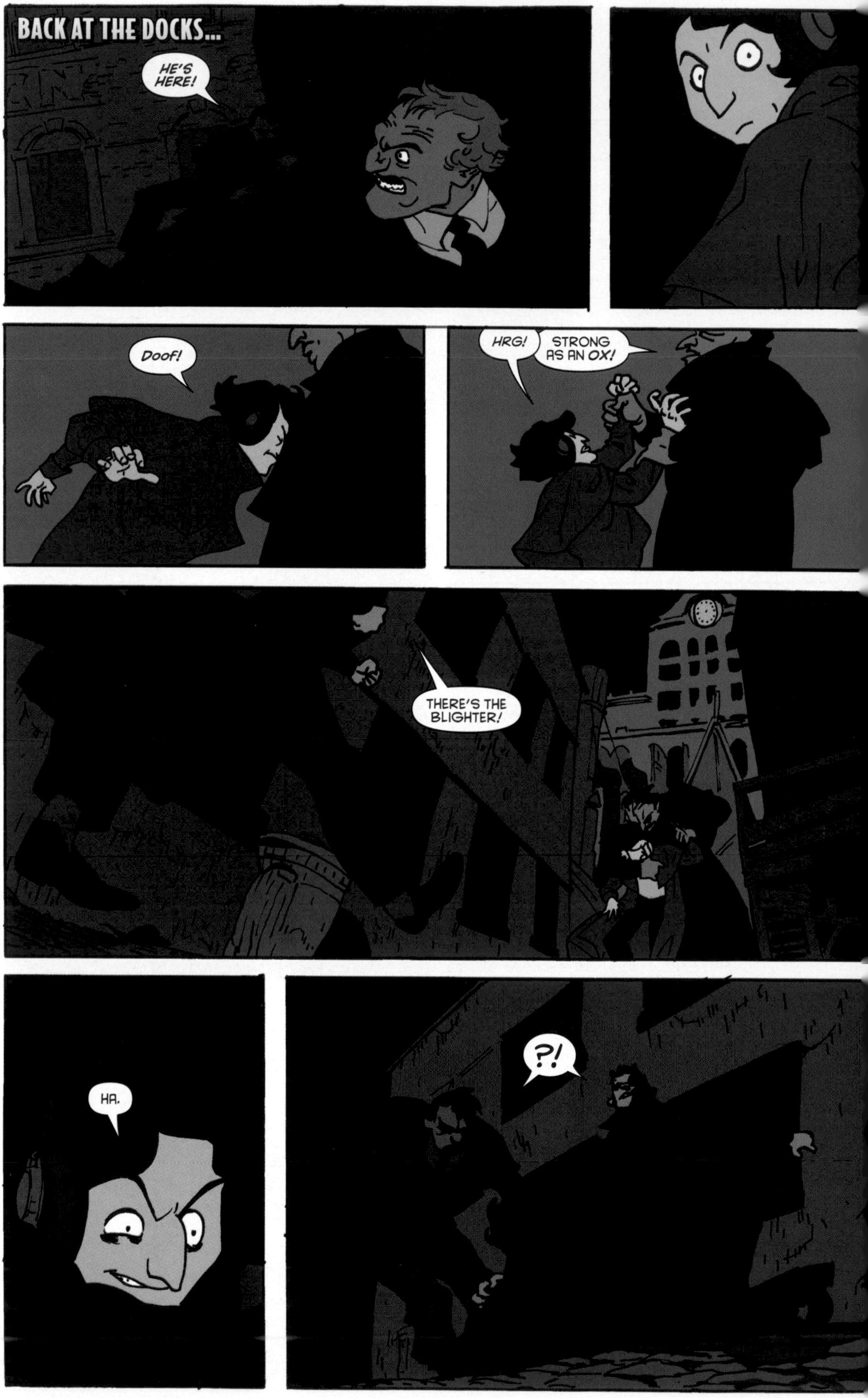
BACK AT THE DOCKS...
HE'S HERE!
Doof!
HRG!
STRONG AS AN OX!
THERE'S THE BLIGHTER!
HA.
?!

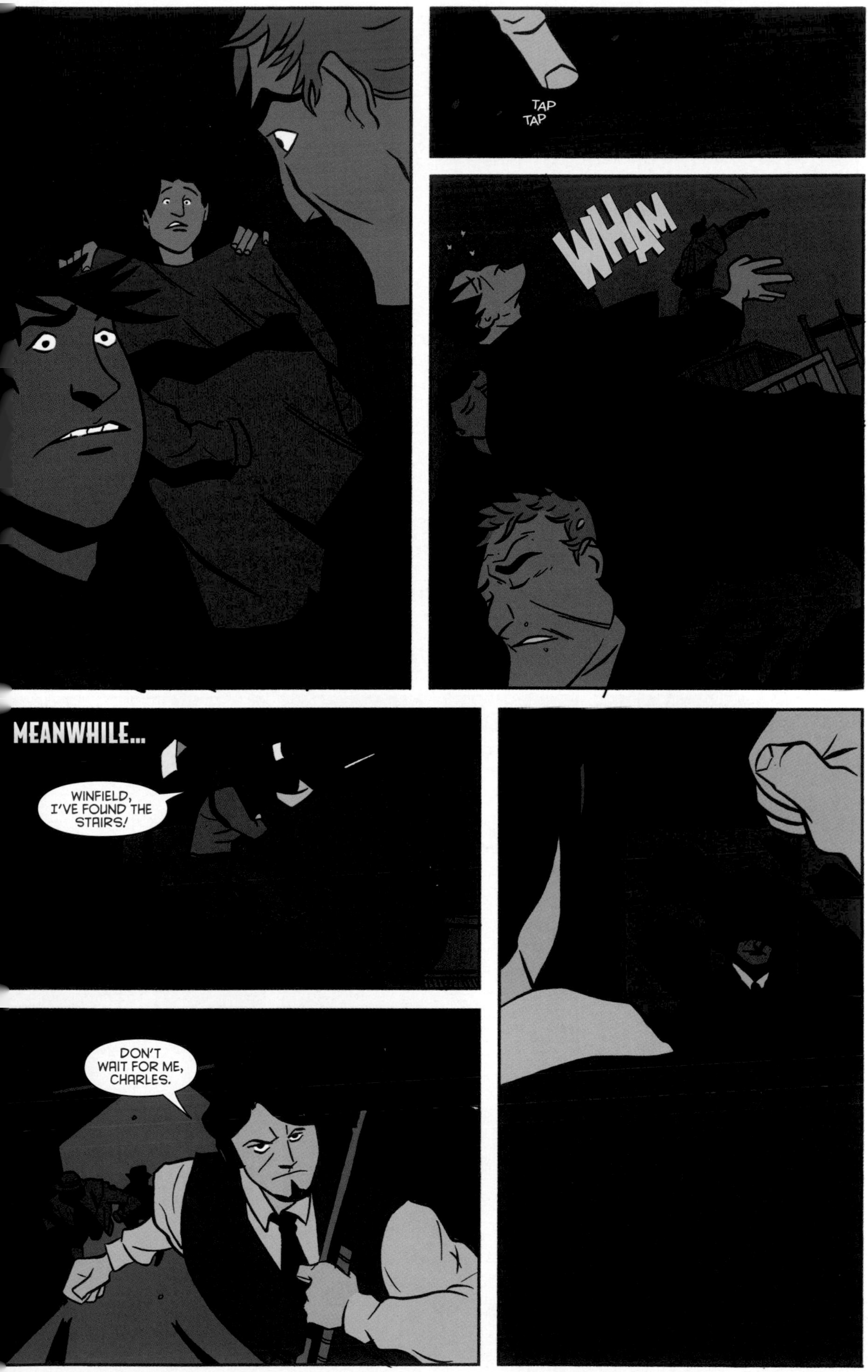
TAP
TAP
WHAM
MEANWHILE...
WINFIELD, I'VE FOUND THE STAIRS!
DON'T WAIT FOR ME, CHARLES.

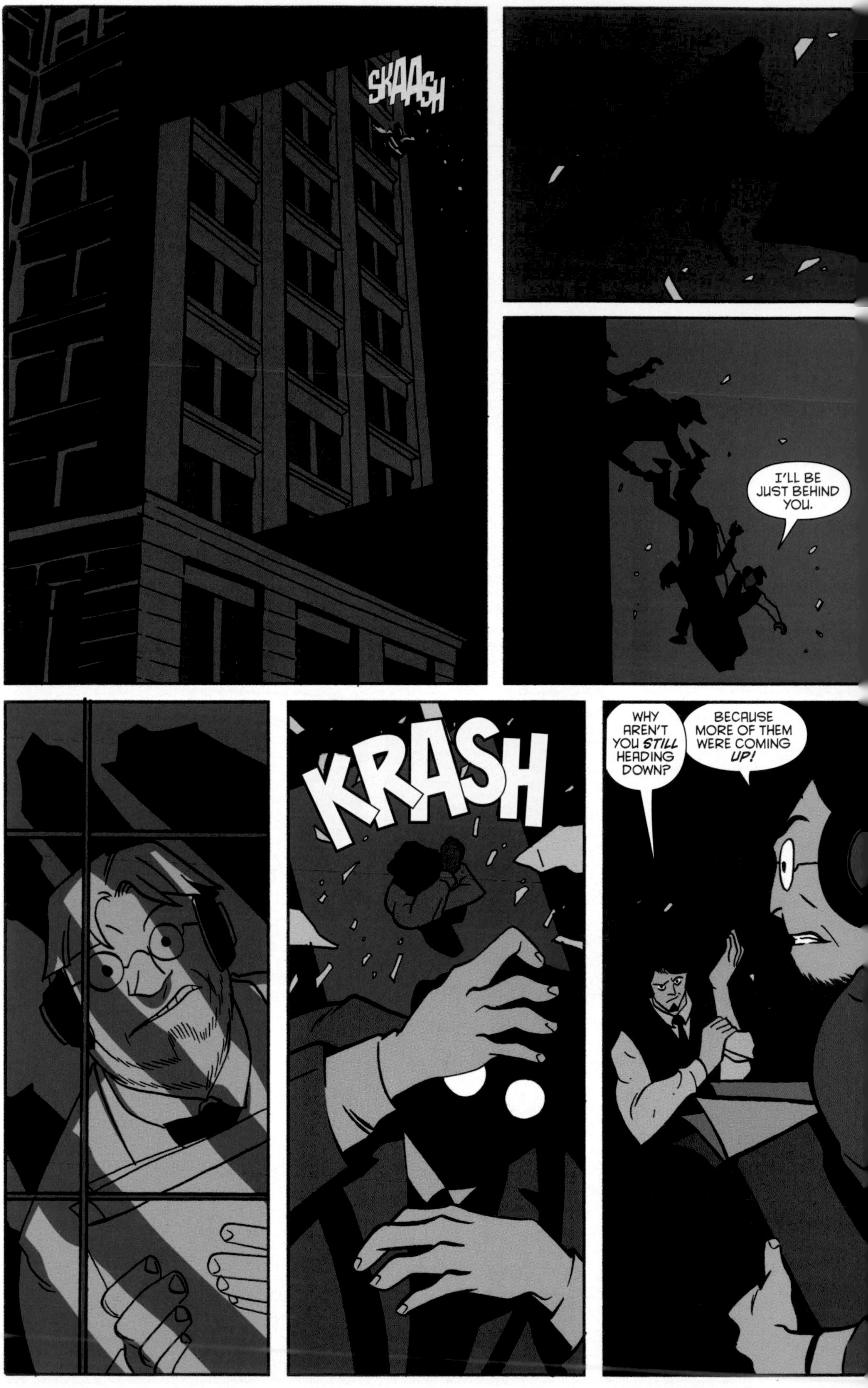
SKAASH
I'LL BE JUST BEHIND YOU.
KRASH
WHY AREN'T YOU STILL HEADING DOWN?
BECAUSE MORE OF THEM WERE COMING UP!

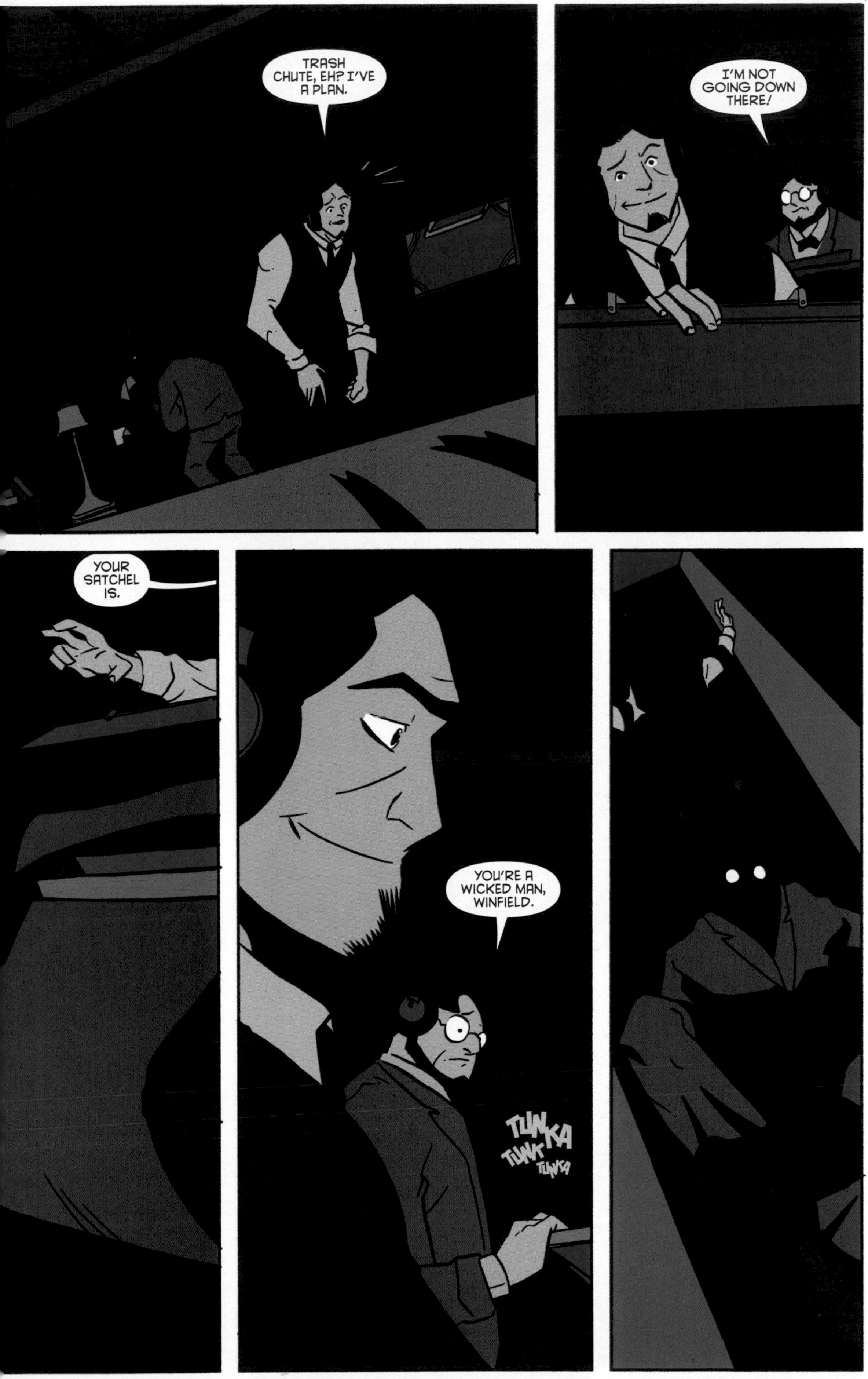
TRASH CHUTE, EH? I'VE A PLAN.
I'M NOT GOING DOWN THERE!
YOUR SATCHEL IS.
YOU'RE A WICKED MAN, WINFIELD.
TUNKA TUNK TUNKA

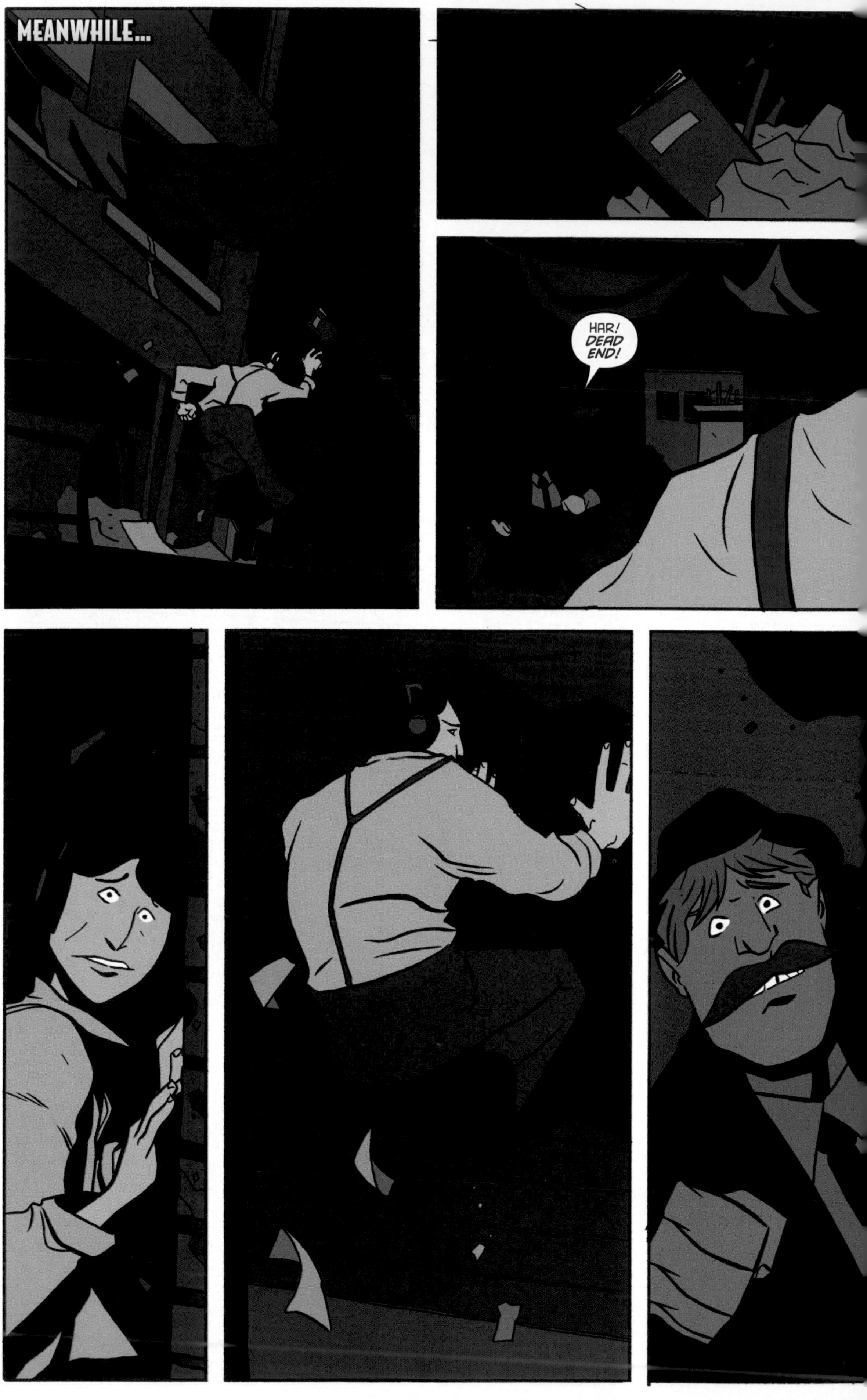
MEANWHILE...
HAR! DEAD END!

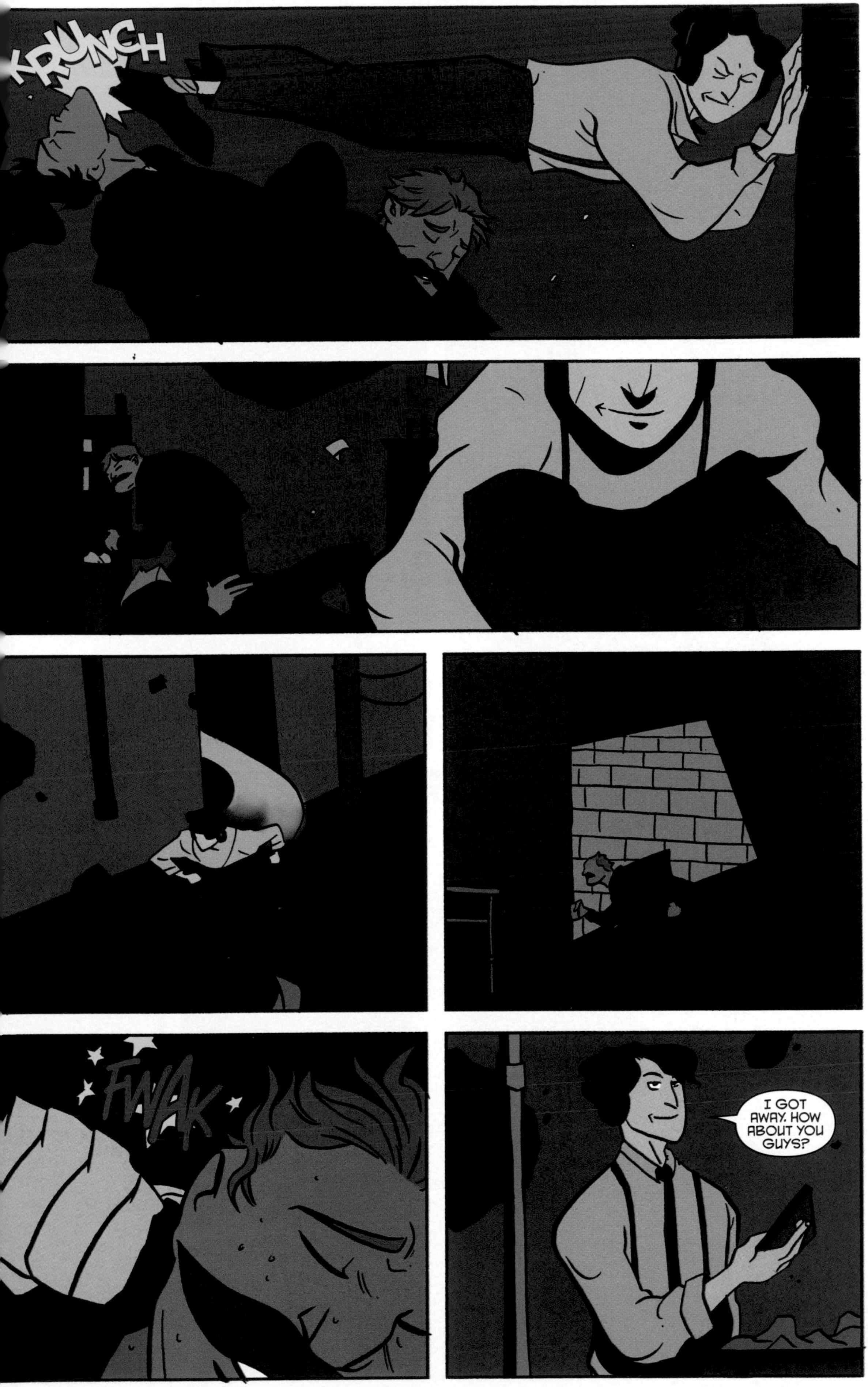
KRUNCH
FWAK
I GOT AWAY. HOW ABOUT YOU GUYS?

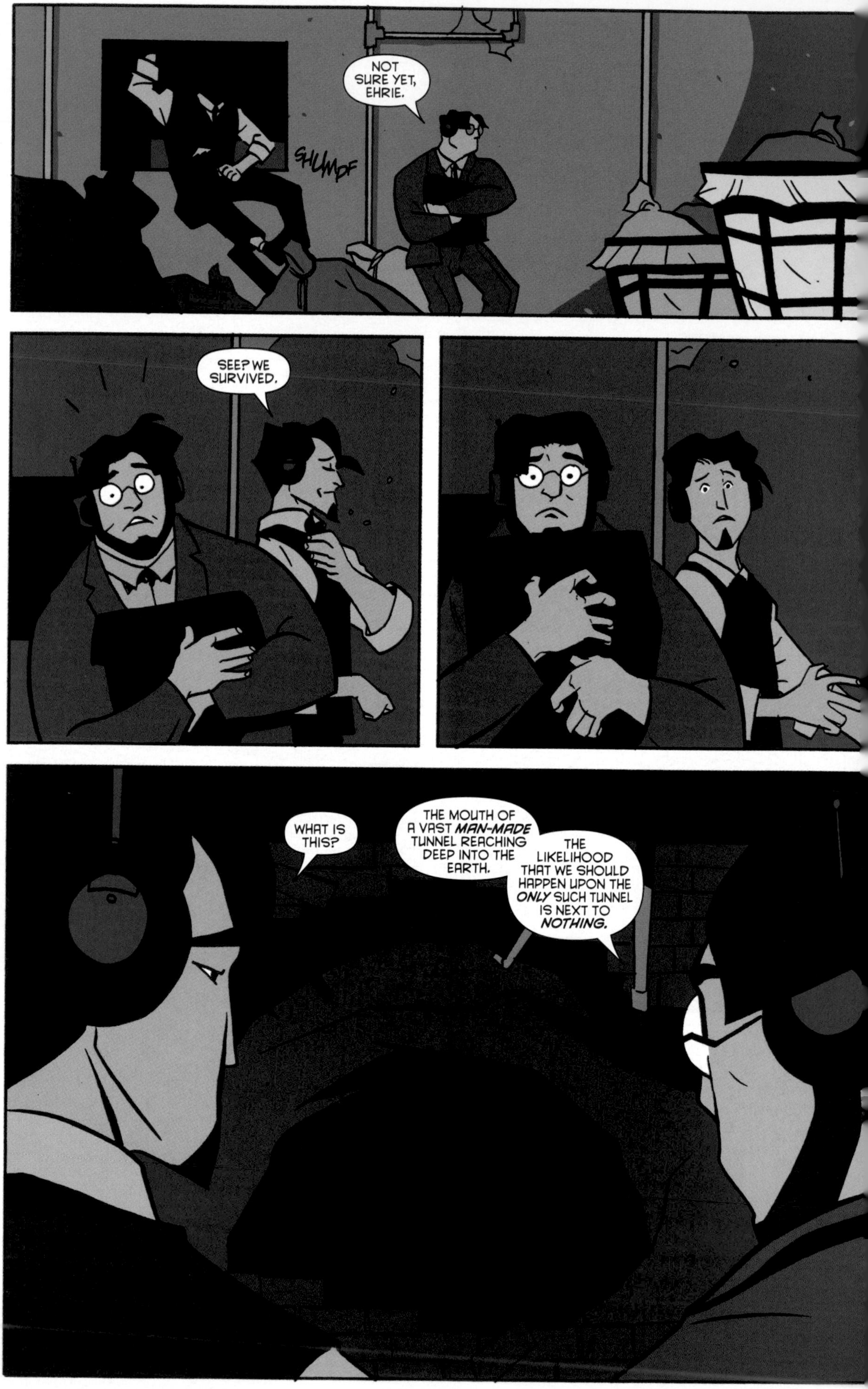
NOT SURE YET, EHRIE.
SHUMPF
SEE? WE SURVIVED.
WHAT IS THIS?
THE MOUTH OF A VAST MAN-MADE TUNNEL REACHING DEEP INTO THE EARTH.
THE LIKELIHOOD THAT WE SHOULD HAPPEN UPON THE ONLY SUCH TUNNEL IS NEXT TO NOTHING.

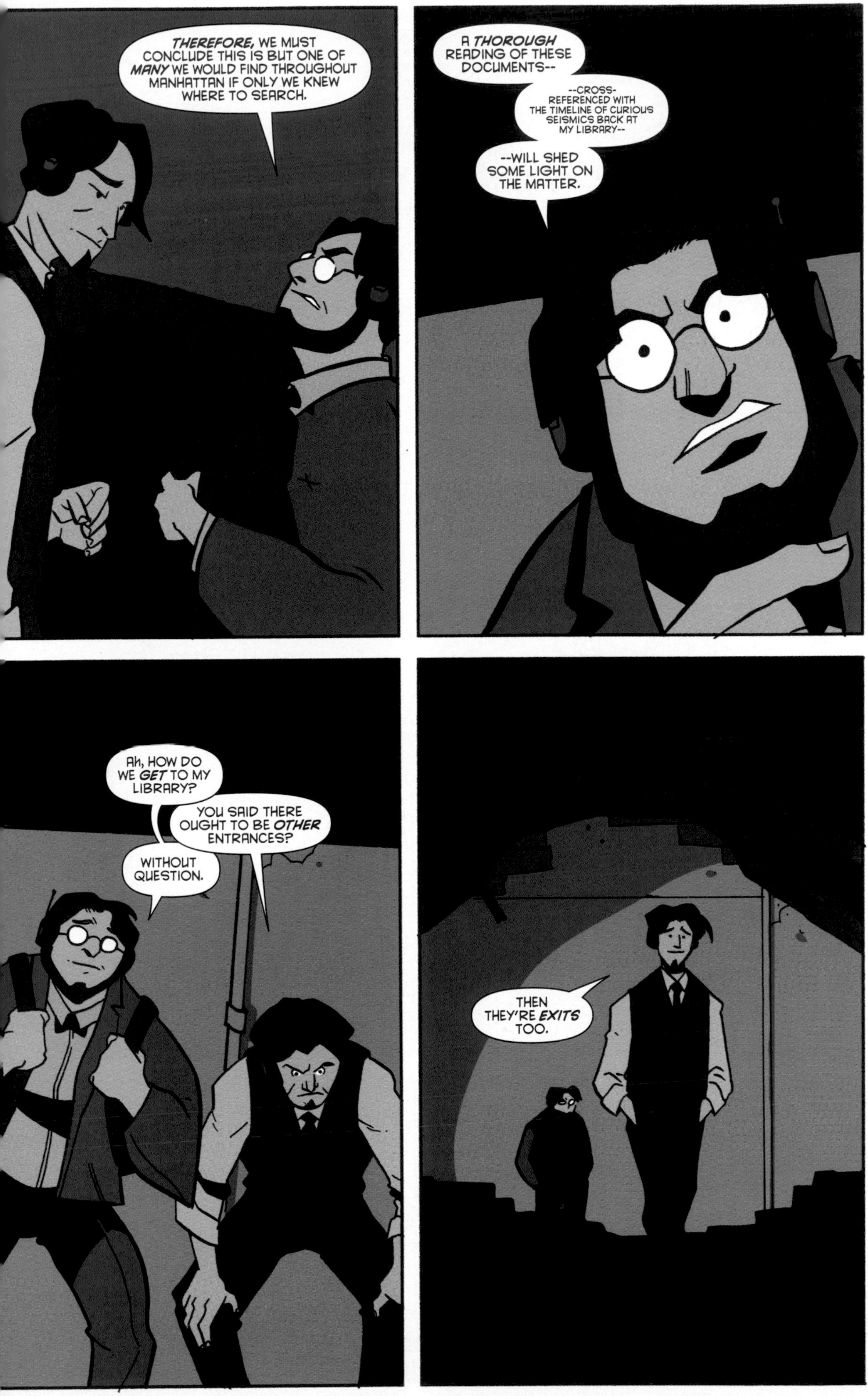
THEREFORE, WE MUST CONCLUDE THIS IS BUT ONE OF MANY WE WOULD FIND THROUGHOUT MANHATTAN IF ONLY WE KNEW WHERE TO SEARCH.
A THOROUGH READING OF THESE DOCUMENTS--
--CROSS-REFERENCED WITH THE TIMELINE OF CURIOUS SEISMICS BACK AT MY LIBRARY--
--WILL SHED SOME LIGHT ON THE MATTER.
Ah, HOW DO WE GET TO MY LIBRARY?
YOU SAID THERE OUGHT TO BE OTHER ENTRANCES?
WITHOUT QUESTION.
THEN THEY'RE EXITS TOO.

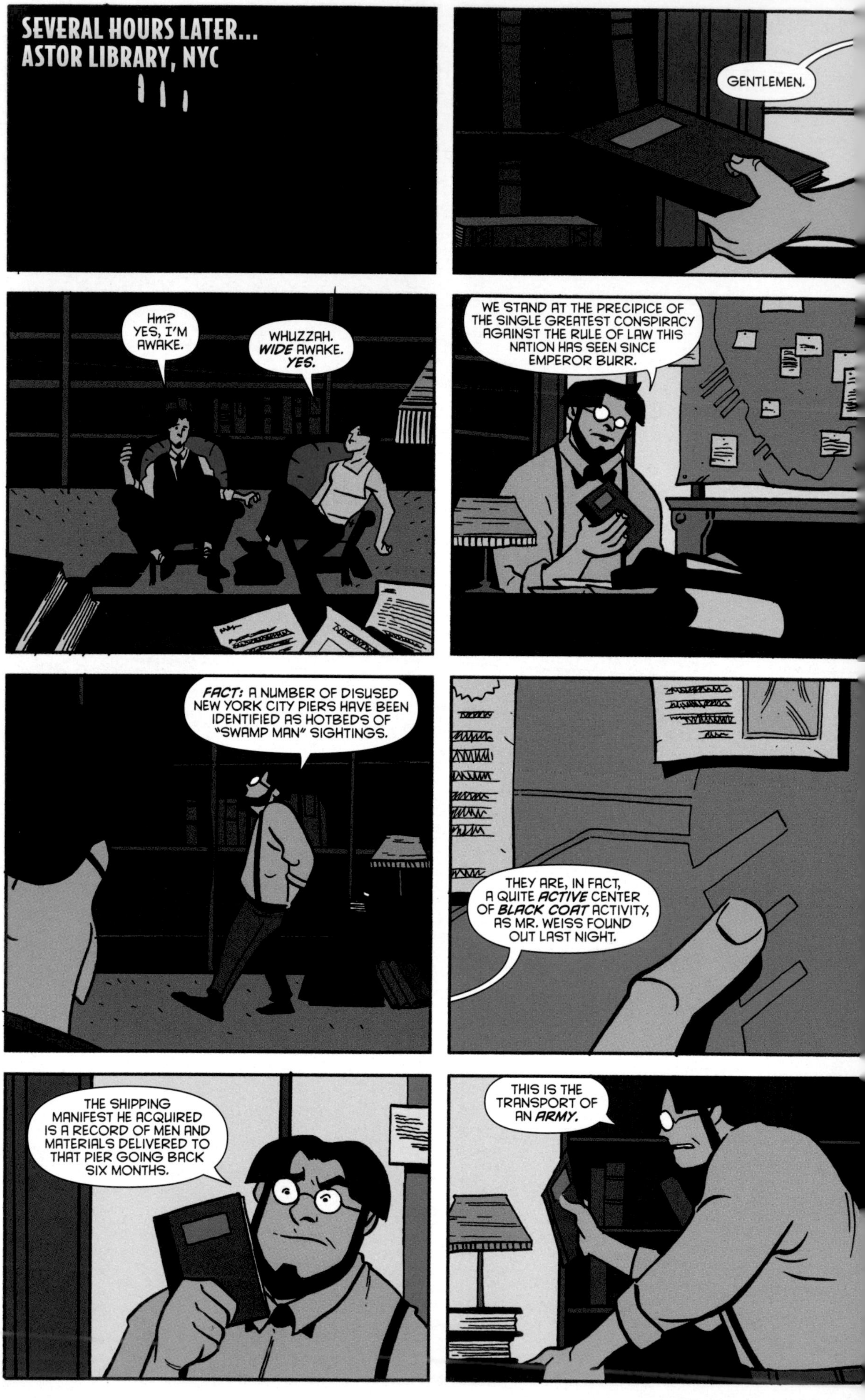

SEVERAL HOURS LATER...
ASTOR LIBRARY, NYC
GENTLEMEN.
Hm? YES, I'M AWAKE.
WHUZZAH. *WIDE* AWAKE. *YES.*
WE STAND AT THE PRECIPICE OF THE SINGLE GREATEST CONSPIRACY AGAINST THE RULE OF LAW THIS NATION HAS SEEN SINCE EMPEROR BURR.
FACT: A NUMBER OF DISUSED NEW YORK CITY PIERS HAVE BEEN IDENTIFIED AS HOTBEDS OF "SWAMP MAN" SIGHTINGS.
THEY ARE, IN FACT, A QUITE *ACTIVE* CENTER OF *BLACK COAT* ACTIVITY, AS MR. WEISS FOUND OUT LAST NIGHT.
THE SHIPPING MANIFEST HE ACQUIRED IS A RECORD OF MEN AND MATERIALS DELIVERED TO THAT PIER GOING BACK SIX MONTHS.
THIS IS THE TRANSPORT OF AN *ARMY.*

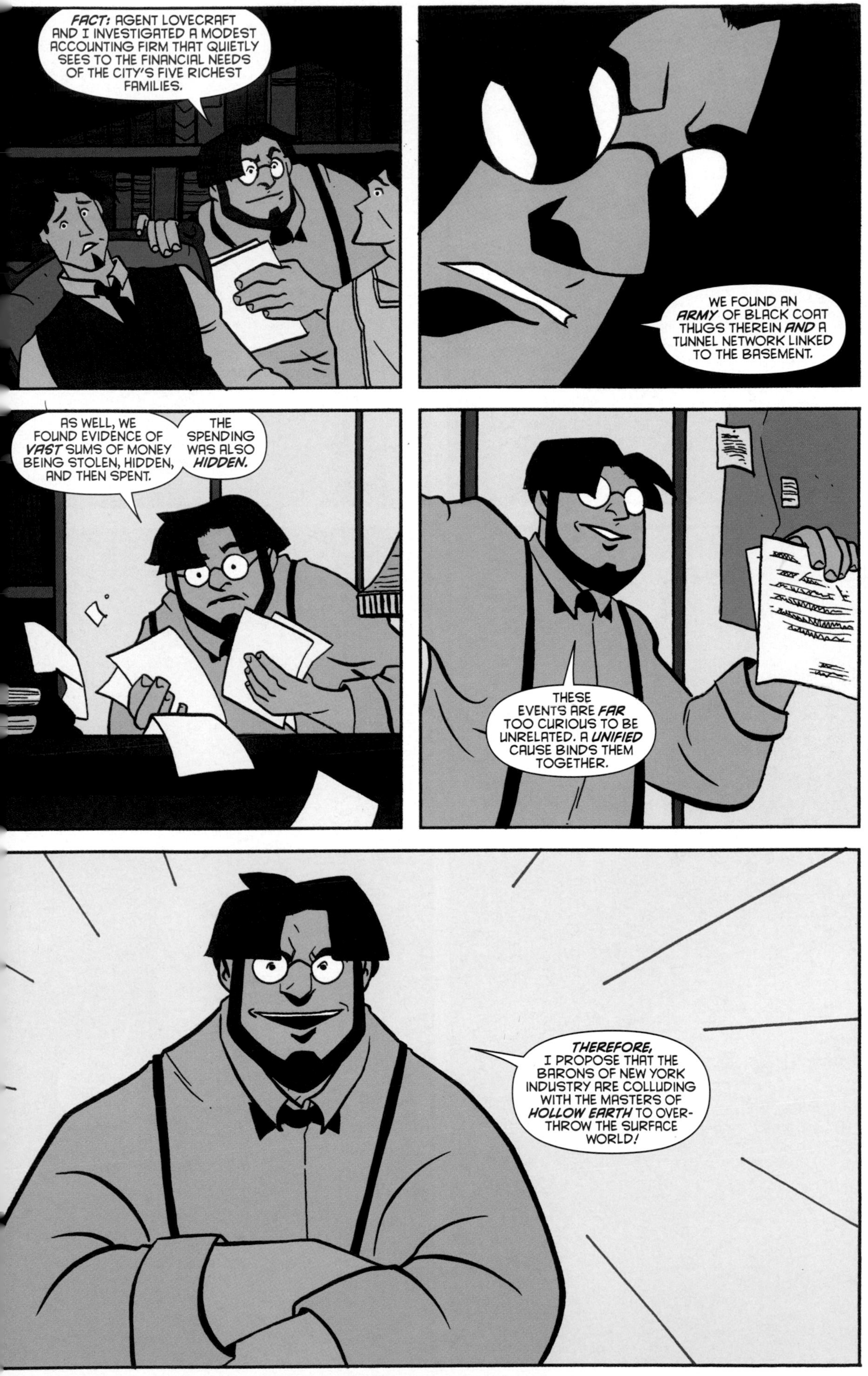

FACT: AGENT LOVECRAFT AND I INVESTIGATED A MODEST ACCOUNTING FIRM THAT QUIETLY SEES TO THE FINANCIAL NEEDS OF THE CITY'S FIVE RICHEST FAMILIES.
WE FOUND AN ARMY OF BLACK COAT THUGS THEREIN AND A TUNNEL NETWORK LINKED TO THE BASEMENT.
AS WELL, WE FOUND EVIDENCE OF VAST SUMS OF MONEY BEING STOLEN, HIDDEN, AND THEN SPENT.
THE SPENDING WAS ALSO HIDDEN.
THESE EVENTS ARE FAR TOO CURIOUS TO BE UNRELATED. A UNIFIED CAUSE BINDS THEM TOGETHER.
THEREFORE, I PROPOSE THAT THE BARONS OF NEW YORK INDUSTRY ARE COLLUDING WITH THE MASTERS OF HOLLOW EARTH TO OVER-THROW THE SURFACE WORLD!

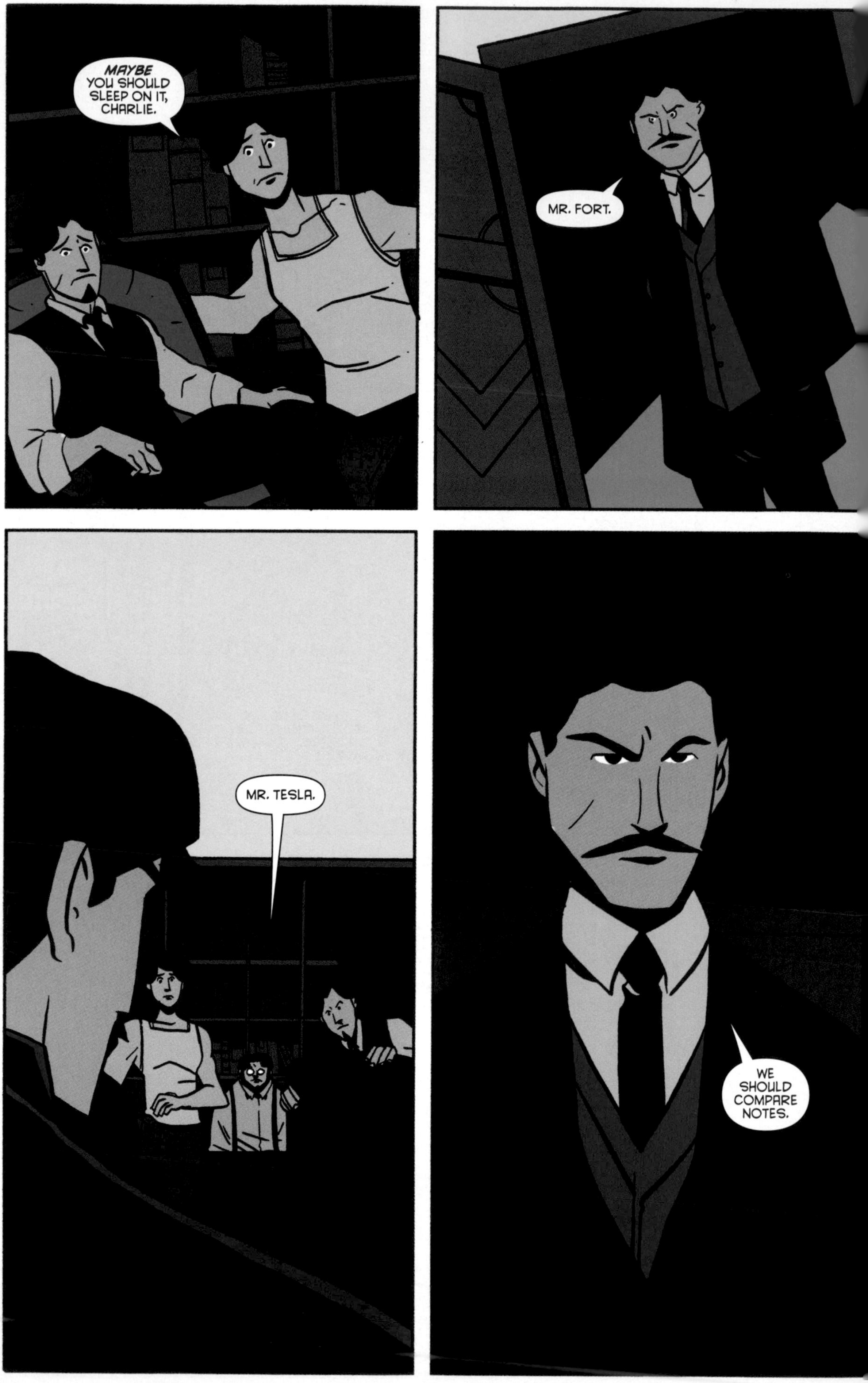
MAYBE YOU SHOULD SLEEP ON IT, CHARLIE.
MR. FORT.
MR. TESLA.
WE SHOULD COMPARE NOTES.

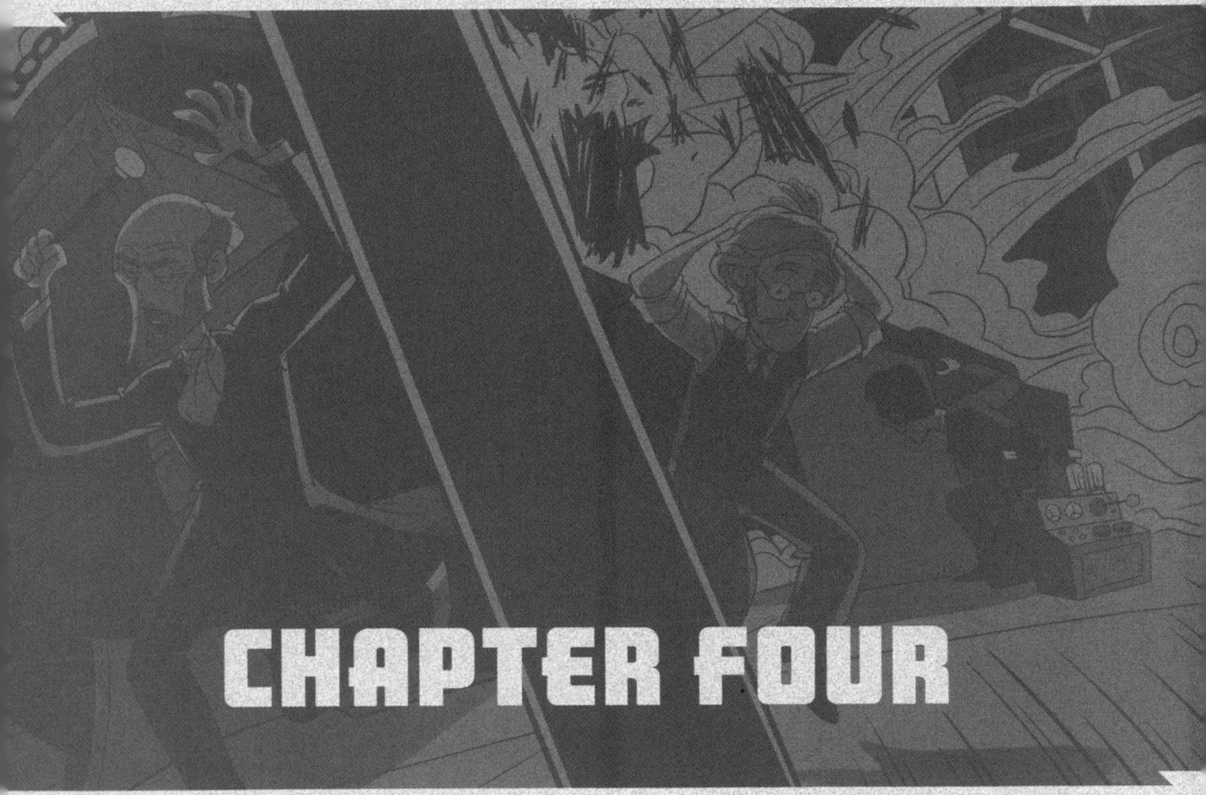

CHAPTER FOUR

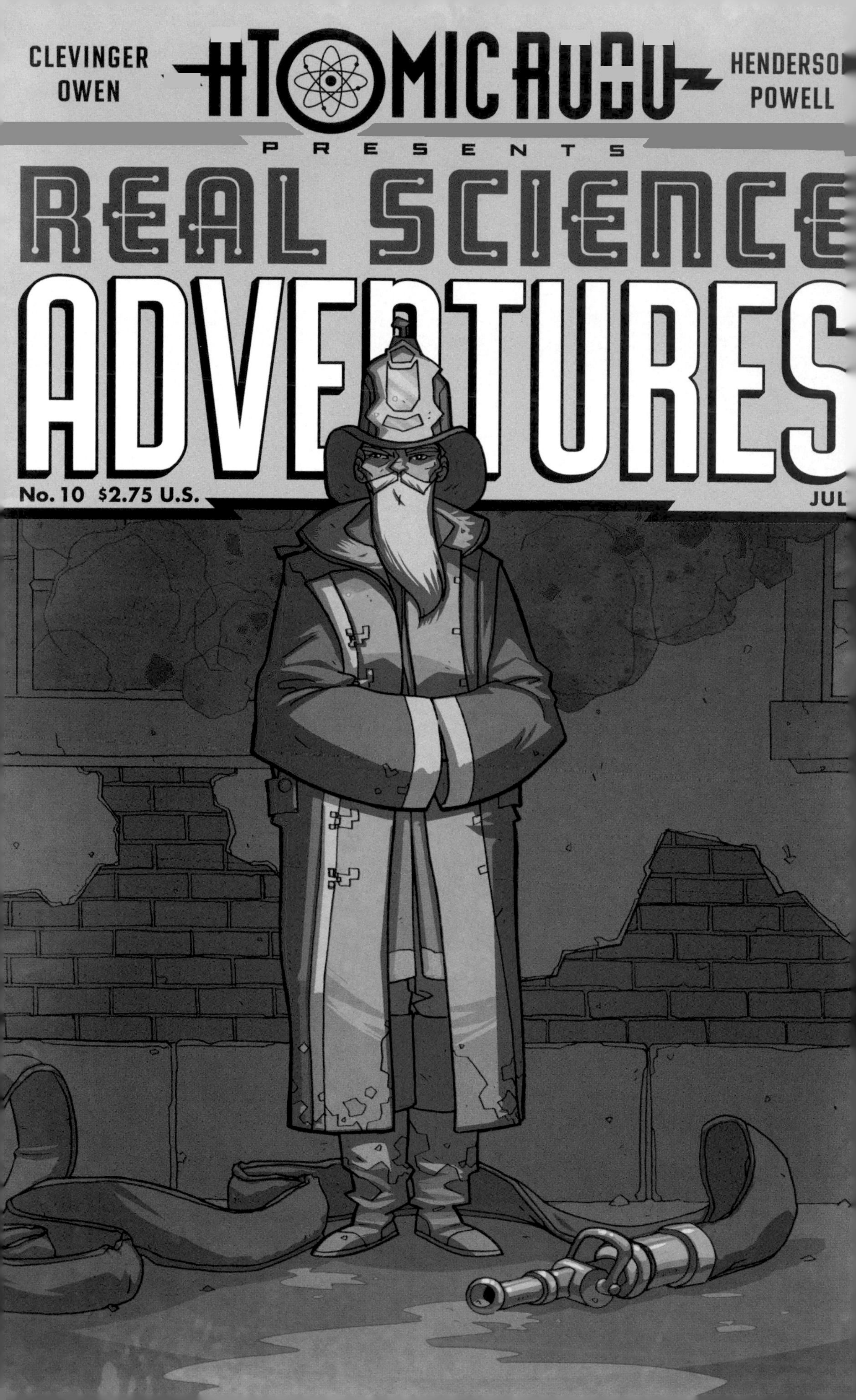
CLEVINGER
OWEN
HENDERSO
POWELL
PRESENTS
REAL SCIENCE
ADVENTURES
No. 10 $2.75 U.S.
JUL

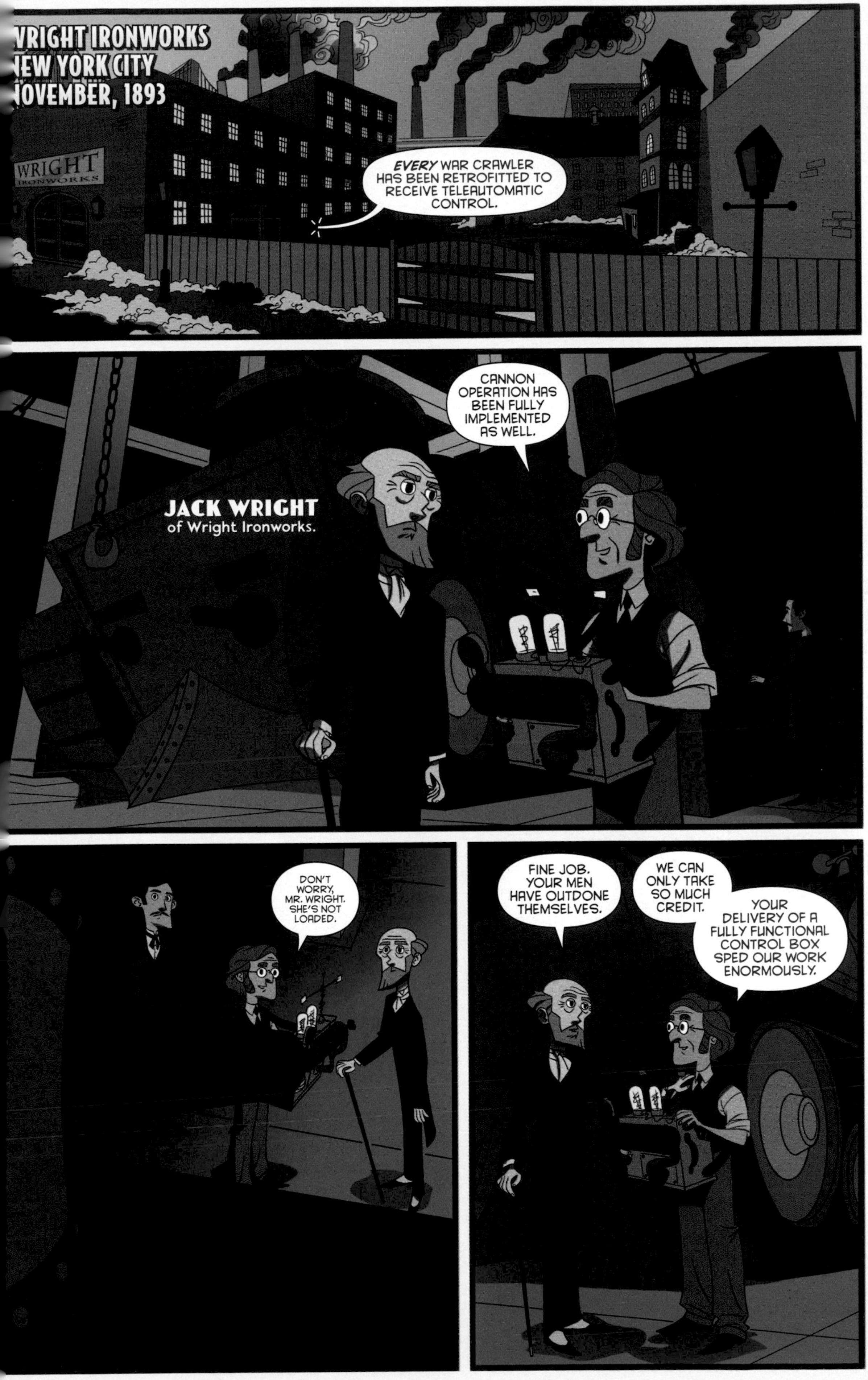
WRIGHT IRONWORKS
NEW YORK CITY
NOVEMBER, 1893
WRIGHT IRONWORKS
EVERY WAR CRAWLER HAS BEEN RETROFITTED TO RECEIVE TELEAUTOMATIC CONTROL.
CANNON OPERATION HAS BEEN FULLY IMPLEMENTED AS WELL.
JACK WRIGHT
of Wright Ironworks.
DON'T WORRY, MR. WRIGHT. SHE'S NOT LOADED.
FINE JOB. YOUR MEN HAVE OUTDONE THEMSELVES.
WE CAN ONLY TAKE SO MUCH CREDIT.
YOUR DELIVERY OF A FULLY FUNCTIONAL CONTROL BOX SPED OUR WORK ENORMOUSLY.

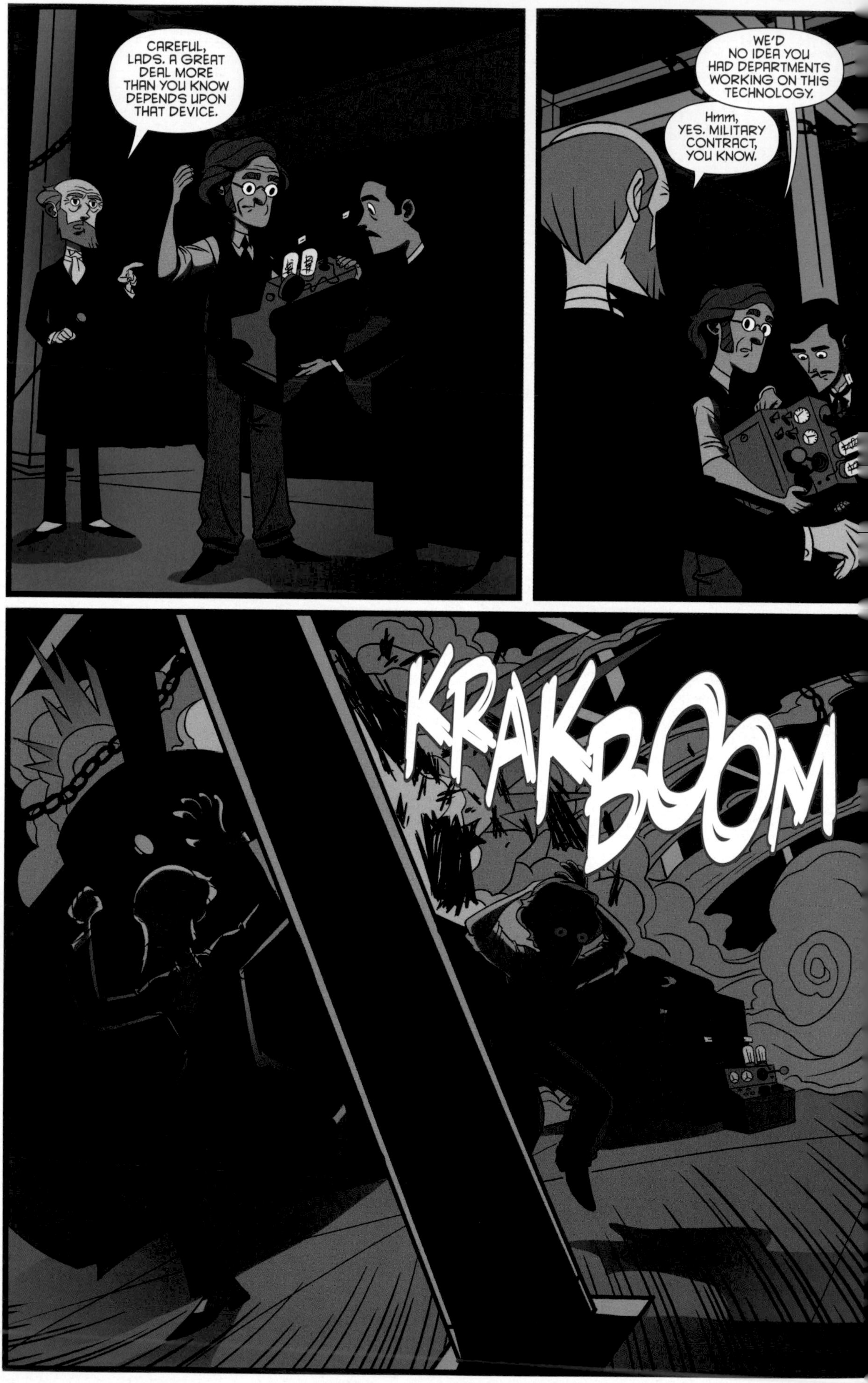
CAREFUL, LADS. A GREAT DEAL MORE THAN YOU KNOW DEPENDS UPON THAT DEVICE.
WE'D NO IDEA YOU HAD DEPARTMENTS WORKING ON THIS TECHNOLOGY.
Hmm, YES. MILITARY CONTRACT, YOU KNOW.
KRAKBOOM

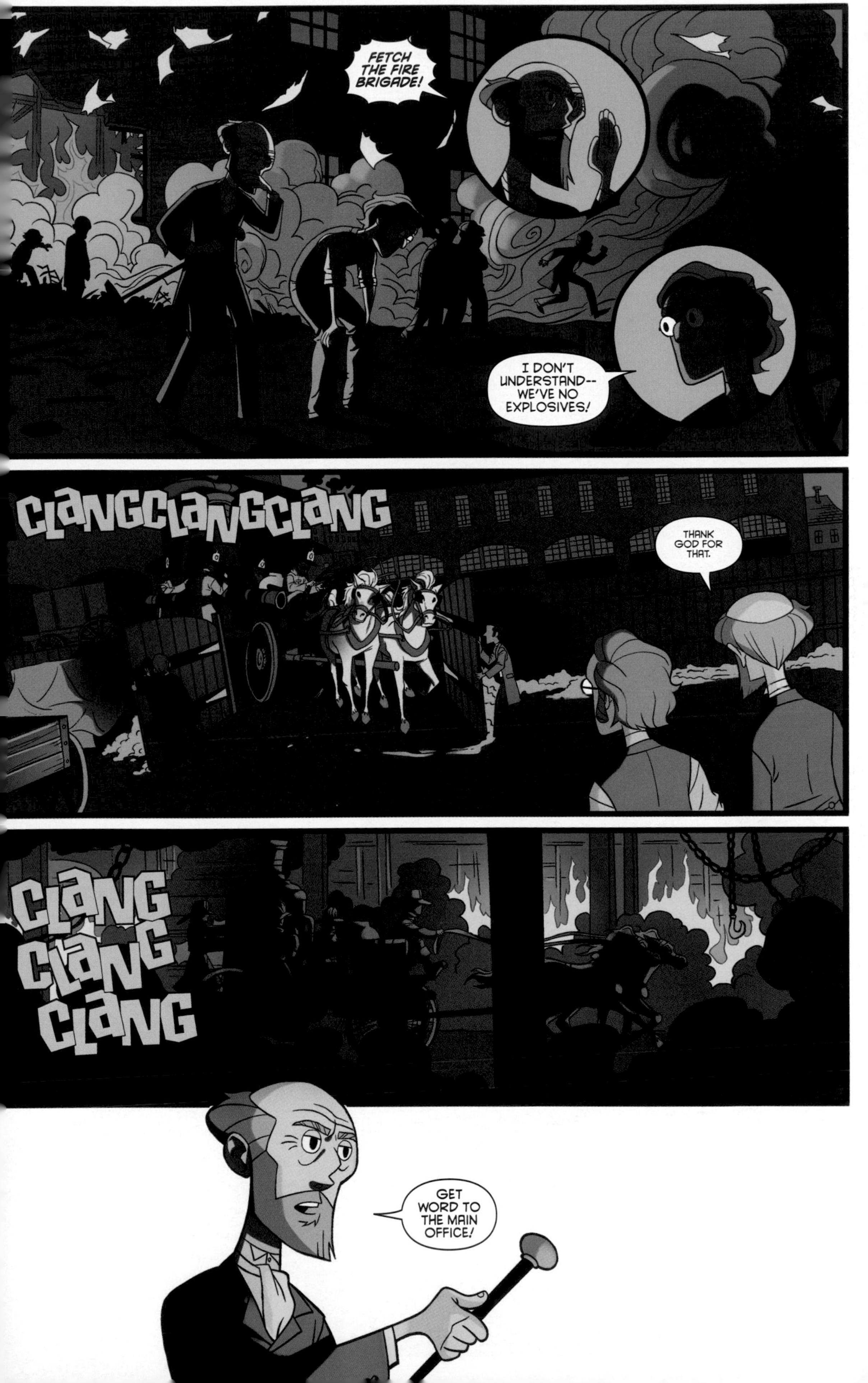
FETCH THE FIRE BRIGADE!
I DON'T UNDERSTAND-- WE'VE NO EXPLOSIVES!
CLANGCLANGCLANG
THANK GOD FOR THAT.
CLANG CLANG CLANG
GET WORD TO THE MAIN OFFICE!

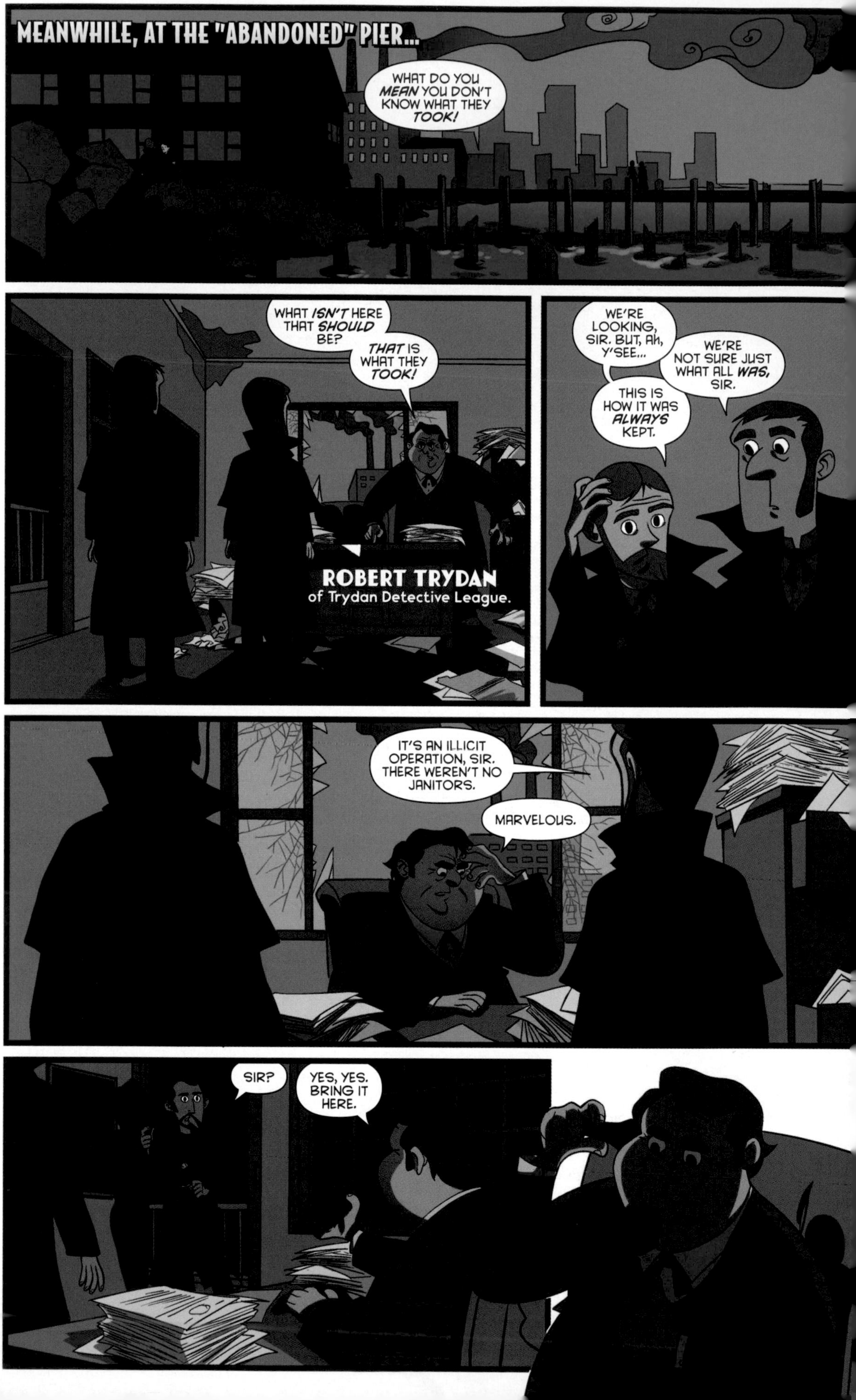
MEANWHILE, AT THE "ABANDONED" PIER...
WHAT DO YOU MEAN YOU DON'T KNOW WHAT THEY TOOK!
WHAT ISN'T HERE THAT SHOULD BE?
THAT IS WHAT THEY TOOK!
ROBERT TRYDAN
of Trydan Detective League.
WE'RE LOOKING, SIR. BUT, AH, Y'SEE...
THIS IS HOW IT WAS ALWAYS KEPT.
WE'RE NOT SURE JUST WHAT ALL WAS, SIR.
IT'S AN ILLICIT OPERATION, SIR. THERE WEREN'T NO JANITORS.
MARVELOUS.
SIR?
YES, YES. BRING IT HERE.

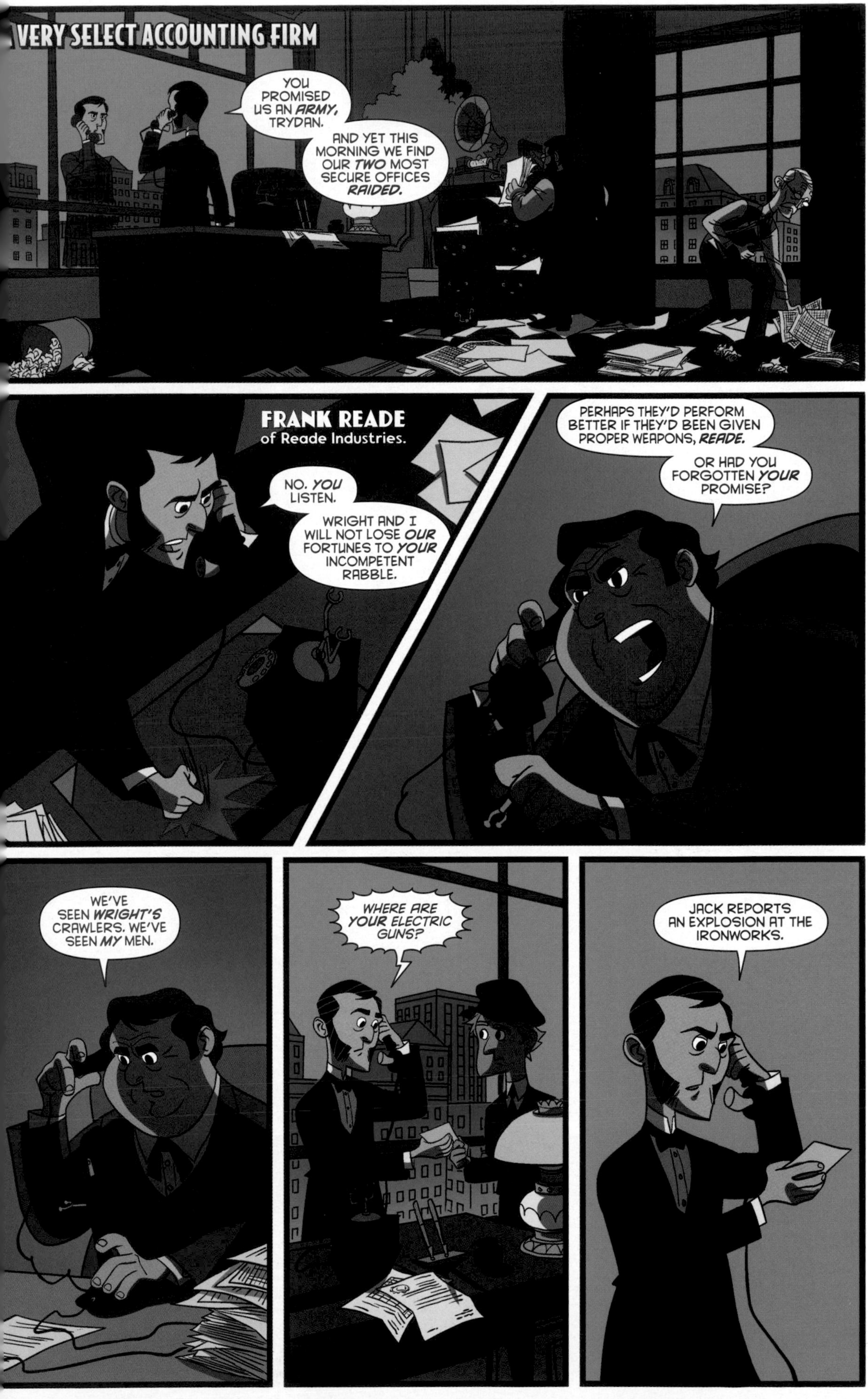
VERY SELECT ACCOUNTING FIRM
YOU PROMISED US AN ARMY, TRYDAN.
AND YET THIS MORNING WE FIND OUR TWO MOST SECURE OFFICES RAIDED.
FRANK READE
of Reade Industries.
NO. YOU LISTEN.
WRIGHT AND I WILL NOT LOSE OUR FORTUNES TO YOUR INCOMPETENT RABBLE.
PERHAPS THEY'D PERFORM BETTER IF THEY'D BEEN GIVEN PROPER WEAPONS, READE.
OR HAD YOU FORGOTTEN YOUR PROMISE?
WE'VE SEEN WRIGHT'S CRAWLERS. WE'VE SEEN MY MEN.
WHERE ARE YOUR ELECTRIC GUNS?
JACK REPORTS AN EXPLOSION AT THE IRONWORKS.

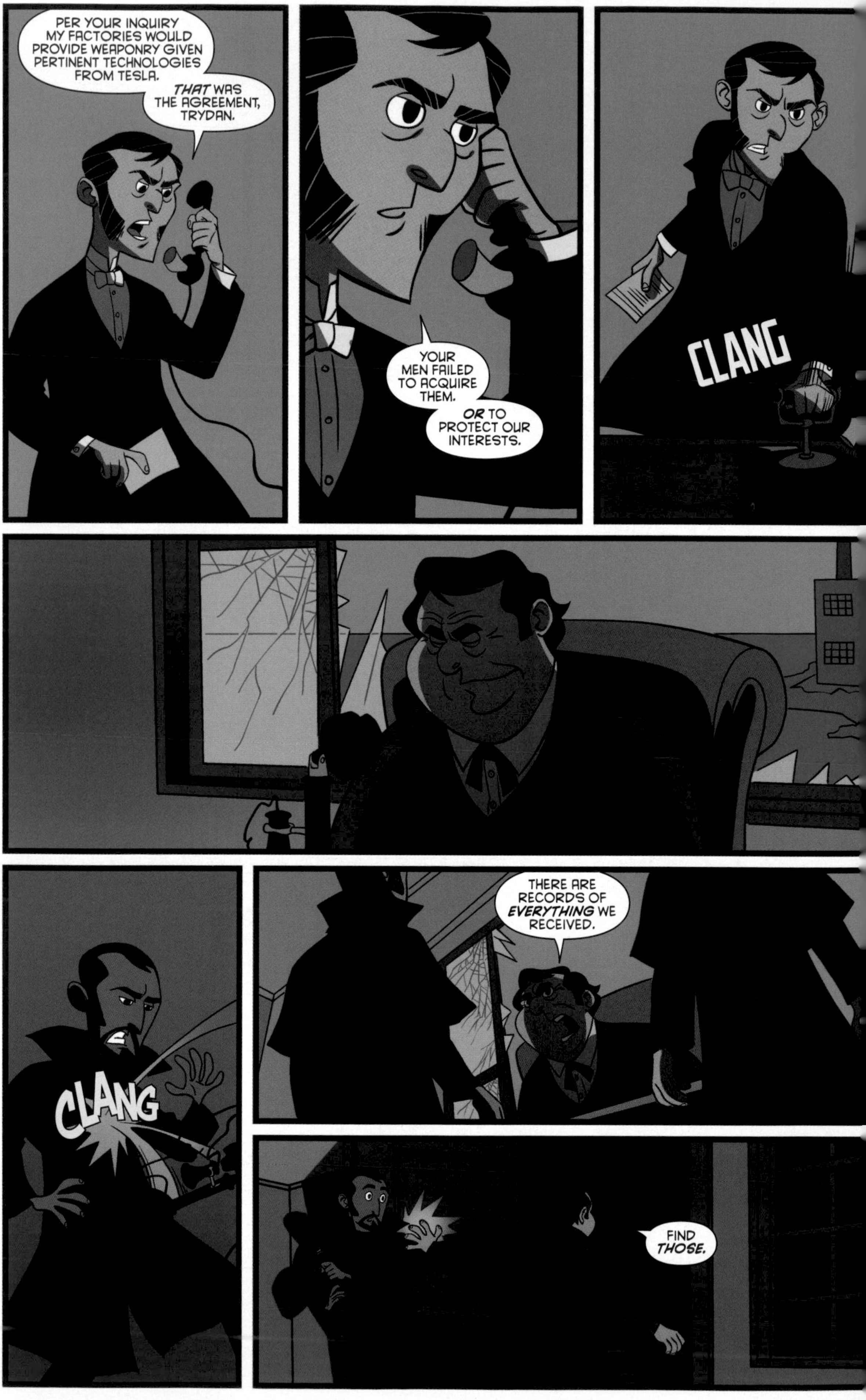
PER YOUR INQUIRY MY FACTORIES WOULD PROVIDE WEAPONRY GIVEN PERTINENT TECHNOLOGIES FROM TESLA.
THAT WAS THE AGREEMENT, TRYDAN.
YOUR MEN FAILED TO ACQUIRE THEM.
OR TO PROTECT OUR INTERESTS.
CLANG
CLANG
THERE ARE RECORDS OF EVERYTHING WE RECEIVED.
FIND THOSE.

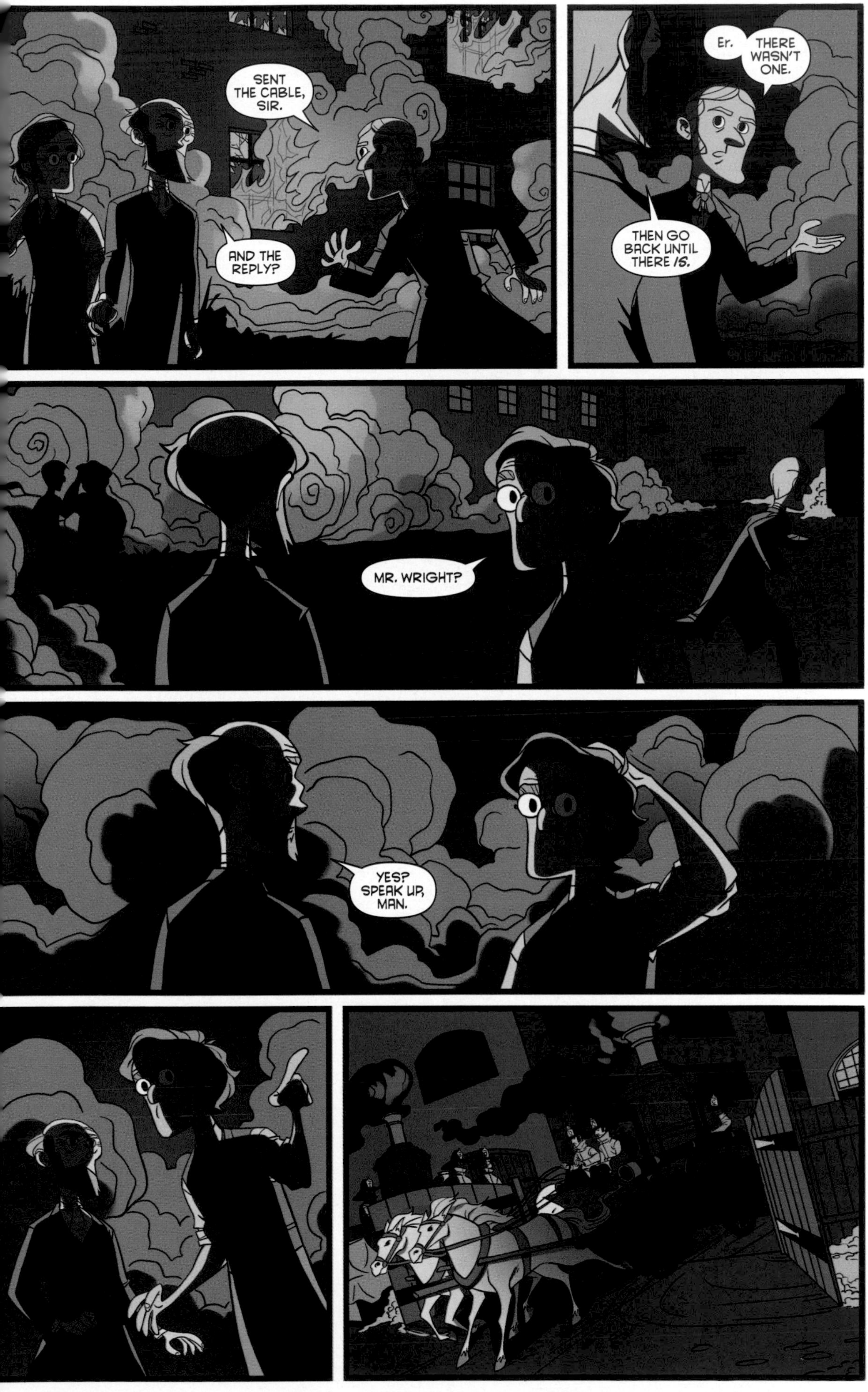
SENT THE CABLE, SIR.
AND THE REPLY?
Er.
THERE WASN'T ONE.
THEN GO BACK UNTIL THERE *IS*.
MR. WRIGHT?
YES? SPEAK UP, MAN.

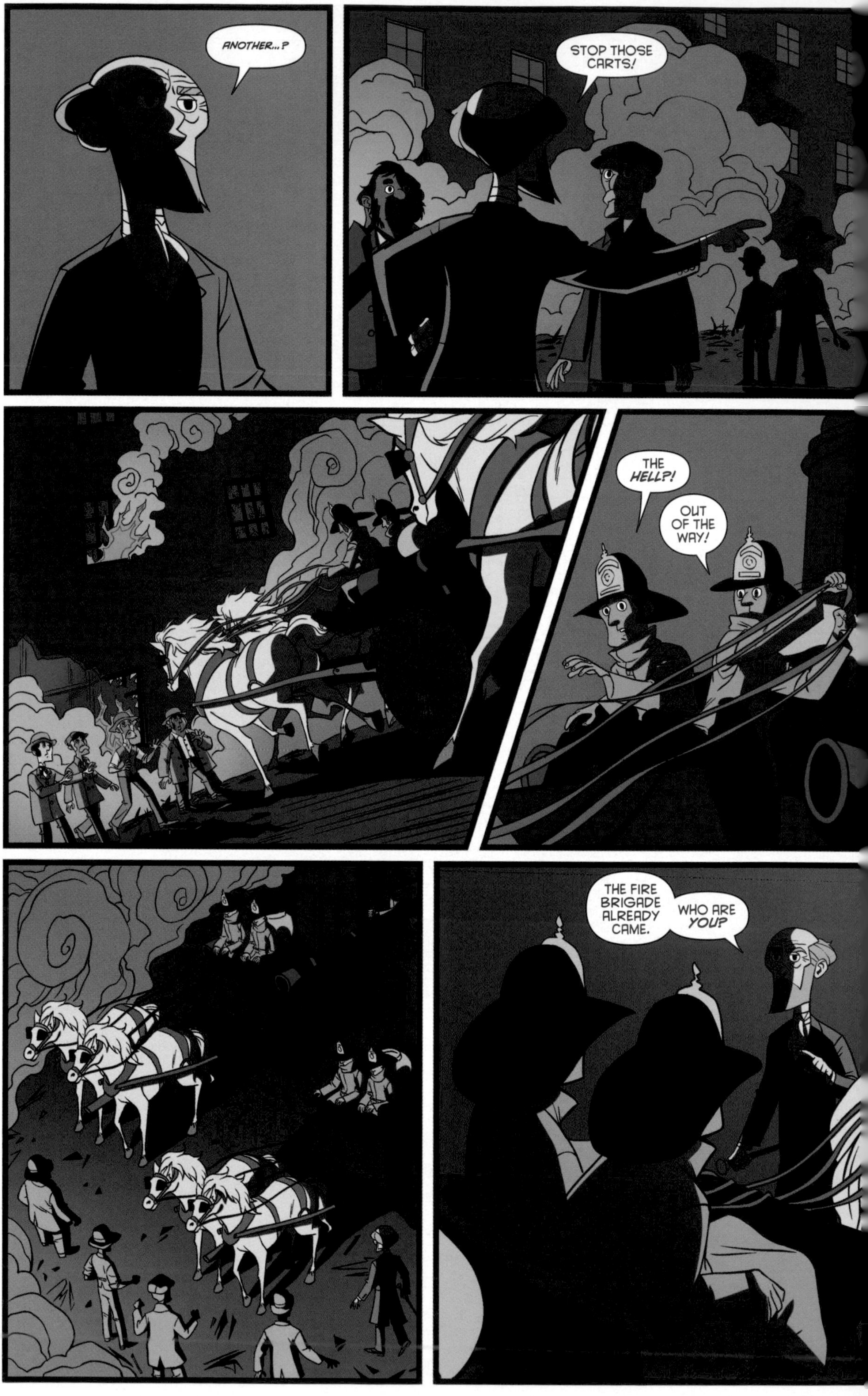
ANOTHER...?
STOP THOSE CARTS!
THE HELL?!
OUT OF THE WAY!
THE FIRE BRIGADE ALREADY CAME.
WHO ARE YOU?

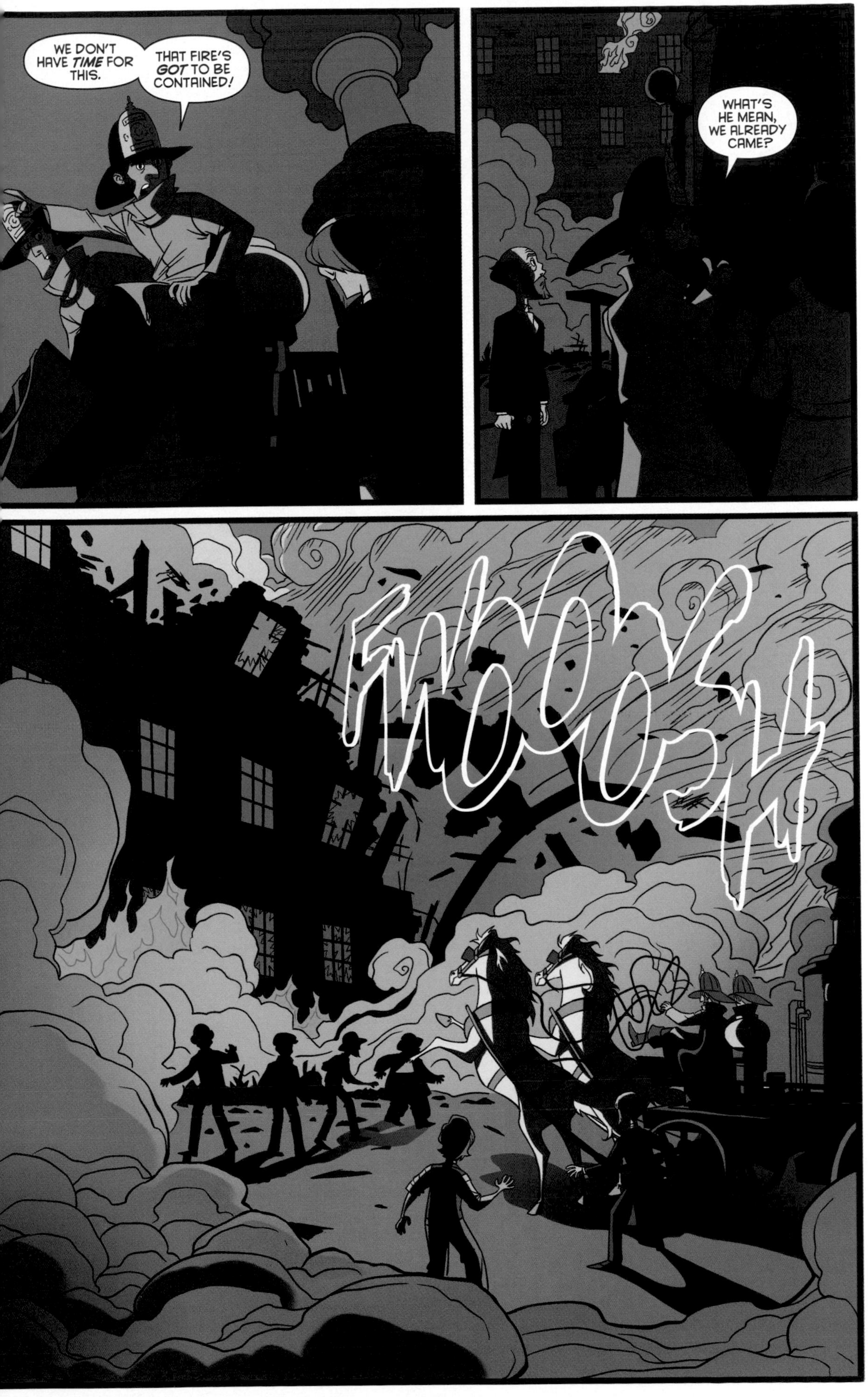
WE DON'T HAVE *TIME* FOR THIS.
THAT FIRE'S *GOT* TO BE CONTAINED!
WHAT'S HE MEAN, WE ALREADY CAME?
FWOOOSH

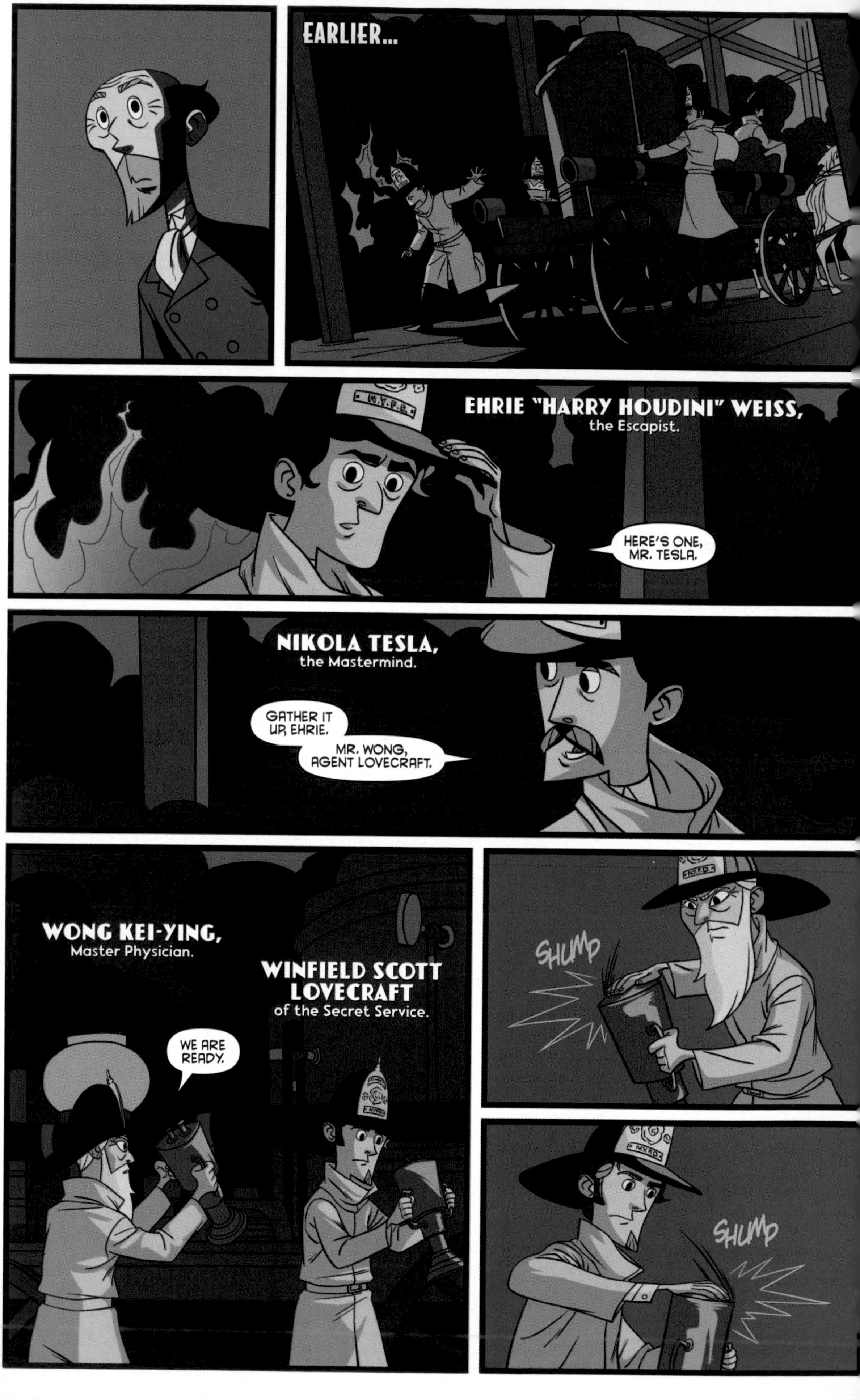
EARLIER...
EHRIE "HARRY HOUDINI" WEISS,
the Escapist.
HERE'S ONE, MR. TESLA.
NIKOLA TESLA,
the Mastermind.
GATHER IT UP, EHRIE.
MR. WONG, AGENT LOVECRAFT.
WONG KEI-YING,
Master Physician.
WINFIELD SCOTT LOVECRAFT
of the Secret Service.
WE ARE READY.
SHUMP
SHUMP

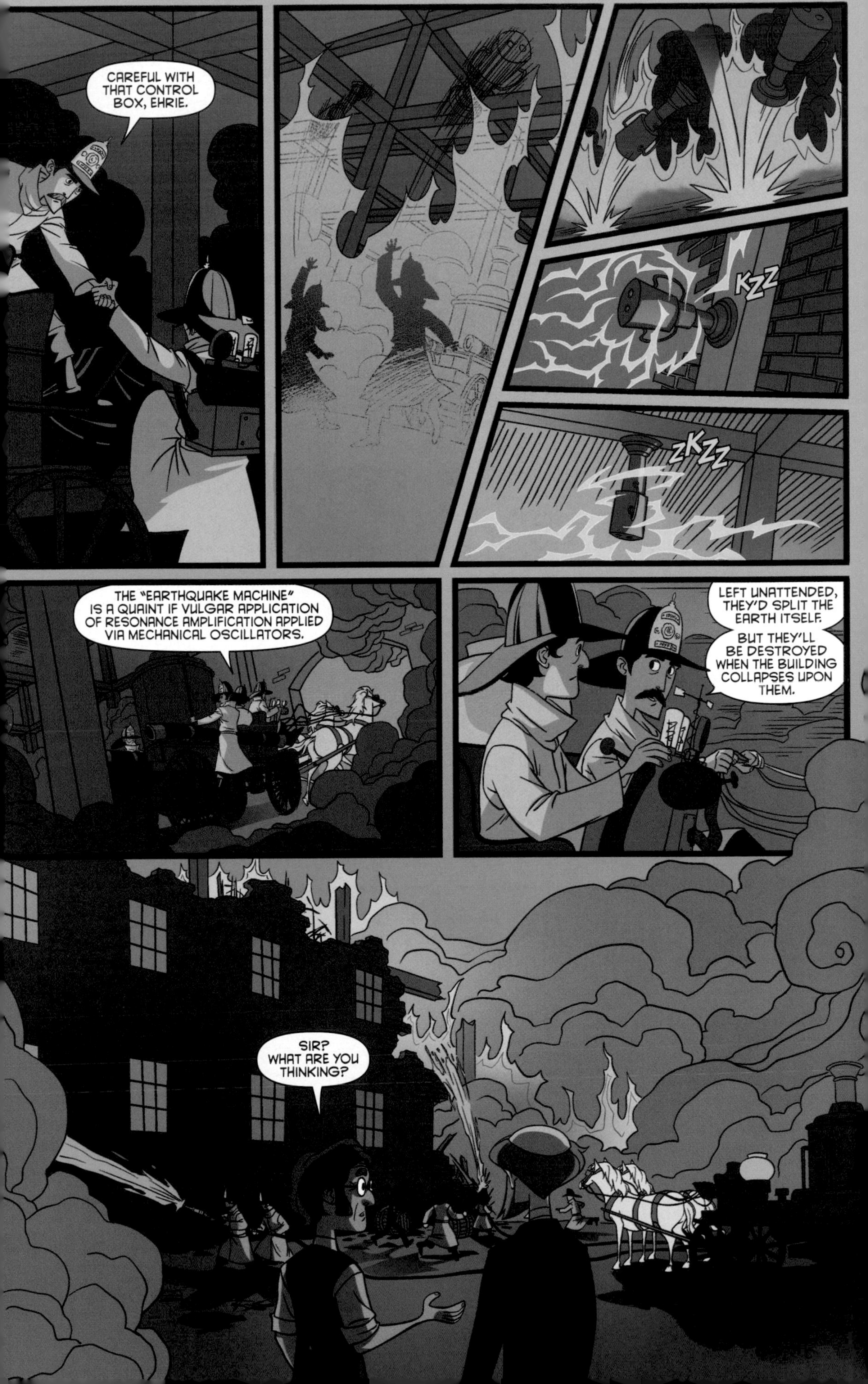
CAREFUL WITH THAT CONTROL BOX, EHRIE.
KZZ
ZKZZ
THE "EARTHQUAKE MACHINE" IS A QUAINT IF VULGAR APPLICATION OF RESONANCE AMPLIFICATION APPLIED VIA MECHANICAL OSCILLATORS.
LEFT UNATTENDED, THEY'D SPLIT THE EARTH ITSELF.
BUT THEY'LL BE DESTROYED WHEN THE BUILDING COLLAPSES UPON THEM.
SIR? WHAT ARE YOU THINKING?

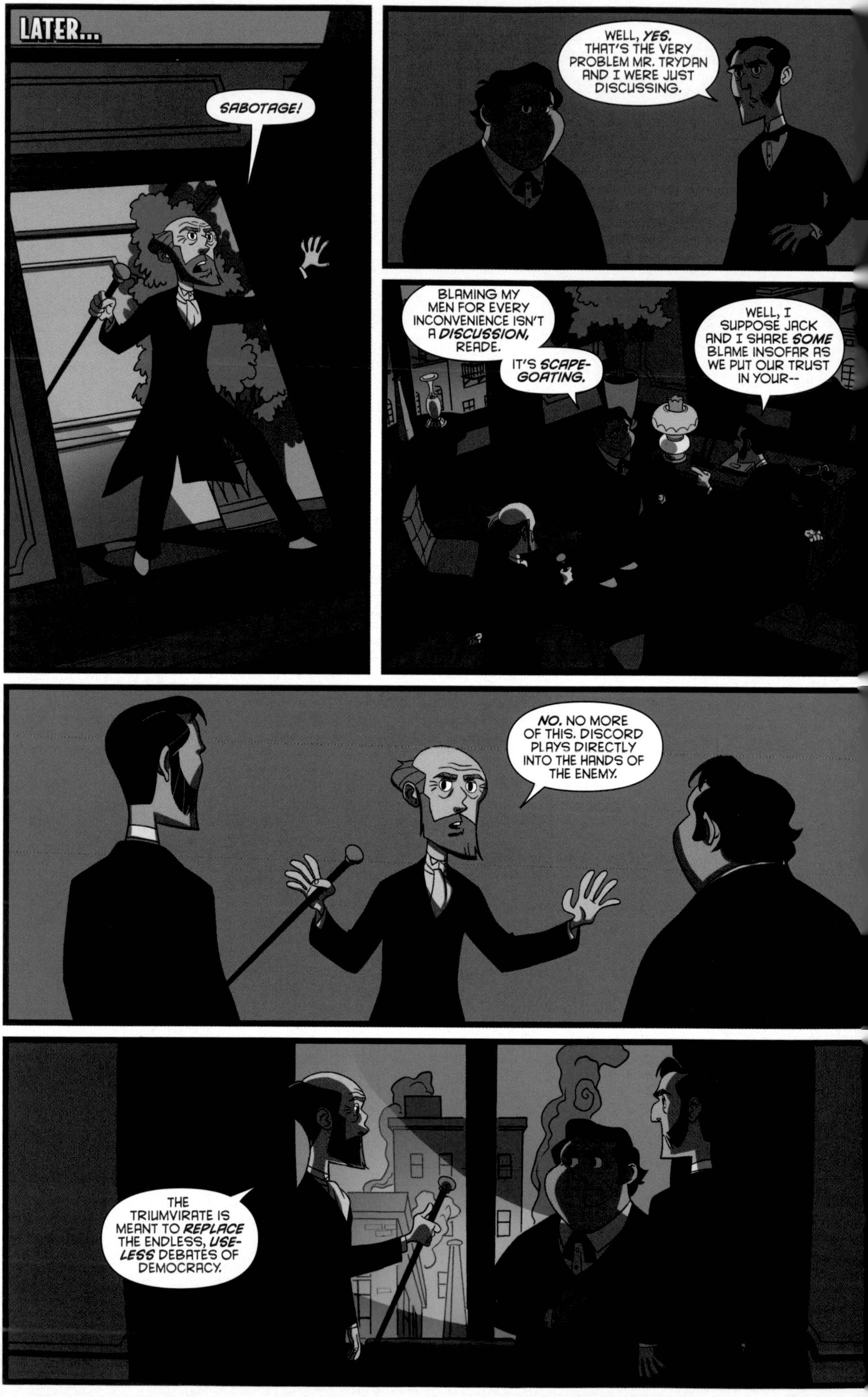
LATER...
SABOTAGE!
WELL, YES. THAT'S THE VERY PROBLEM MR. TRYDAN AND I WERE JUST DISCUSSING.
BLAMING MY MEN FOR EVERY INCONVENIENCE ISN'T A DISCUSSION, READE.
IT'S SCAPE-GOATING.
WELL, I SUPPOSE JACK AND I SHARE SOME BLAME INSOFAR AS WE PUT OUR TRUST IN YOUR--
NO. NO MORE OF THIS. DISCORD PLAYS DIRECTLY INTO THE HANDS OF THE ENEMY.
THE TRIUMVIRATE IS MEANT TO REPLACE THE ENDLESS, USE-LESS DEBATES OF DEMOCRACY.

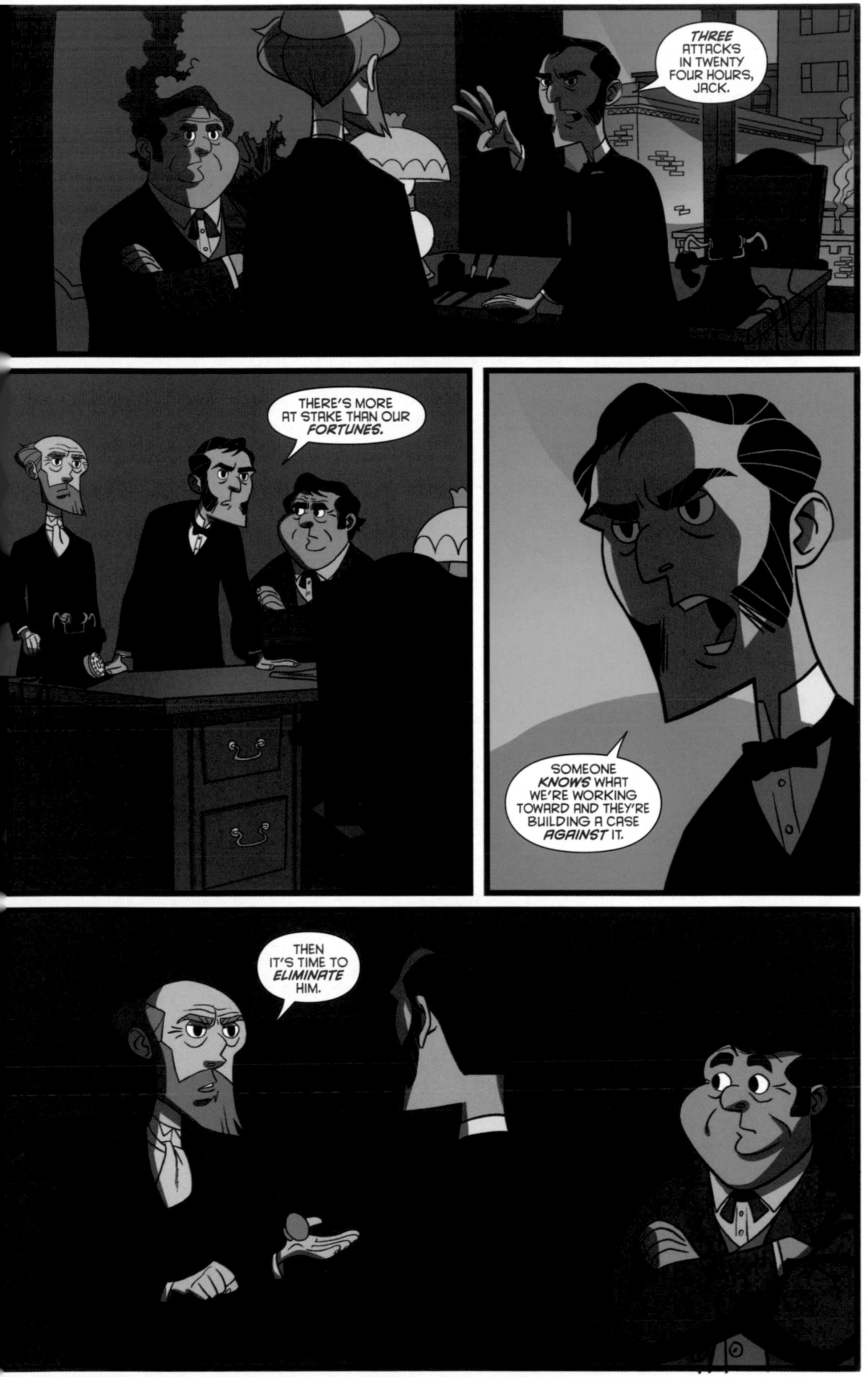
THREE ATTACKS IN TWENTY FOUR HOURS, JACK.
THERE'S MORE AT STAKE THAN OUR FORTUNES.
SOMEONE KNOWS WHAT WE'RE WORKING TOWARD AND THEY'RE BUILDING A CASE AGAINST IT.
THEN IT'S TIME TO ELIMINATE HIM.

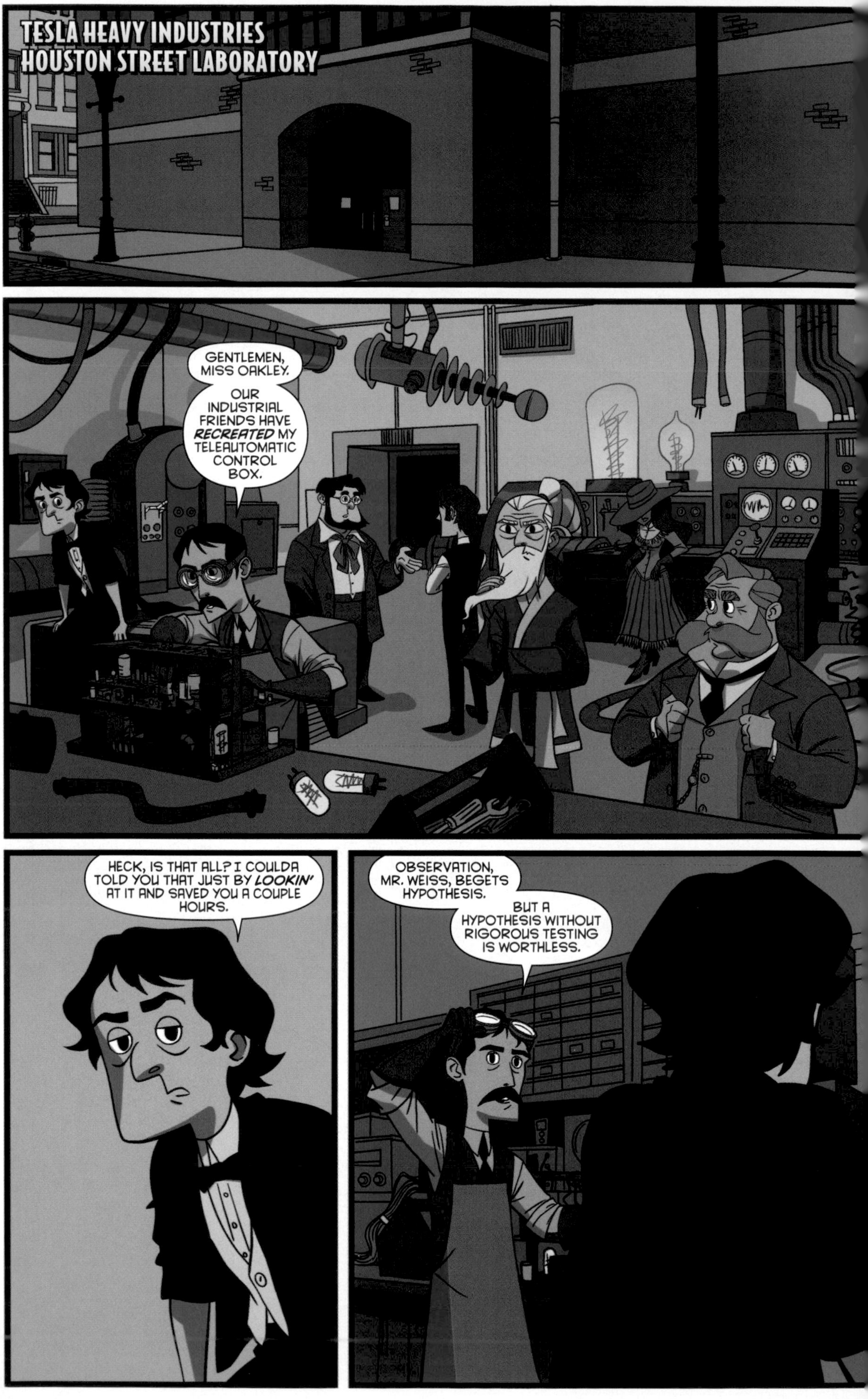

TESLA HEAVY INDUSTRIES
HOUSTON STREET LABORATORY
GENTLEMEN, MISS OAKLEY.
OUR INDUSTRIAL FRIENDS HAVE *RECREATED* MY TELEAUTOMATIC CONTROL BOX.
HECK, IS THAT ALL? I COULDA TOLD YOU THAT JUST BY *LOOKIN'* AT IT AND SAVED YOU A COUPLE HOURS.
OBSERVATION, MR. WEISS, BEGETS HYPOTHESIS.
BUT A HYPOTHESIS WITHOUT RIGOROUS TESTING IS WORTHLESS.

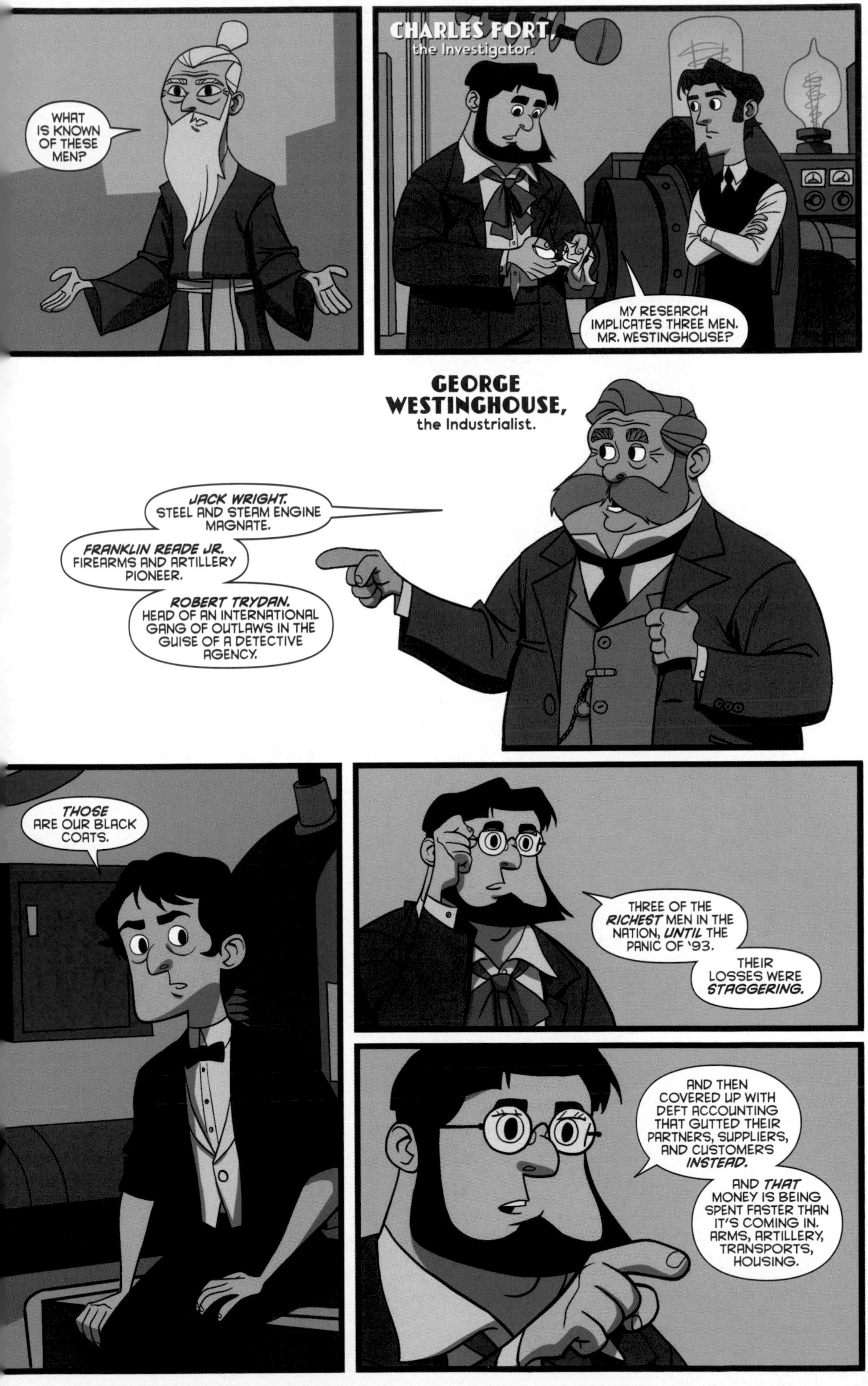

WHAT IS KNOWN OF THESE MEN?
CHARLES FORT, the Investigator.
MY RESEARCH IMPLICATES THREE MEN. MR. WESTINGHOUSE?
GEORGE WESTINGHOUSE, the Industrialist.
JACK WRIGHT. STEEL AND STEAM ENGINE MAGNATE.
FRANKLIN READE JR. FIREARMS AND ARTILLERY PIONEER.
ROBERT TRYDAN. HEAD OF AN INTERNATIONAL GANG OF OUTLAWS IN THE GUISE OF A DETECTIVE AGENCY.
THOSE ARE OUR BLACK COATS.
THREE OF THE RICHEST MEN IN THE NATION, UNTIL THE PANIC OF '93.
THEIR LOSSES WERE STAGGERING.
AND THEN COVERED UP WITH DEFT ACCOUNTING THAT GUTTED THEIR PARTNERS, SUPPLIERS, AND CUSTOMERS INSTEAD.
AND THAT MONEY IS BEING SPENT FASTER THAN IT'S COMING IN. ARMS, ARTILLERY, TRANSPORTS, HOUSING.

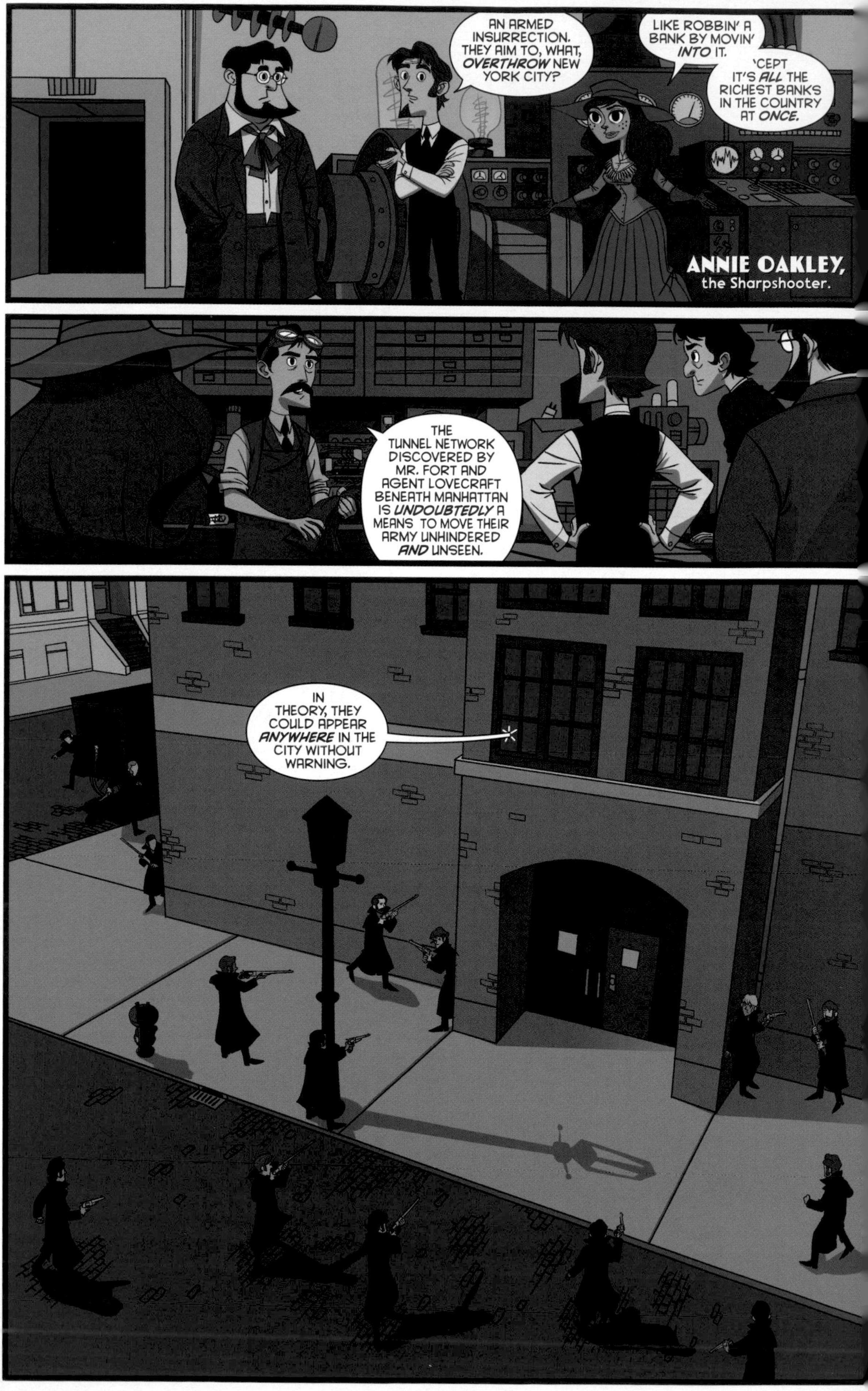
AN ARMED INSURRECTION. THEY AIM TO, WHAT, *OVERTHROW* NEW YORK CITY?
LIKE ROBBIN' A BANK BY MOVIN' *INTO* IT.
'CEPT IT'S *ALL* THE RICHEST BANKS IN THE COUNTRY AT *ONCE.*
ANNIE OAKLEY, the Sharpshooter.
THE TUNNEL NETWORK DISCOVERED BY MR. FORT AND AGENT LOVECRAFT BENEATH MANHATTAN IS *UNDOUBTEDLY* A MEANS TO MOVE THEIR ARMY UNHINDERED *AND* UNSEEN.
IN THEORY, THEY COULD APPEAR *ANYWHERE* IN THE CITY WITHOUT WARNING.

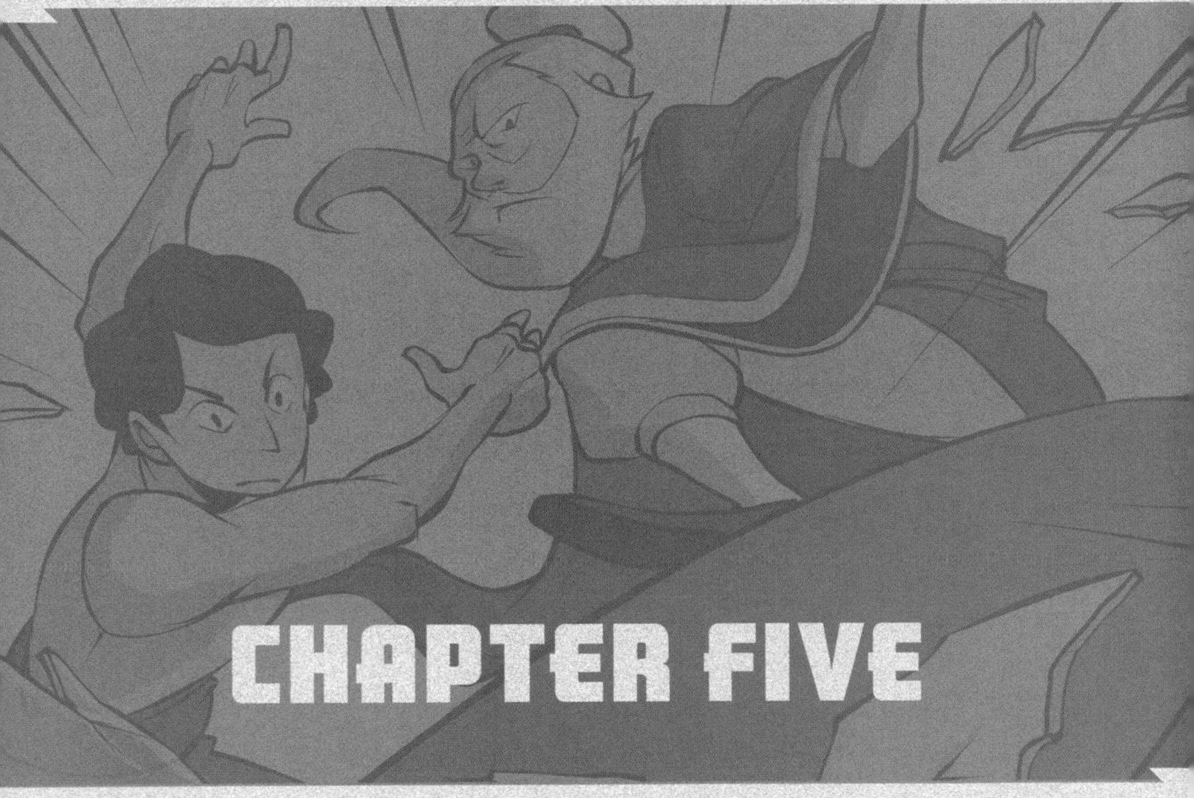

CHAPTER FIVE

CLEVINGER
ENDURO

ATOMIC ROBO

PRESENTS

HENDERSO
POWELL

REAL SCIENCE ADVENTURES

No. 11 $2.75 U.S.

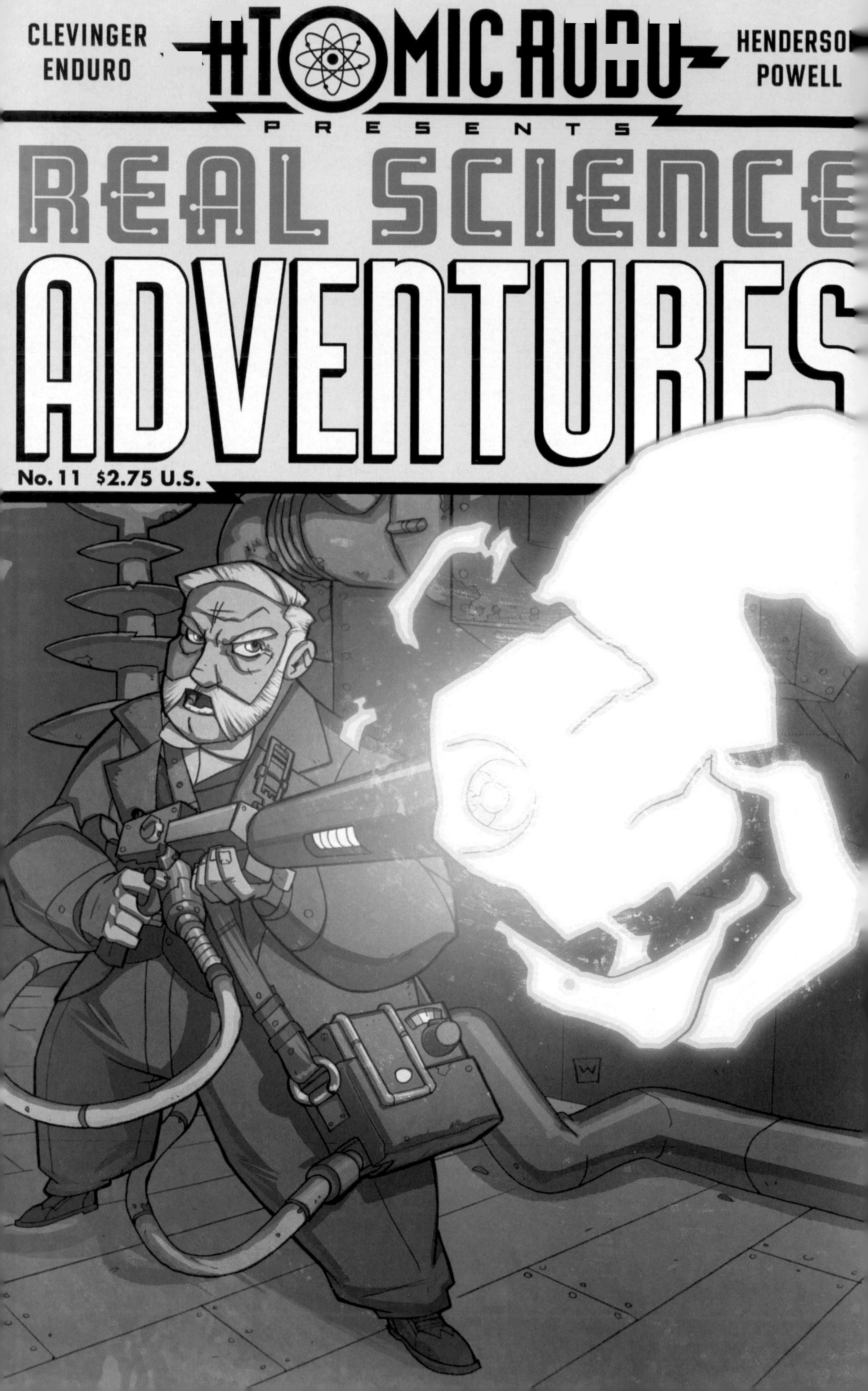

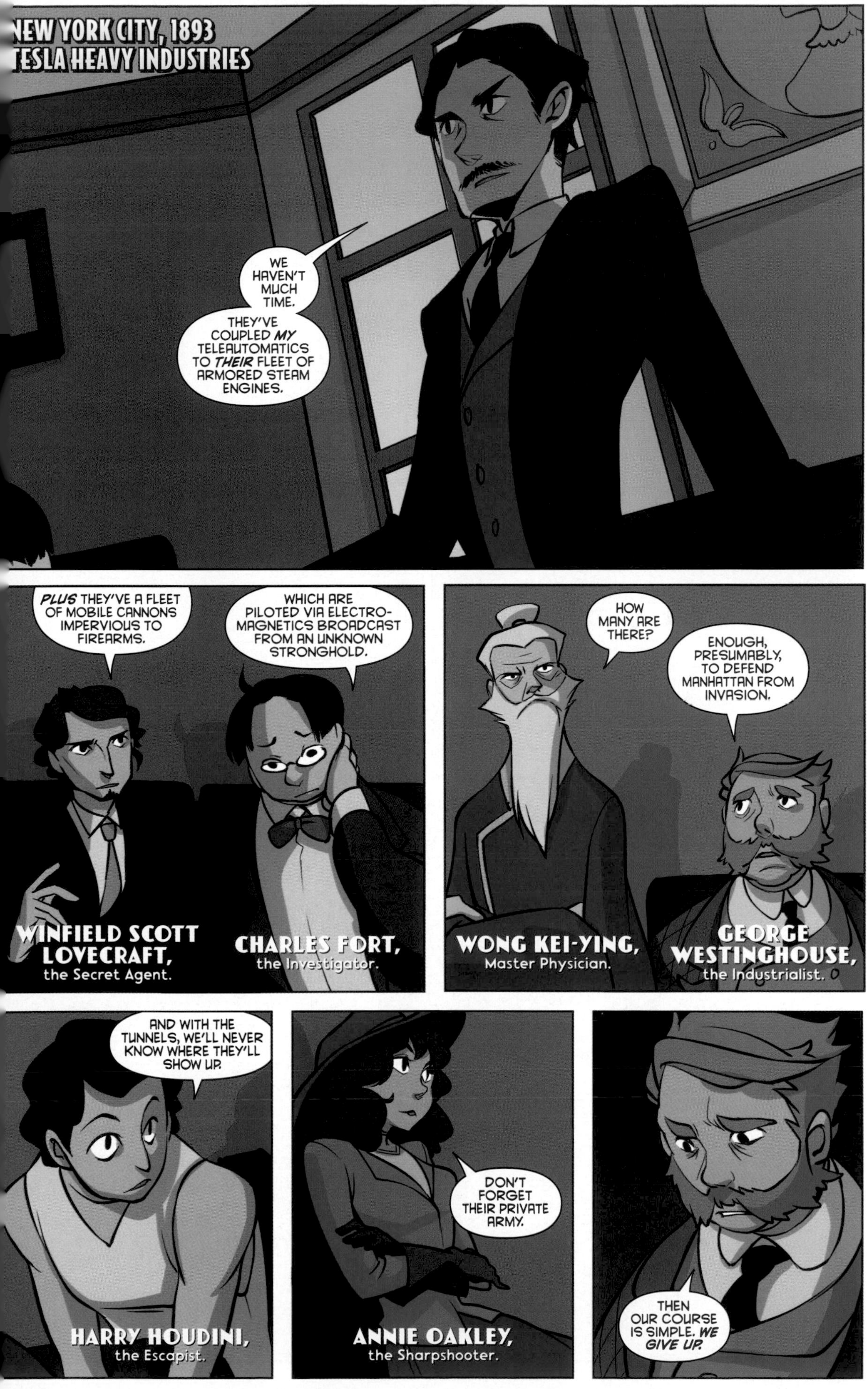
NEW YORK CITY, 1893
TESLA HEAVY INDUSTRIES
WE HAVEN'T MUCH TIME.
THEY'VE COUPLED *MY* TELEAUTOMATICS TO *THEIR* FLEET OF ARMORED STEAM ENGINES.
PLUS THEY'VE A FLEET OF MOBILE CANNONS IMPERVIOUS TO FIREARMS.
WHICH ARE PILOTED VIA ELECTRO-MAGNETICS BROADCAST FROM AN UNKNOWN STRONGHOLD.
WINFIELD SCOTT LOVECRAFT, the Secret Agent.
CHARLES FORT, the Investigator.
HOW MANY ARE THERE?
ENOUGH, PRESUMABLY, TO DEFEND MANHATTAN FROM INVASION.
WONG KEI-YING, Master Physician.
GEORGE WESTINGHOUSE, the Industrialist.
AND WITH THE TUNNELS, WE'LL NEVER KNOW WHERE THEY'LL SHOW UP.
HARRY HOUDINI, the Escapist.
DON'T FORGET THEIR PRIVATE ARMY.
ANNIE OAKLEY, the Sharpshooter.
THEN OUR COURSE IS SIMPLE. *WE GIVE UP.*

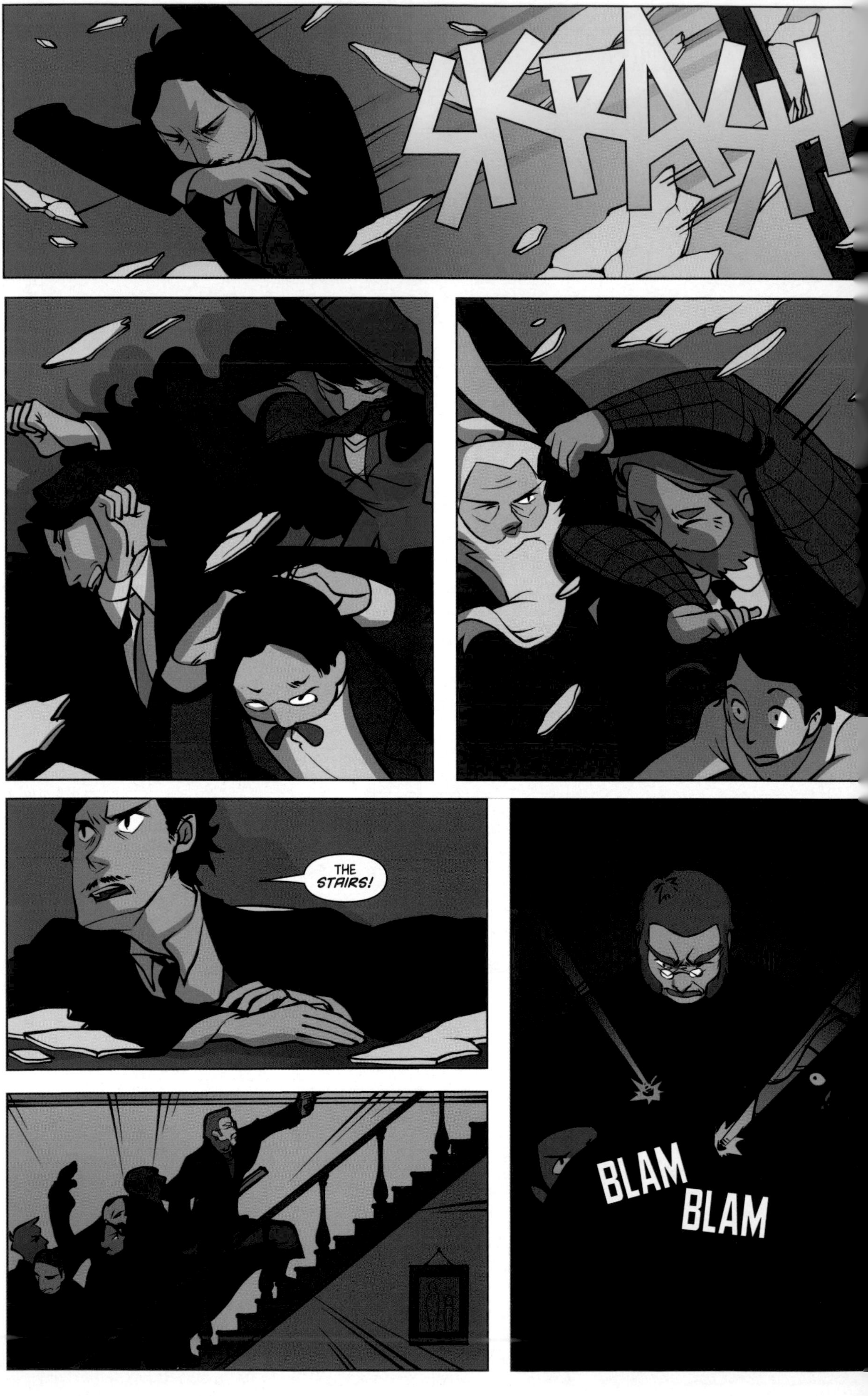
KRAAASH
THE STAIRS!
BLAM
BLAM

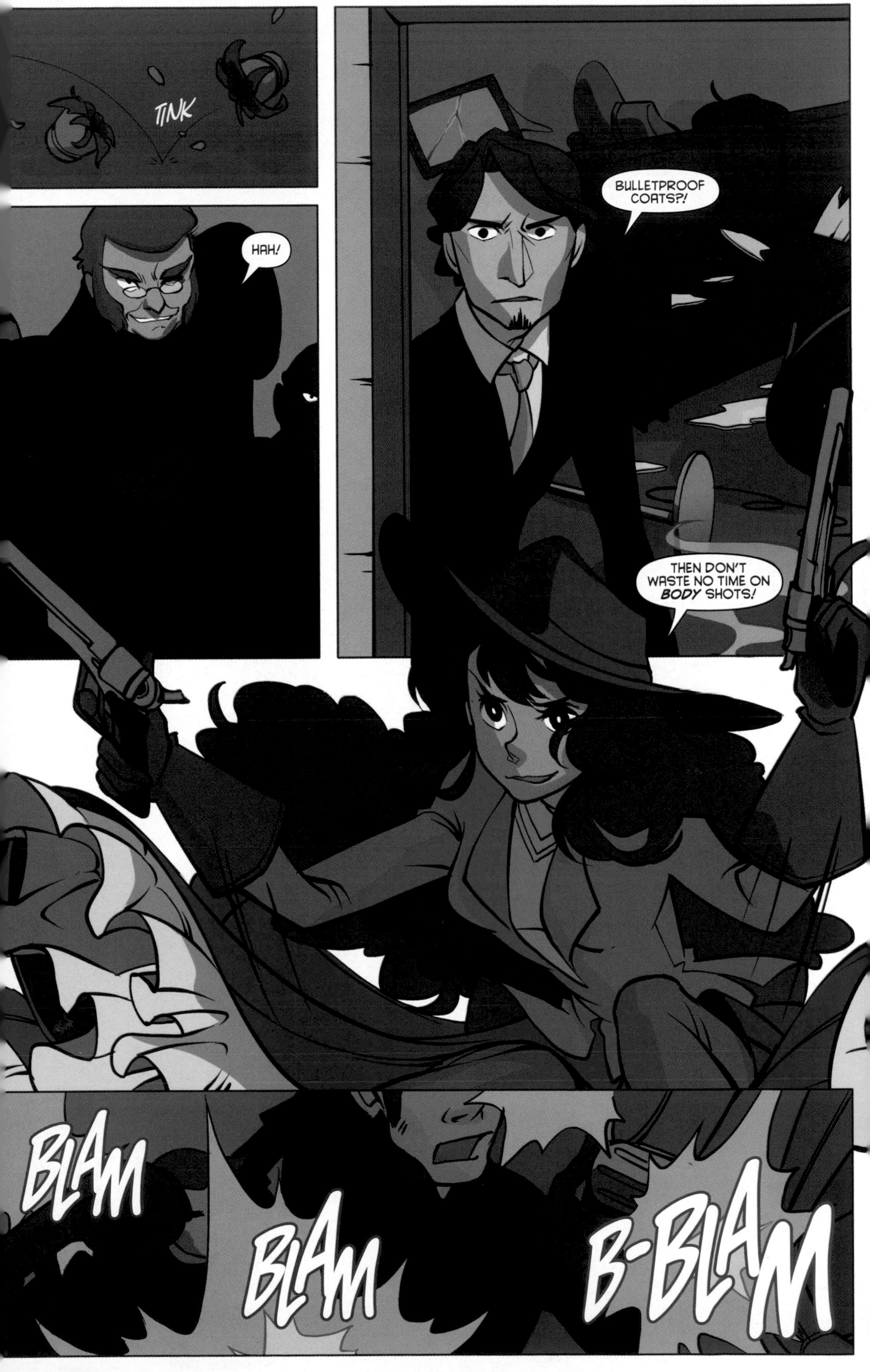
TINK
HAH!
BULLETPROOF COATS?!
THEN DON'T WASTE NO TIME ON *BODY* SHOTS!
BLAM
BLAM
B-BLAM

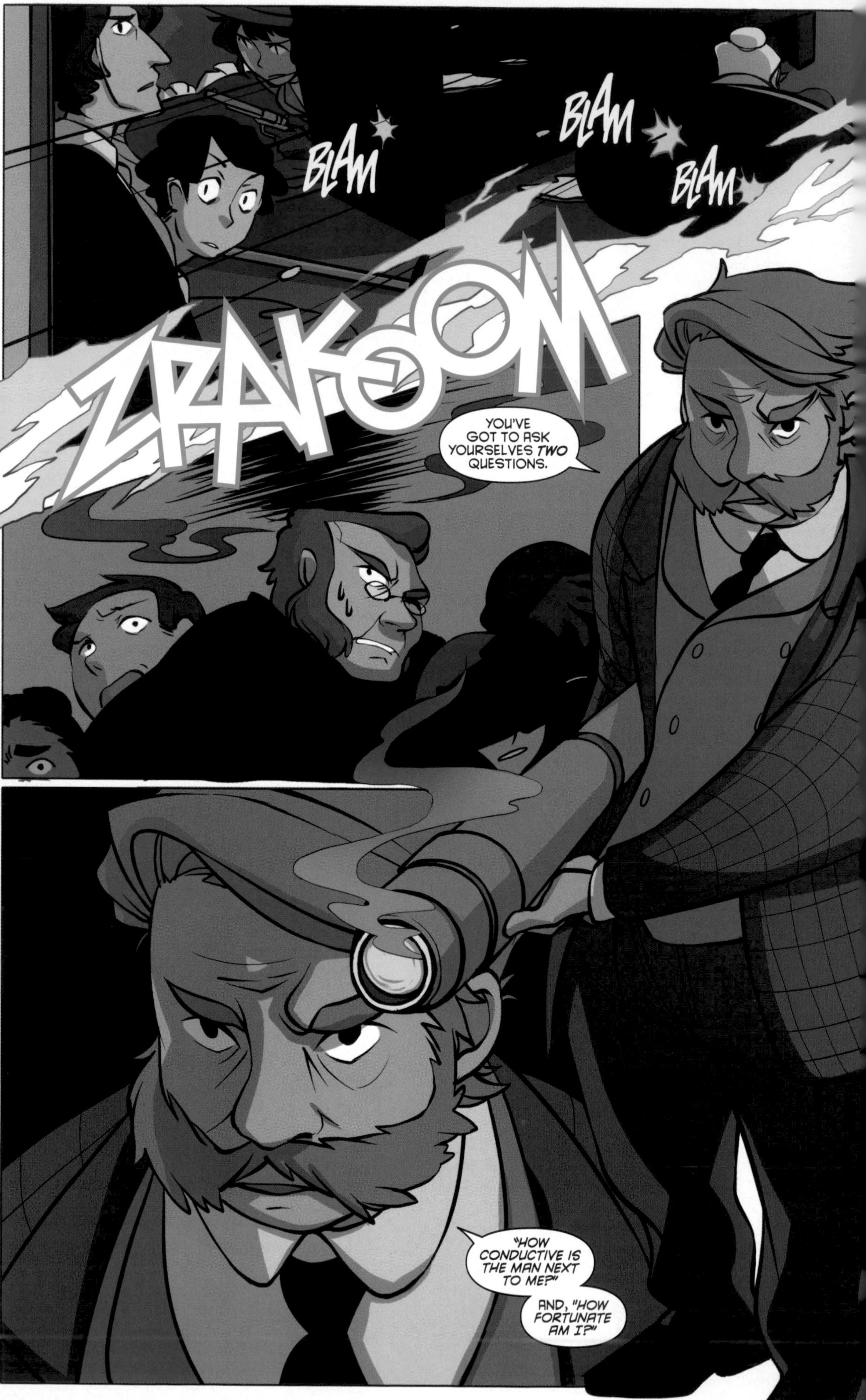
BLAM
BLAM
BLAM
ZRAKOOM
YOU'VE GOT TO ASK YOURSELVES *TWO* QUESTIONS.
"HOW CONDUCTIVE IS THE MAN NEXT TO ME?"
AND, "HOW FORTUNATE AM I?"

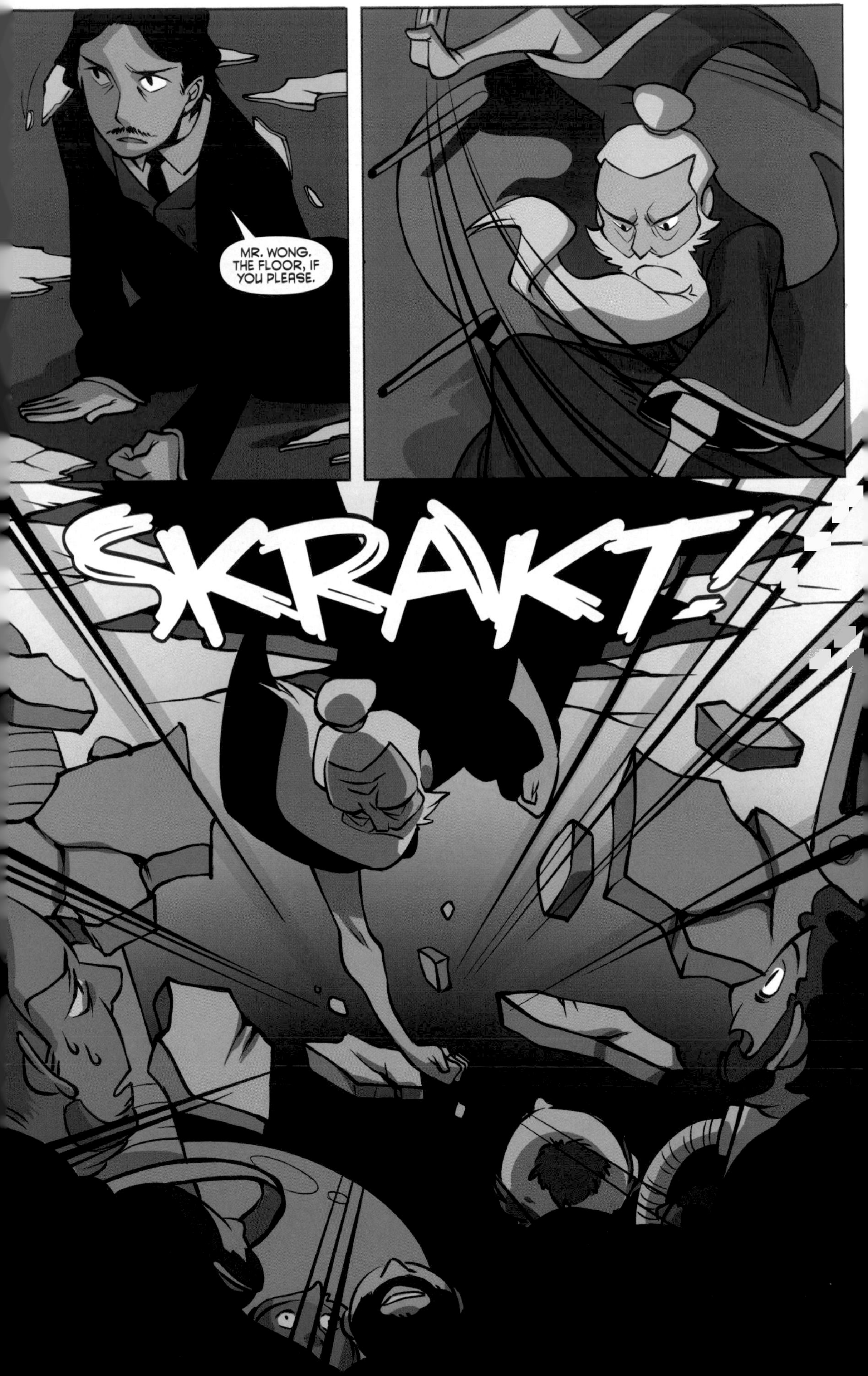
MR. WONG. THE FLOOR, IF YOU PLEASE.
SKRAKT!

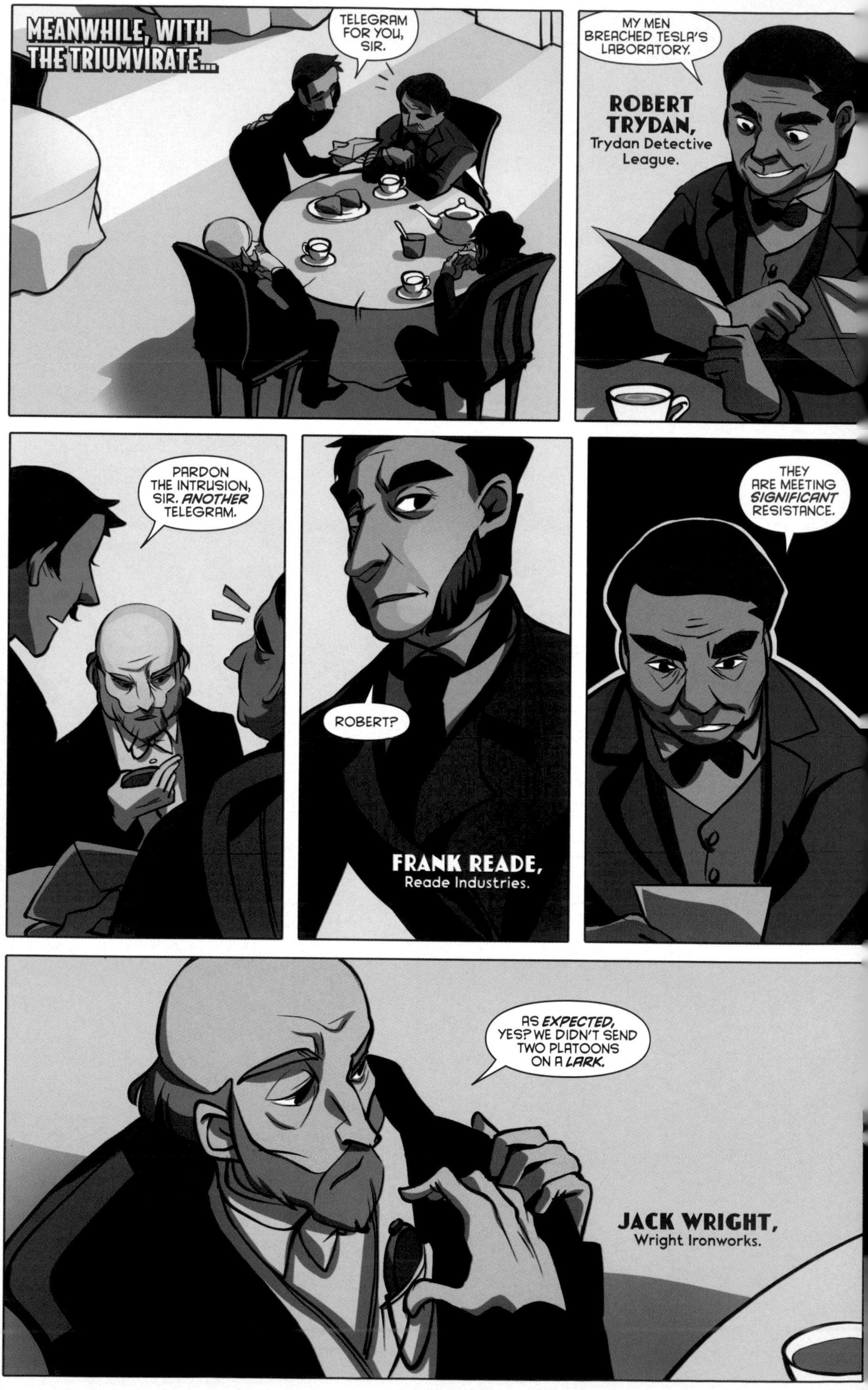
MEANWHILE, WITH THE TRIUMVIRATE...
TELEGRAM FOR YOU, SIR.
MY MEN BREACHED TESLA'S LABORATORY.
ROBERT TRYDAN,
Trydan Detective League.
PARDON THE INTRUSION, SIR. *ANOTHER* TELEGRAM.
ROBERT?
FRANK READE,
Reade Industries.
THEY ARE MEETING *SIGNIFICANT* RESISTANCE.
AS *EXPECTED,* YES? WE DIDN'T SEND TWO PLATOONS ON A *LARK.*
JACK WRIGHT,
Wright Ironworks.

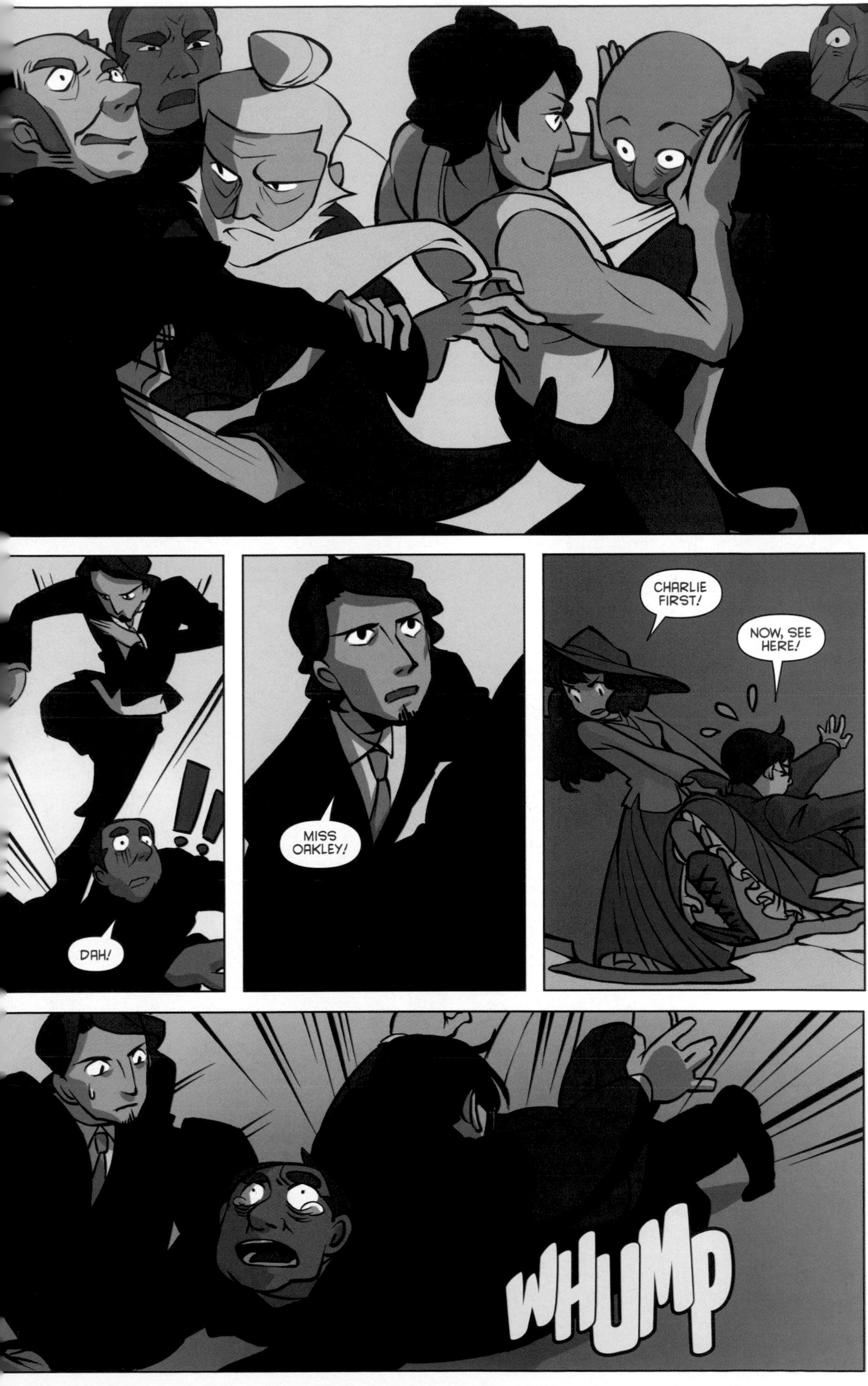
DAH!
MISS OAKLEY!
CHARLIE FIRST!
NOW, SEE HERE!
WHUMP

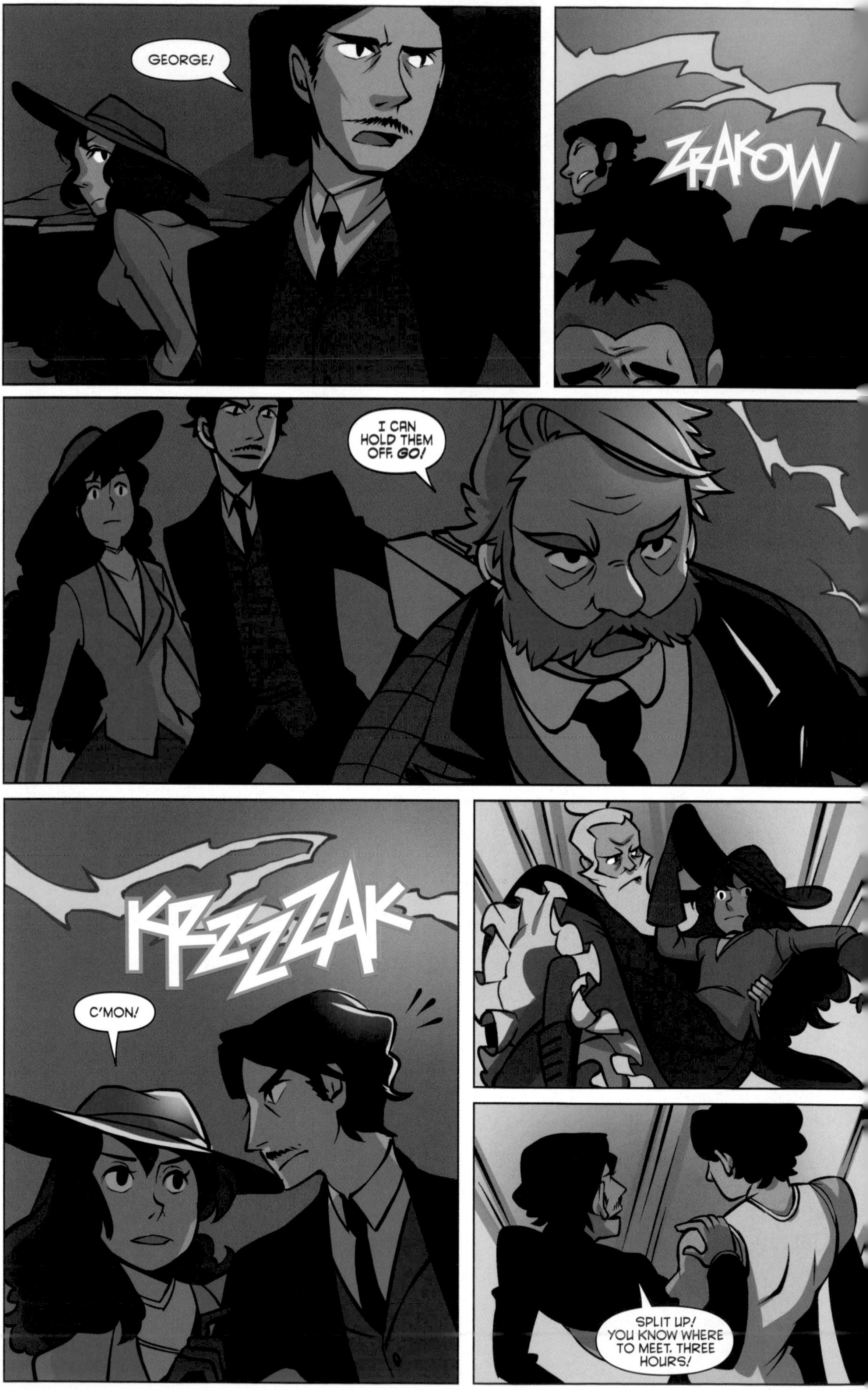
GEORGE!
ZRAKOW
I CAN HOLD THEM OFF. GO!
KRZZZZAK
C'MON!
SPLIT UP! YOU KNOW WHERE TO MEET. THREE HOURS!

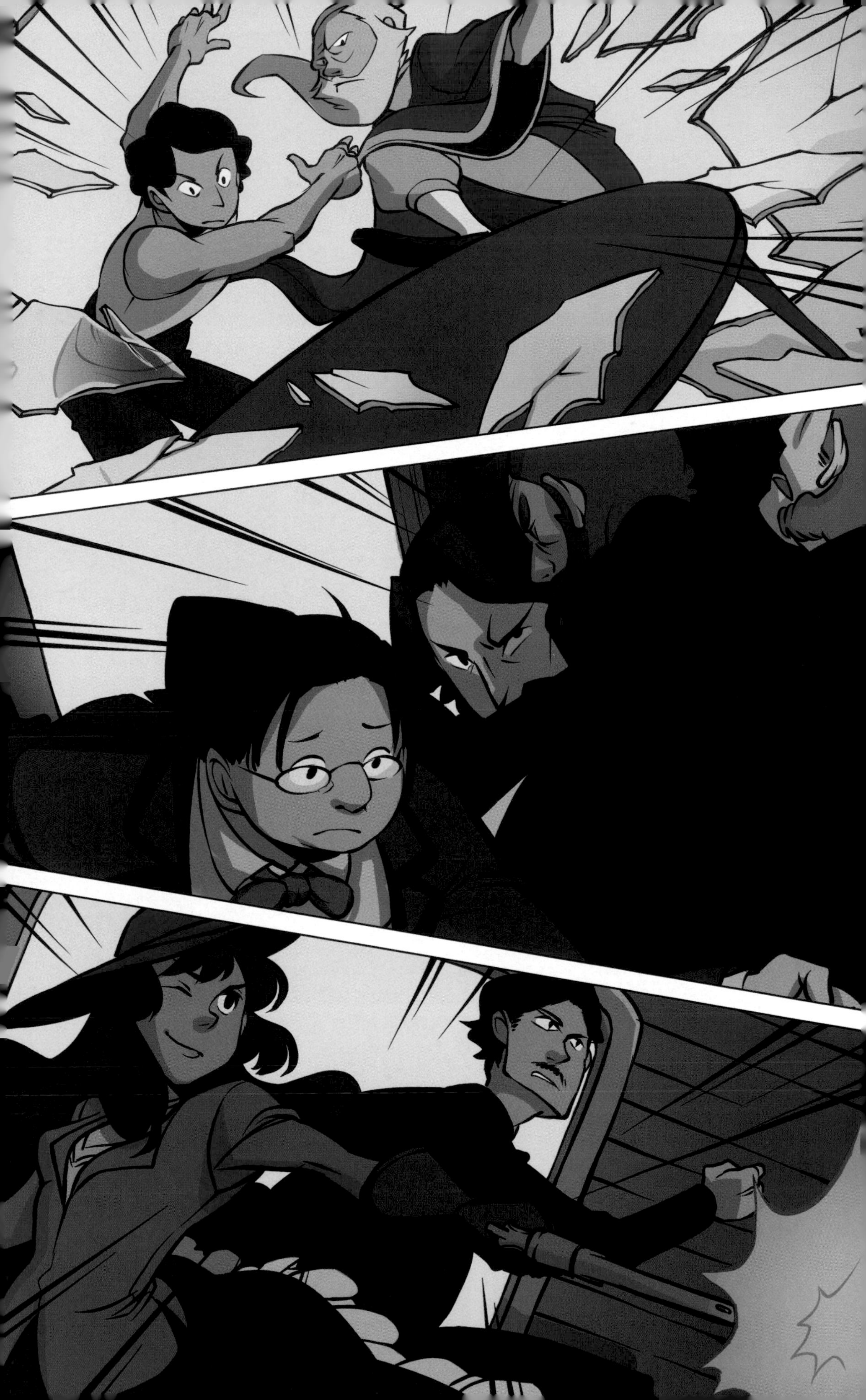

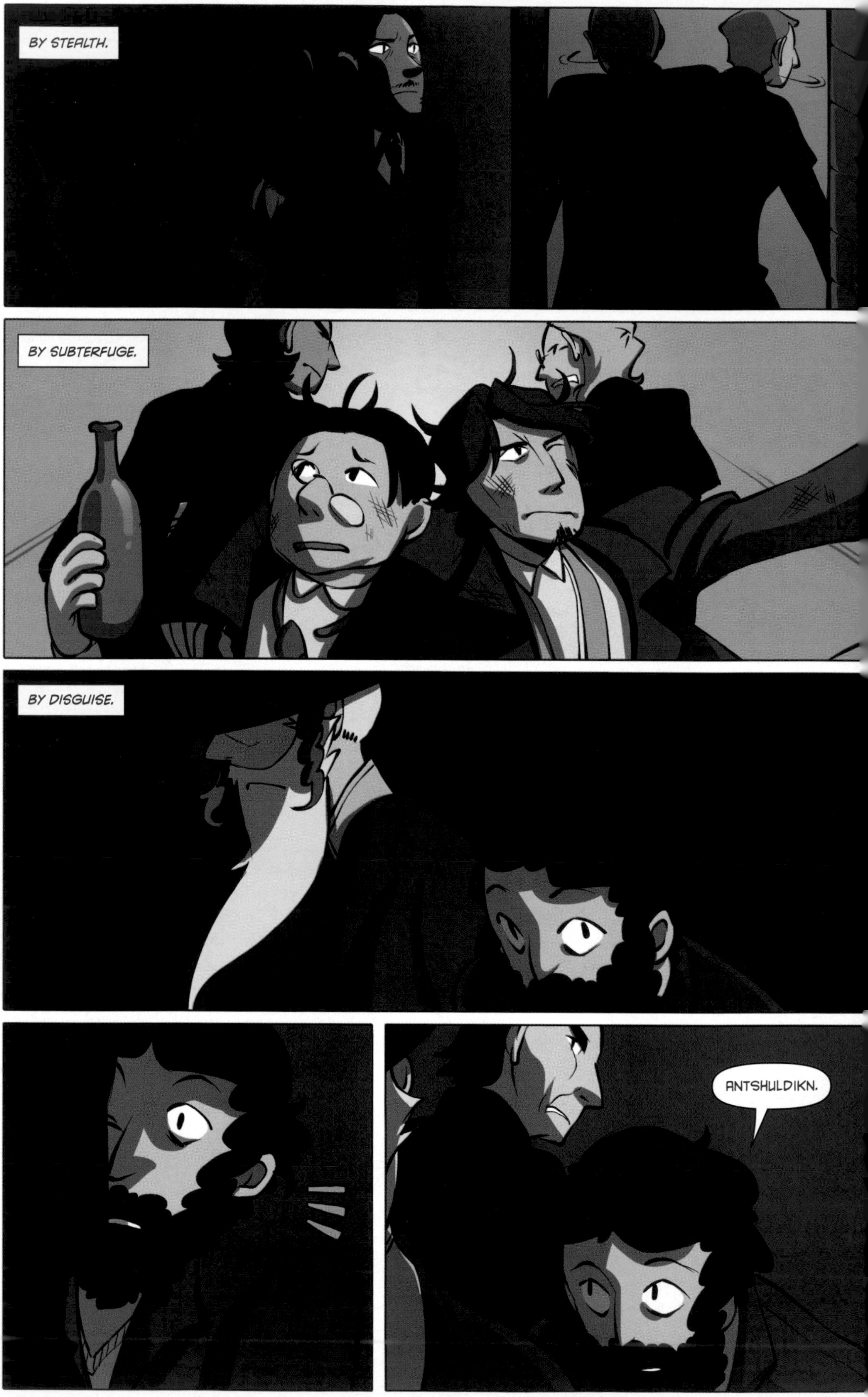
BY STEALTH.
BY SUBTERFUGE.
BY DISGUISE.
ANTSHULDIKN.

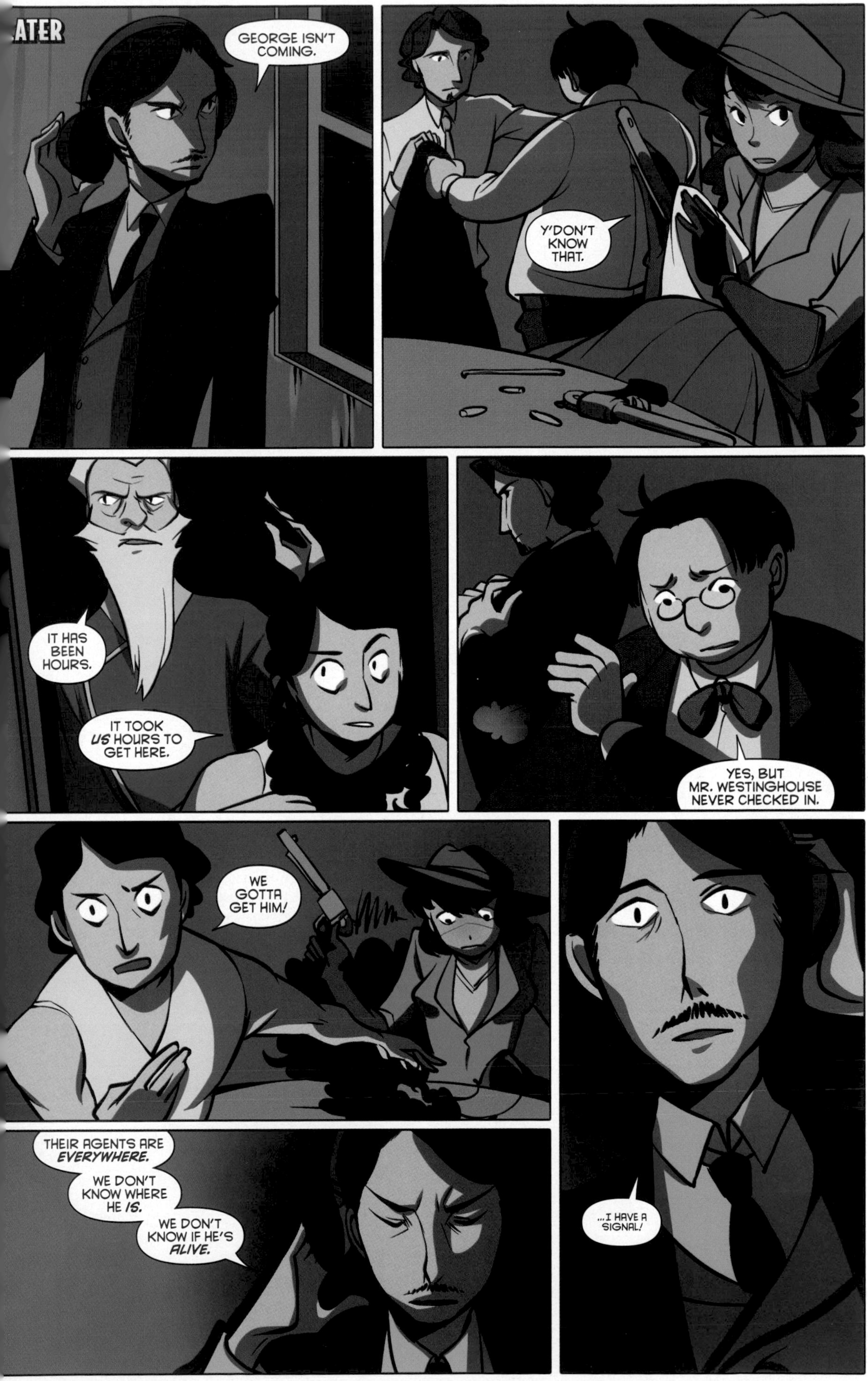
LATER
GEORGE ISN'T COMING.
Y'DON'T KNOW THAT.
IT HAS BEEN HOURS.
IT TOOK *US* HOURS TO GET HERE.
YES, BUT MR. WESTINGHOUSE NEVER CHECKED IN.
WE GOTTA GET HIM!
THEIR AGENTS ARE *EVERYWHERE.*
WE DON'T KNOW WHERE HE *IS.*
WE DON'T KNOW IF HE'S *ALIVE.*
...I HAVE A SIGNAL!

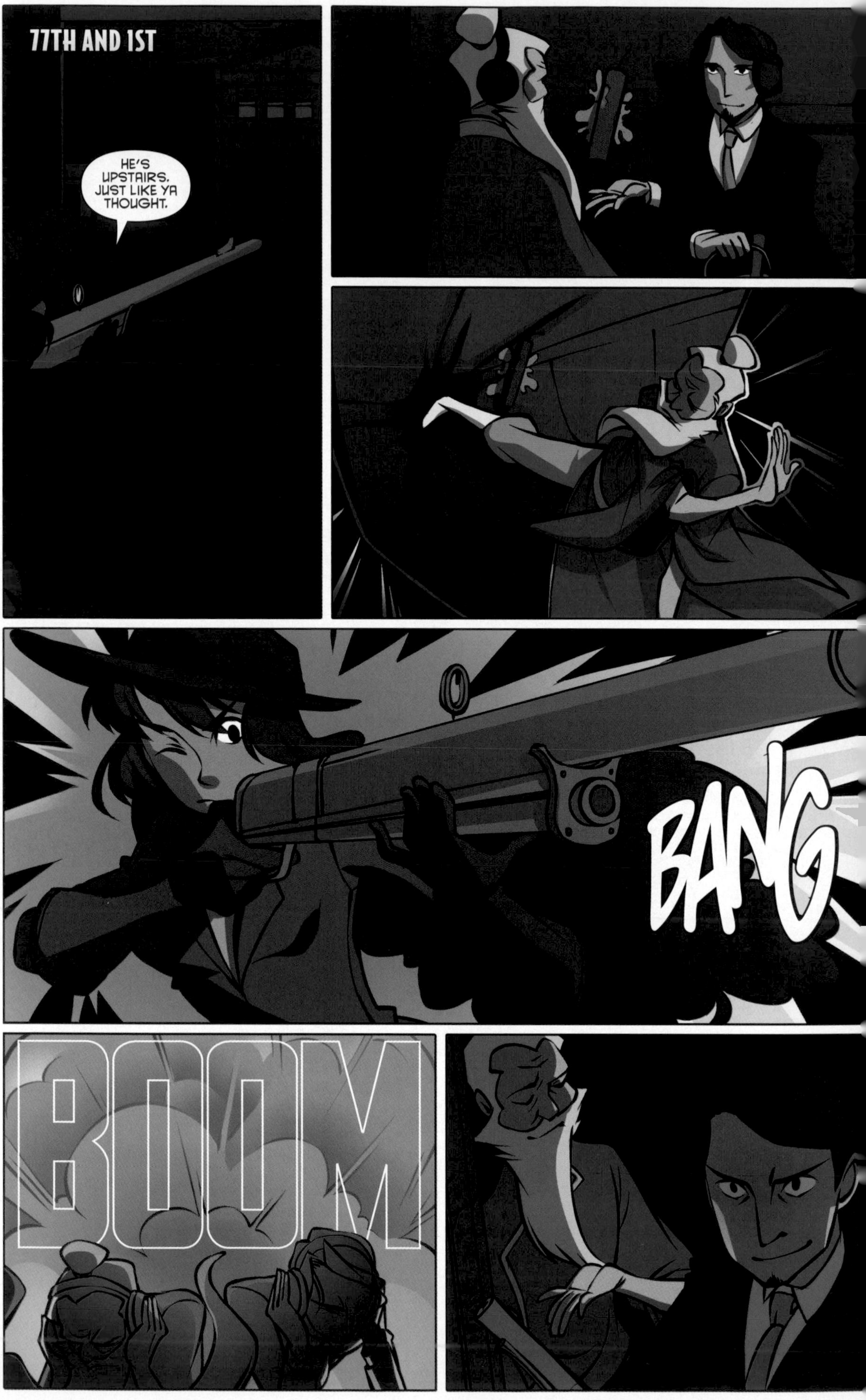
77TH AND 1ST
HE'S UPSTAIRS. JUST LIKE YA THOUGHT.
BANG
BOOM

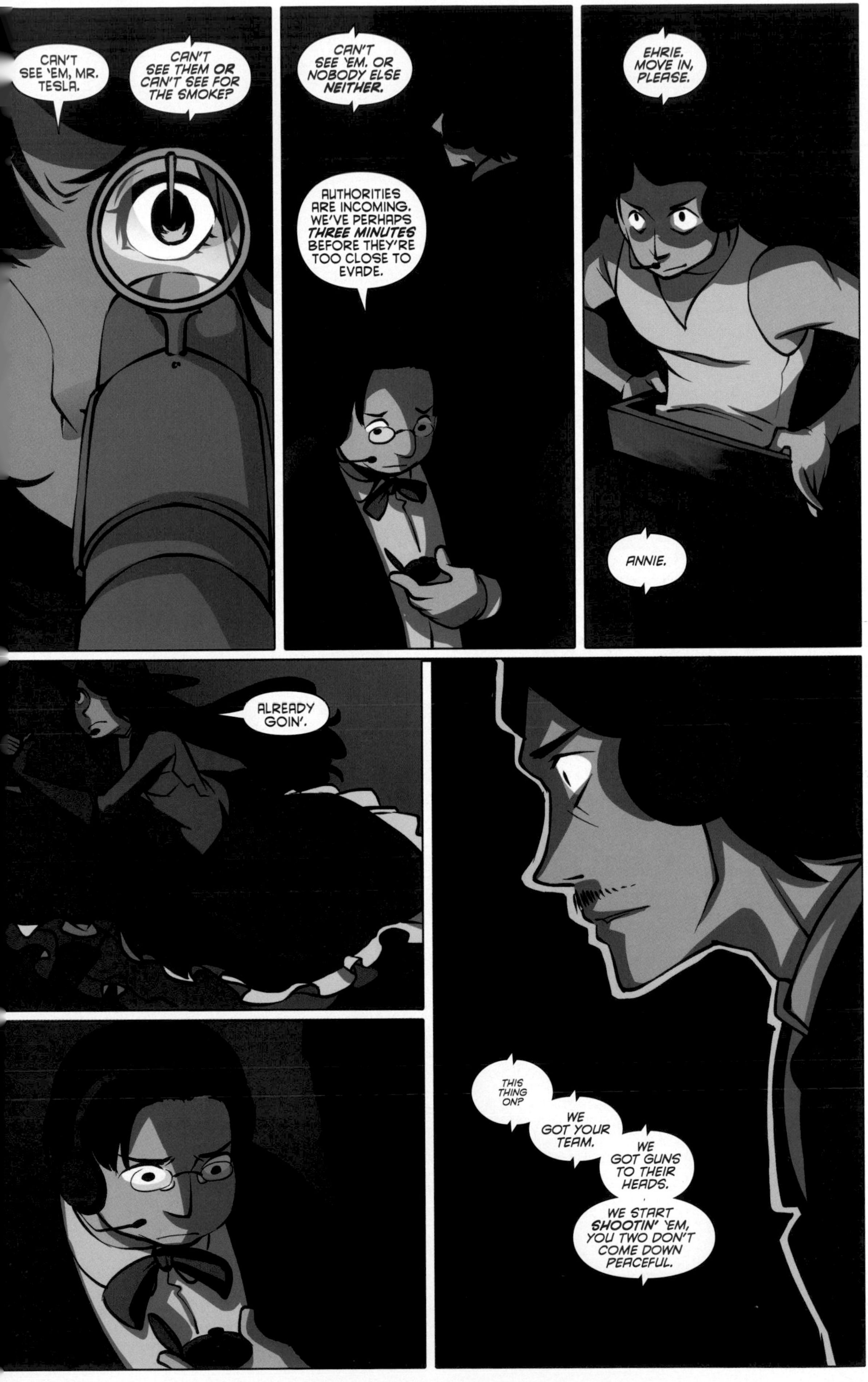
CAN'T SEE 'EM, MR. TESLA.
CAN'T SEE THEM OR CAN'T SEE FOR THE SMOKE?
CAN'T SEE 'EM. OR NOBODY ELSE NEITHER.
AUTHORITIES ARE INCOMING. WE'VE PERHAPS THREE MINUTES BEFORE THEY'RE TOO CLOSE TO EVADE.
EHRIE. MOVE IN, PLEASE.
ANNIE.
ALREADY GOIN'.
THIS THING ON?
WE GOT YOUR TEAM.
WE GOT GUNS TO THEIR HEADS.
WE START SHOOTIN' 'EM, YOU TWO DON'T COME DOWN PEACEFUL.

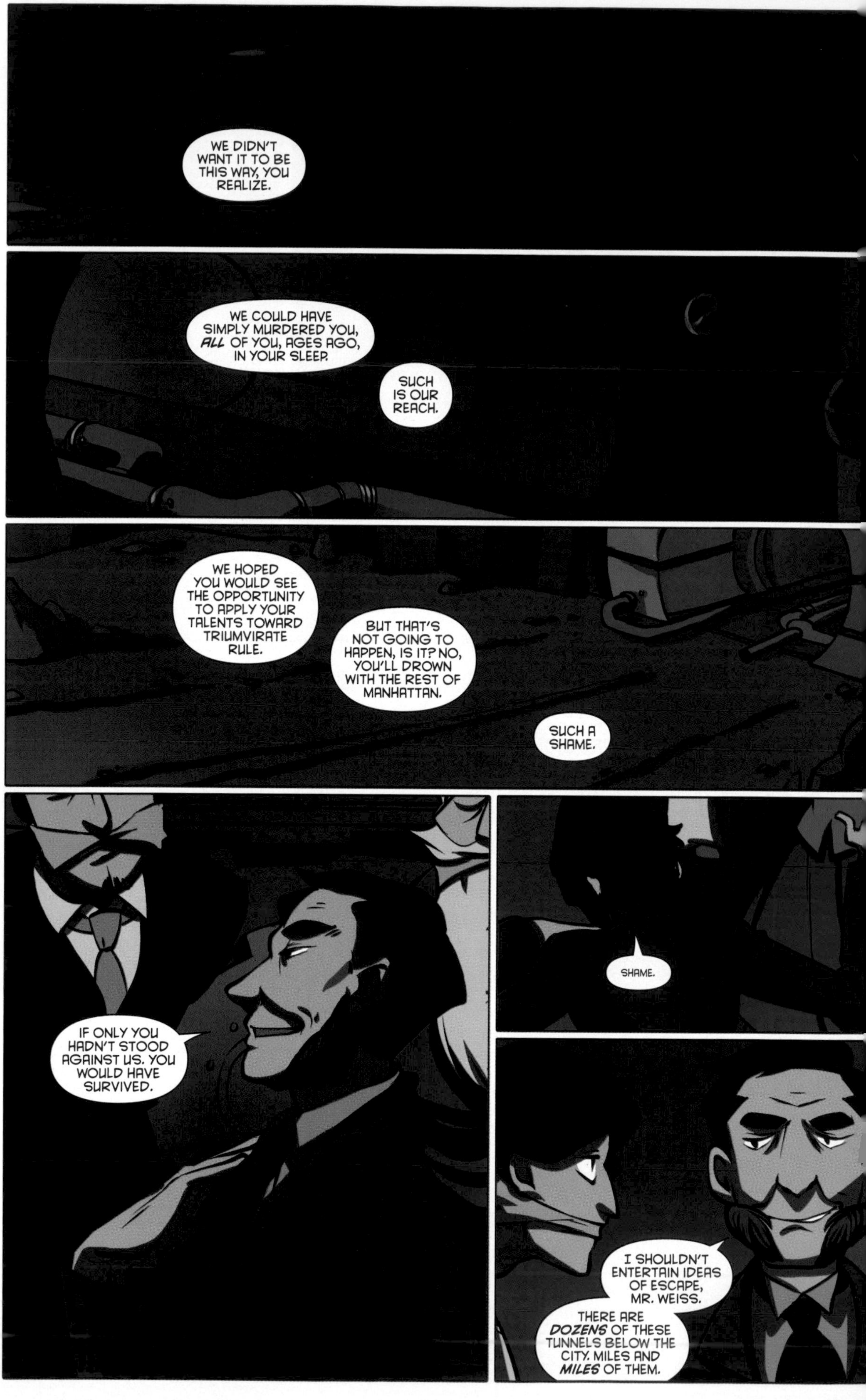
WE DIDN'T WANT IT TO BE THIS WAY, YOU REALIZE.
WE COULD HAVE SIMPLY MURDERED YOU, ALL OF YOU, AGES AGO, IN YOUR SLEEP.
SUCH IS OUR REACH.
WE HOPED YOU WOULD SEE THE OPPORTUNITY TO APPLY YOUR TALENTS TOWARD TRIUMVIRATE RULE.
BUT THAT'S NOT GOING TO HAPPEN, IS IT? NO, YOU'LL DROWN WITH THE REST OF MANHATTAN.
SUCH A SHAME.
IF ONLY YOU HADN'T STOOD AGAINST US. YOU WOULD HAVE SURVIVED.
SHAME.
I SHOULDN'T ENTERTAIN IDEAS OF ESCAPE, MR. WEISS.
THERE ARE DOZENS OF THESE TUNNELS BELOW THE CITY. MILES AND MILES OF THEM.

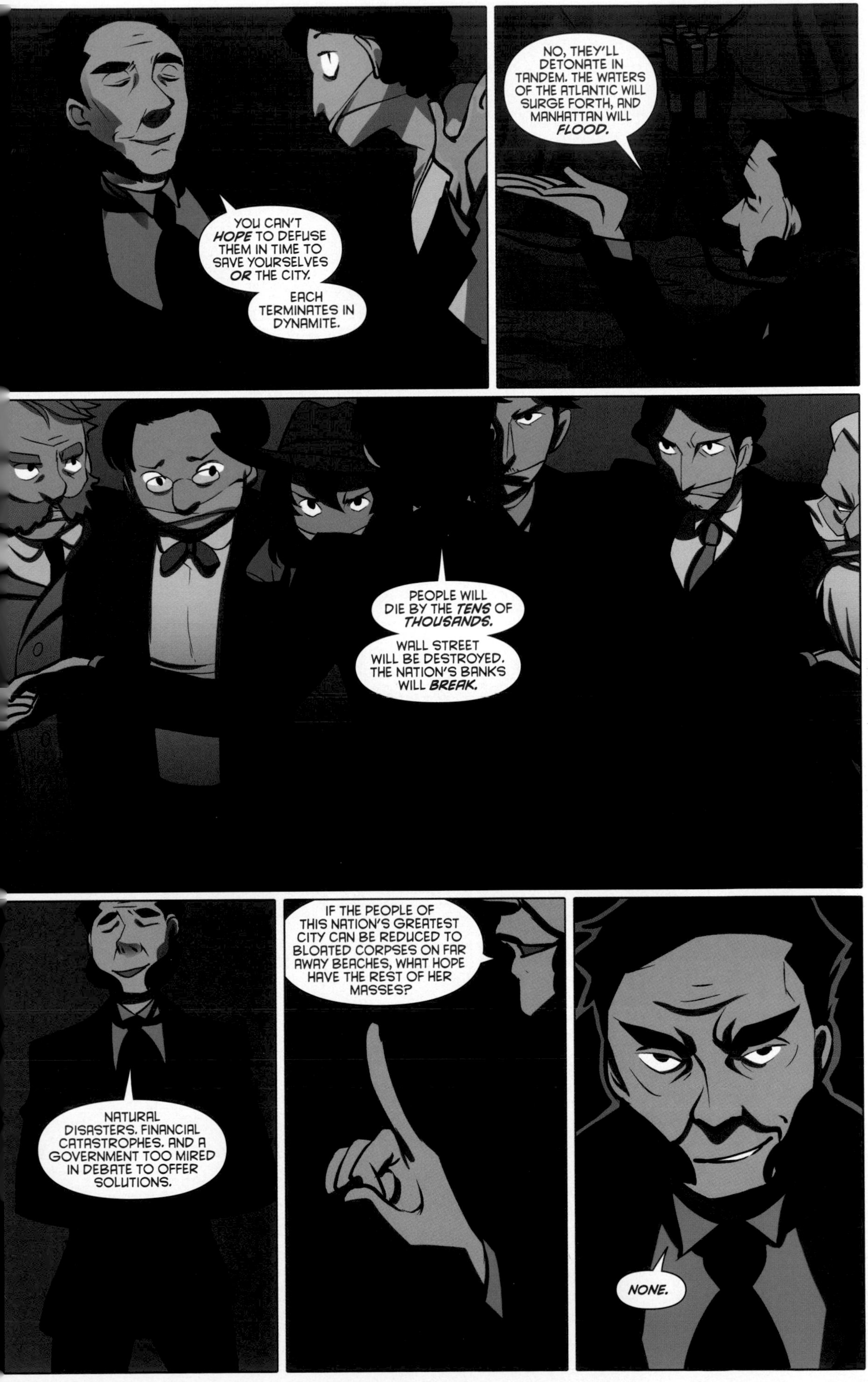
YOU CAN'T HOPE TO DEFUSE THEM IN TIME TO SAVE YOURSELVES OR THE CITY.
EACH TERMINATES IN DYNAMITE.
NO, THEY'LL DETONATE IN TANDEM. THE WATERS OF THE ATLANTIC WILL SURGE FORTH, AND MANHATTAN WILL FLOOD.
PEOPLE WILL DIE BY THE TENS OF THOUSANDS.
WALL STREET WILL BE DESTROYED. THE NATION'S BANKS WILL BREAK.
NATURAL DISASTERS. FINANCIAL CATASTROPHES. AND A GOVERNMENT TOO MIRED IN DEBATE TO OFFER SOLUTIONS.
IF THE PEOPLE OF THIS NATION'S GREATEST CITY CAN BE REDUCED TO BLOATED CORPSES ON FAR AWAY BEACHES, WHAT HOPE HAVE THE REST OF HER MASSES?
NONE.

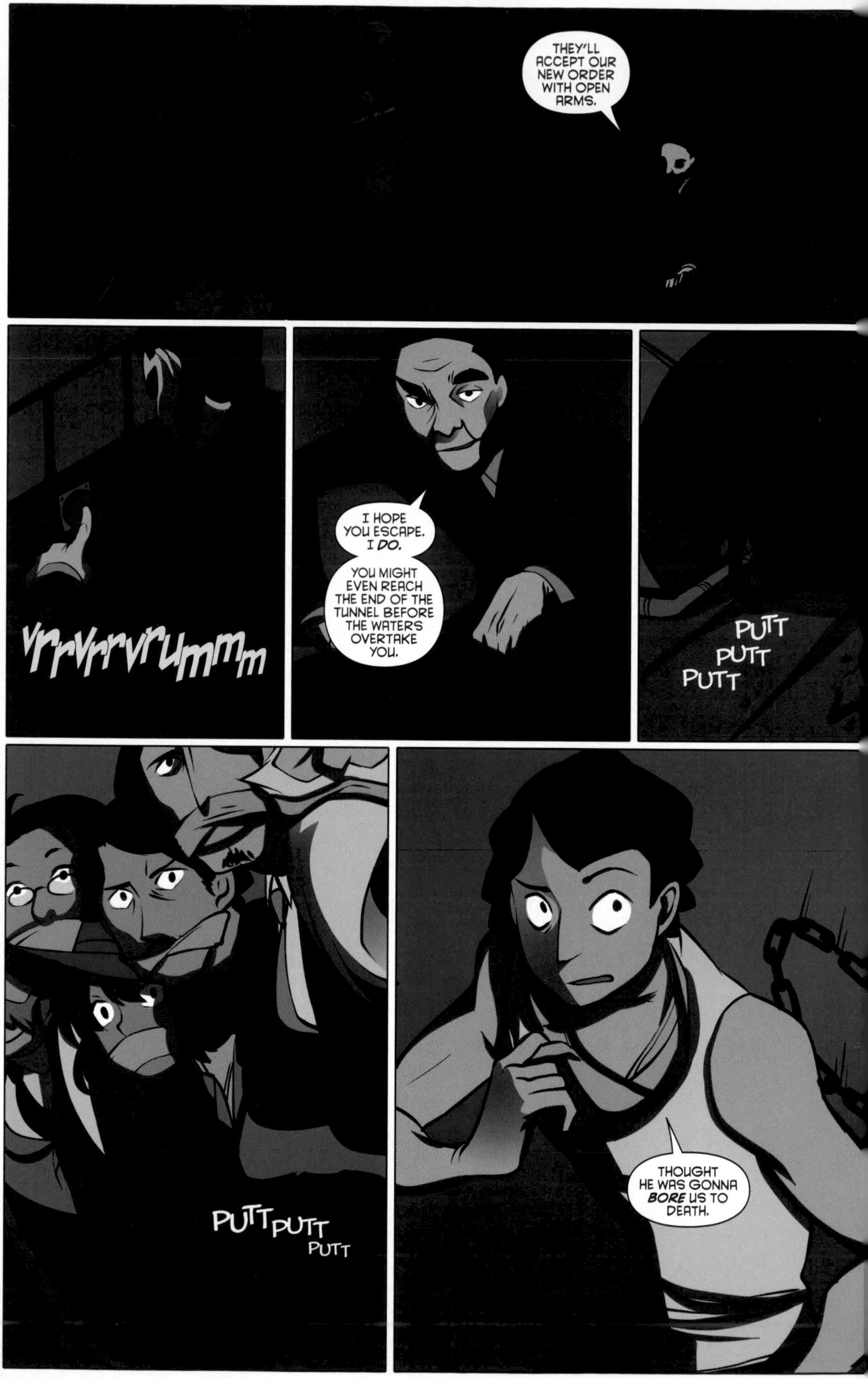
THEY'LL ACCEPT OUR NEW ORDER WITH OPEN ARMS.
vrrrvrrrvrummmm
I HOPE YOU ESCAPE. I DO.
YOU MIGHT EVEN REACH THE END OF THE TUNNEL BEFORE THE WATERS OVERTAKE YOU.
PUTT PUTT PUTT
PUTT PUTT PUTT
THOUGHT HE WAS GONNA BORE US TO DEATH.

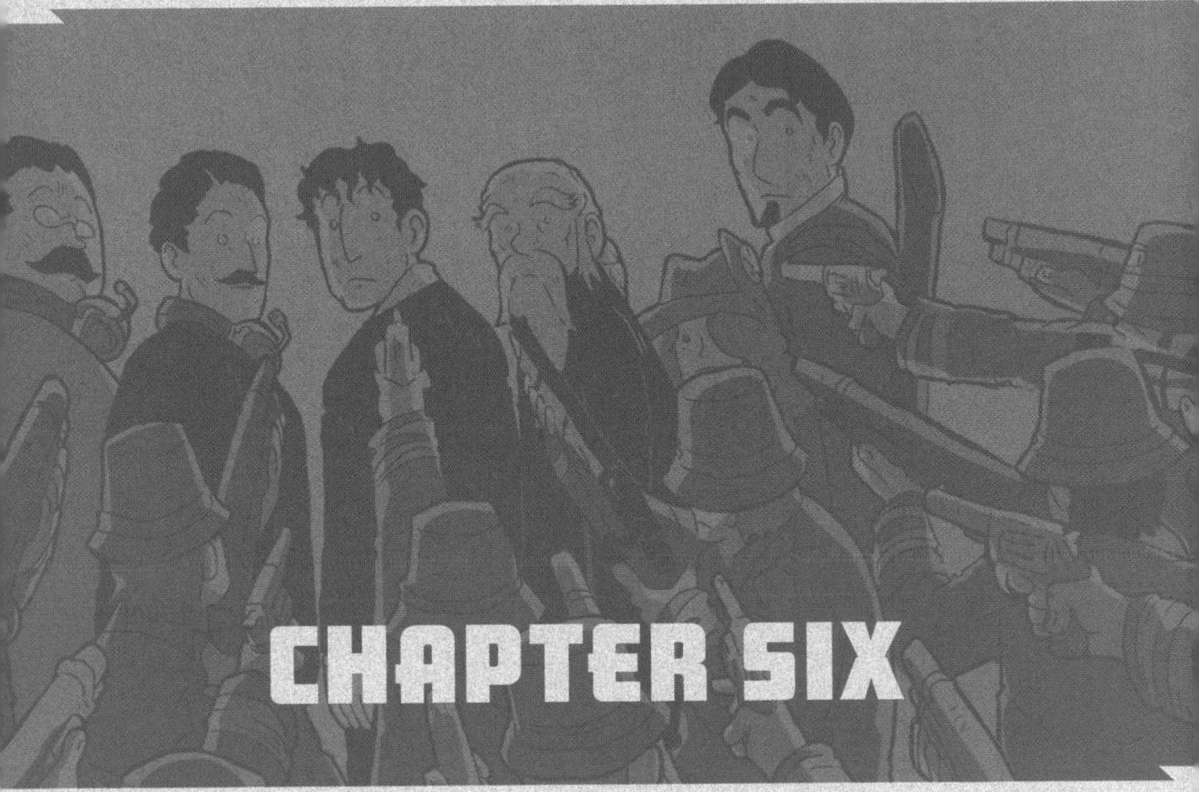

CHAPTER SIX

CLEVINGER
PENMAN

HENDERSON
POWELL

HTOMIC ROBO

PRESENTS

REAL SCIENCE
ADVENTURES

No. 12 $2.75

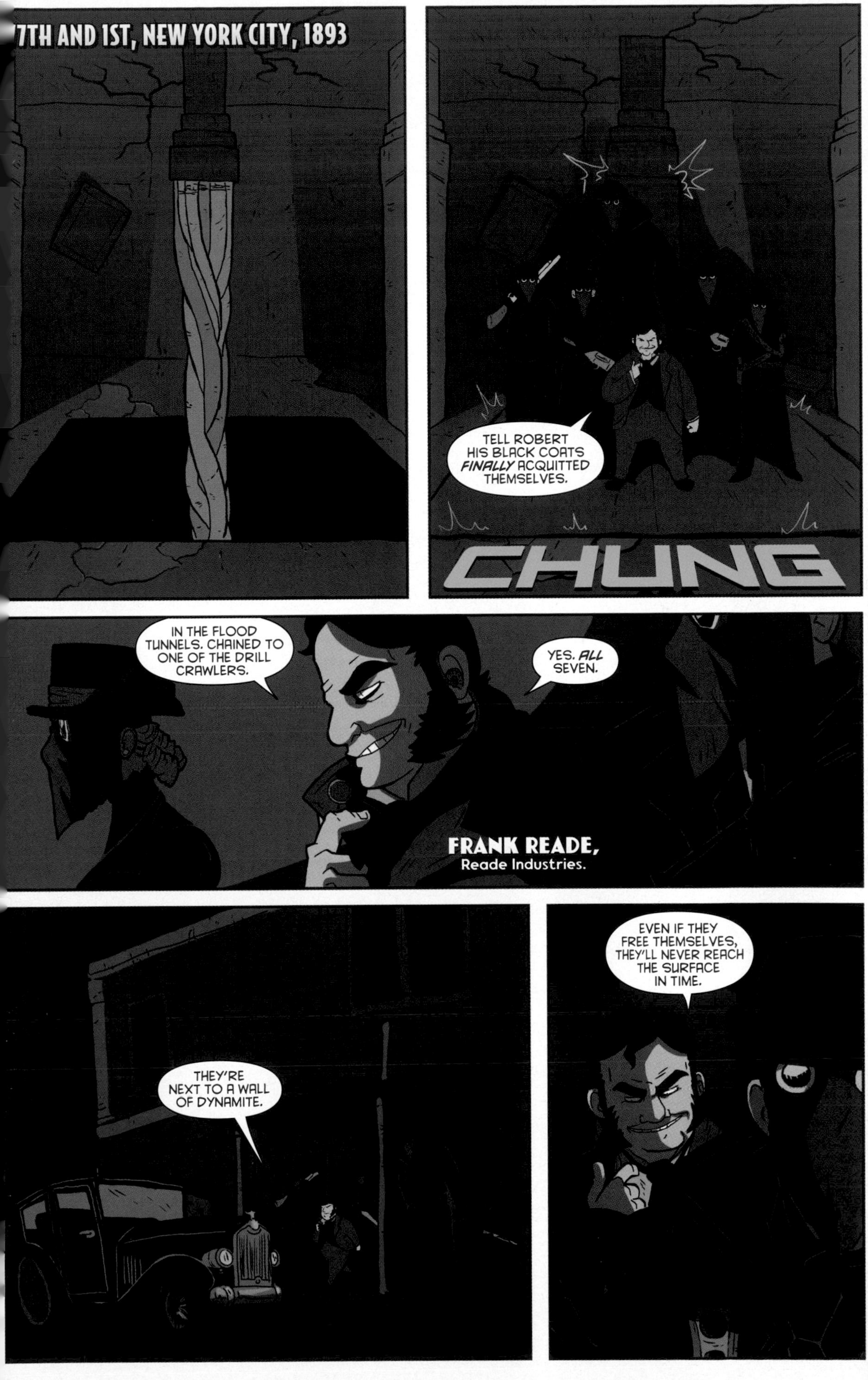
7TH AND 1ST, NEW YORK CITY, 1893
TELL ROBERT HIS BLACK COATS FINALLY ACQUITTED THEMSELVES.
CHUNG
IN THE FLOOD TUNNELS. CHAINED TO ONE OF THE DRILL CRAWLERS.
YES. ALL SEVEN.
FRANK READE, Reade Industries.
THEY'RE NEXT TO A WALL OF DYNAMITE.
EVEN IF THEY FREE THEMSELVES, THEY'LL NEVER REACH THE SURFACE IN TIME.

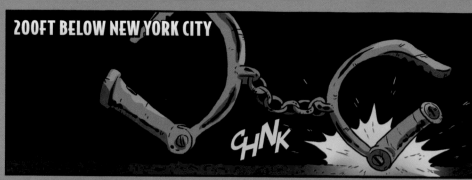

CHNK

APOLOGIES, EVERYONE. OUR CAPTURE WAS A NECESSARY INDIGNITY TO LEARN THE FULL SCOPE OF THEIR PLANS.

NIKOLA TESLA,
the Mastermind.

HARRY HOUDINI,
the Escapist.

I NEVER *IMAGINED* THEIR AMBITIONS COULD REACH SO FAR AS *NATIONAL CONQUEST.*

NOR *SHOULD* YOU HAVE. THAT YOU CANNOT THINK LIKE A VILLAIN SPEAKS TO THE NATURE OF YOUR GENIUS.

WONG KEI-YING,
Master Physician.

FOUND A GUN 'N SEVEN BULLETS.

FIVE OF THEM FIT.

IT *WILL* GO IN REVERSE. IF WE CAN GET IT STARTED, WE CAN GET OUT.

CHARLES FORT,
the Investigator.

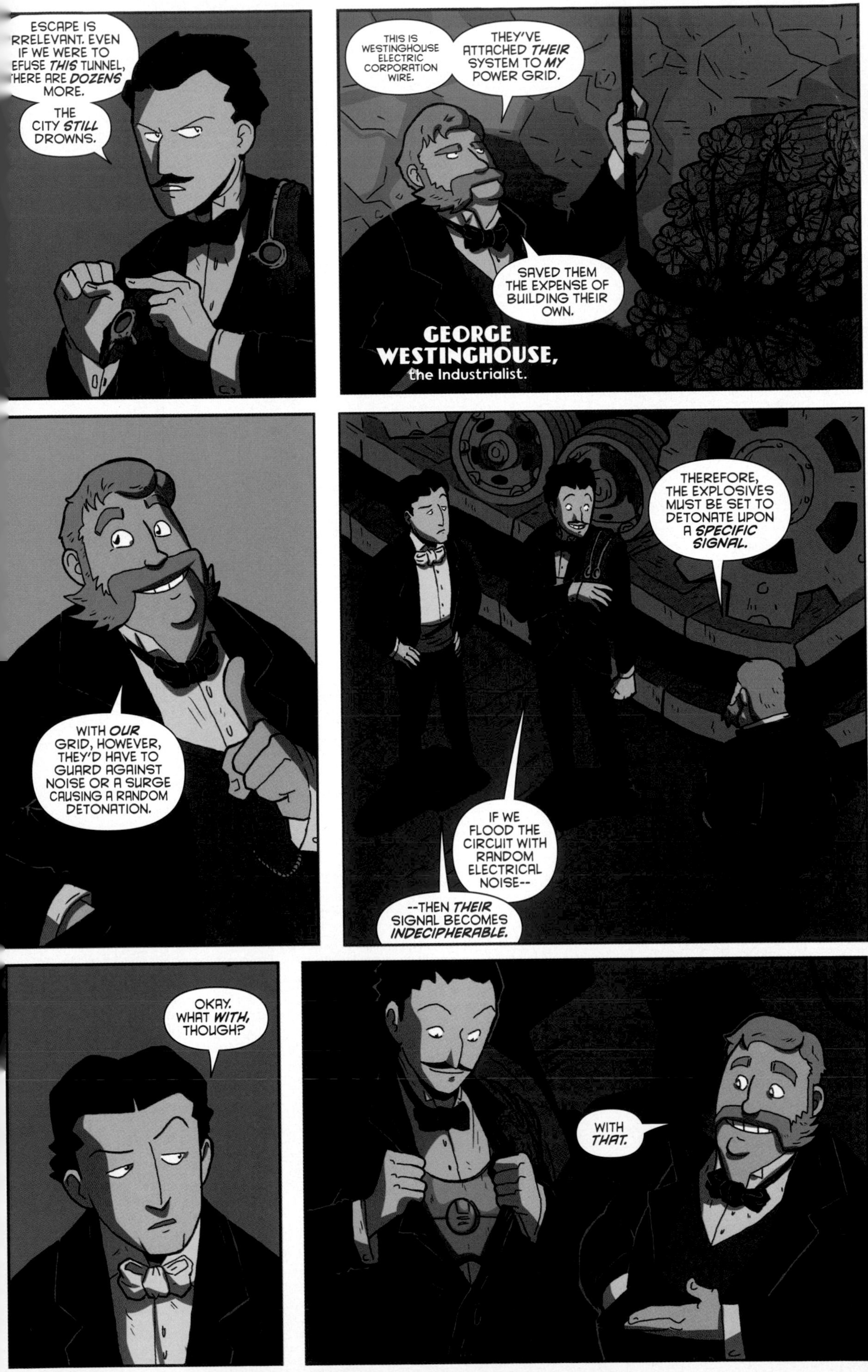
ESCAPE IS RRELEVANT. EVEN IF WE WERE TO EFUSE THIS TUNNEL, HERE ARE DOZENS MORE.
THE CITY STILL DROWNS.
THIS IS WESTINGHOUSE ELECTRIC CORPORATION WIRE.
THEY'VE ATTACHED THEIR SYSTEM TO MY POWER GRID.
SAVED THEM THE EXPENSE OF BUILDING THEIR OWN.
GEORGE WESTINGHOUSE, the Industrialist.
WITH OUR GRID, HOWEVER, THEY'D HAVE TO GUARD AGAINST NOISE OR A SURGE CAUSING A RANDOM DETONATION.
THEREFORE, THE EXPLOSIVES MUST BE SET TO DETONATE UPON A SPECIFIC SIGNAL.
IF WE FLOOD THE CIRCUIT WITH RANDOM ELECTRICAL NOISE--
--THEN THEIR SIGNAL BECOMES INDECIPHERABLE.
OKAY. WHAT WITH, THOUGH?
WITH THAT.

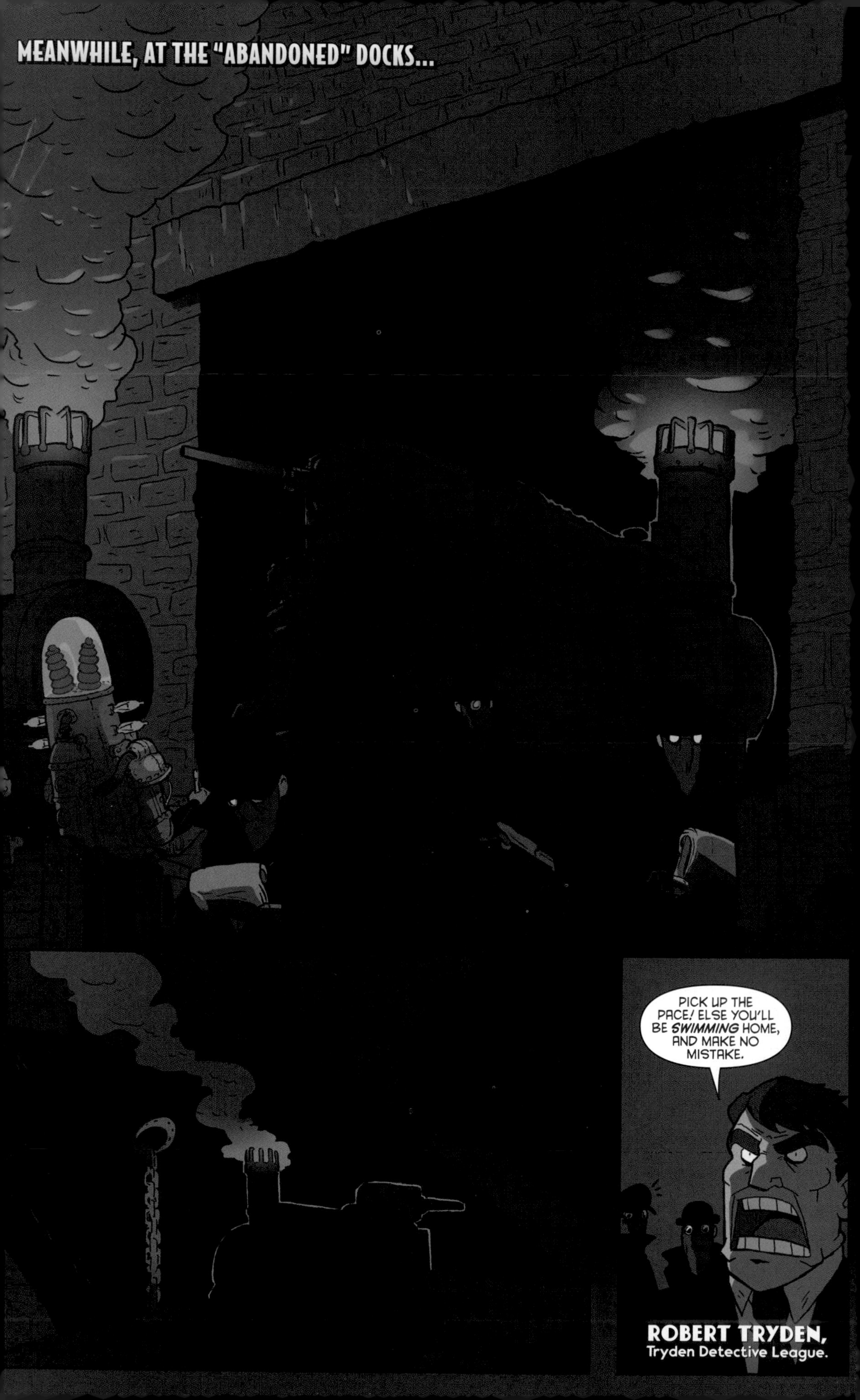
MEANWHILE, AT THE "ABANDONED" DOCKS...
PICK UP THE PACE! ELSE YOU'LL BE *SWIMMING* HOME, AND MAKE NO MISTAKE.
ROBERT TRYDEN,
Tryden Detective League.

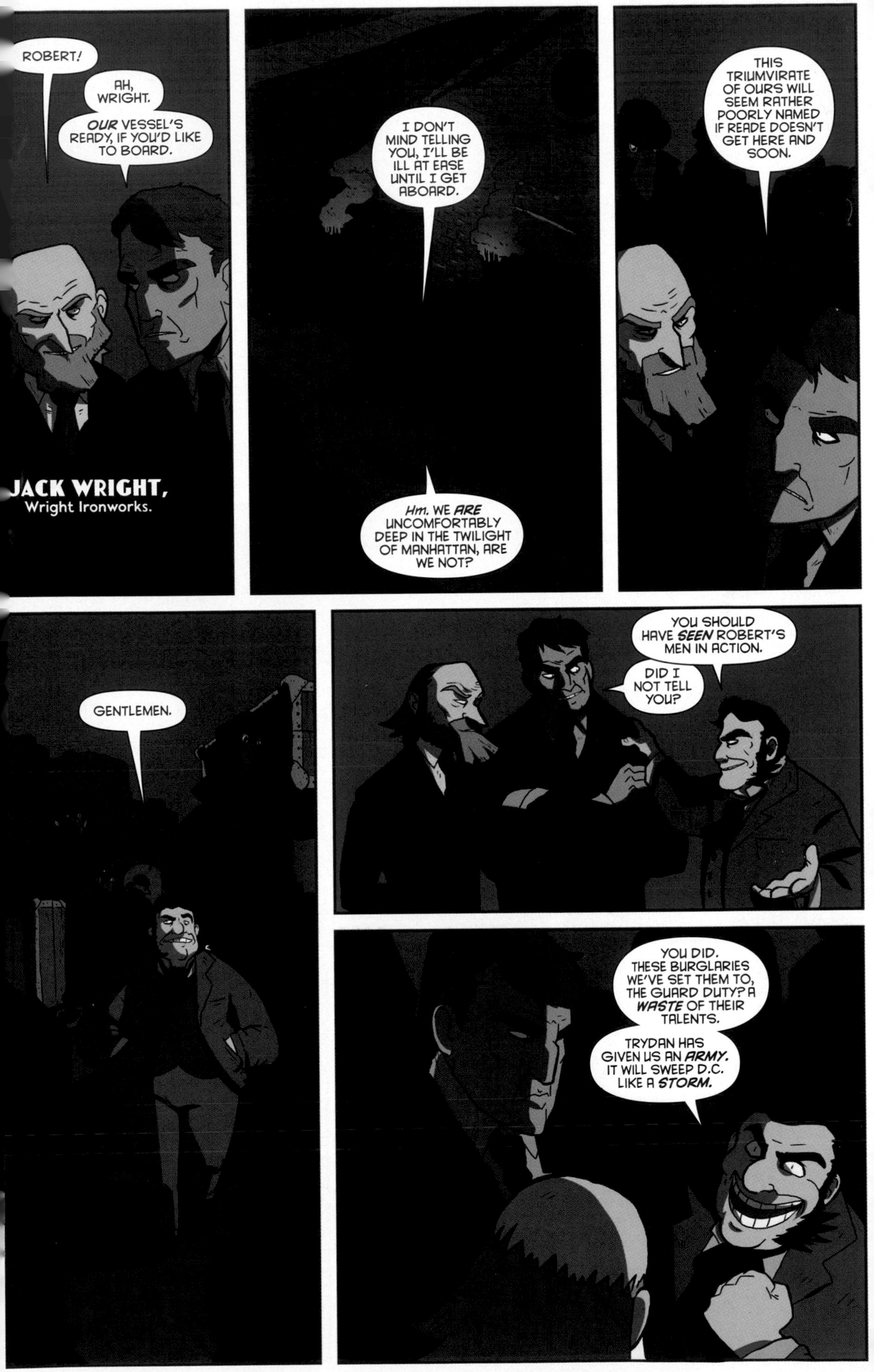

ROBERT!
AH, WRIGHT.
OUR VESSEL'S READY, IF YOU'D LIKE TO BOARD.
JACK WRIGHT,
Wright Ironworks.
I DON'T MIND TELLING YOU, I'LL BE ILL AT EASE UNTIL I GET ABOARD.
Hm. WE ARE UNCOMFORTABLY DEEP IN THE TWILIGHT OF MANHATTAN, ARE WE NOT?
THIS TRIUMVIRATE OF OURS WILL SEEM RATHER POORLY NAMED IF READE DOESN'T GET HERE AND SOON.
GENTLEMEN.
YOU SHOULD HAVE SEEN ROBERT'S MEN IN ACTION.
DID I NOT TELL YOU?
YOU DID. THESE BURGLARIES WE'VE SET THEM TO, THE GUARD DUTY? A WASTE OF THEIR TALENTS.
TRYDAN HAS GIVEN US AN ARMY. IT WILL SWEEP D.C. LIKE A STORM.

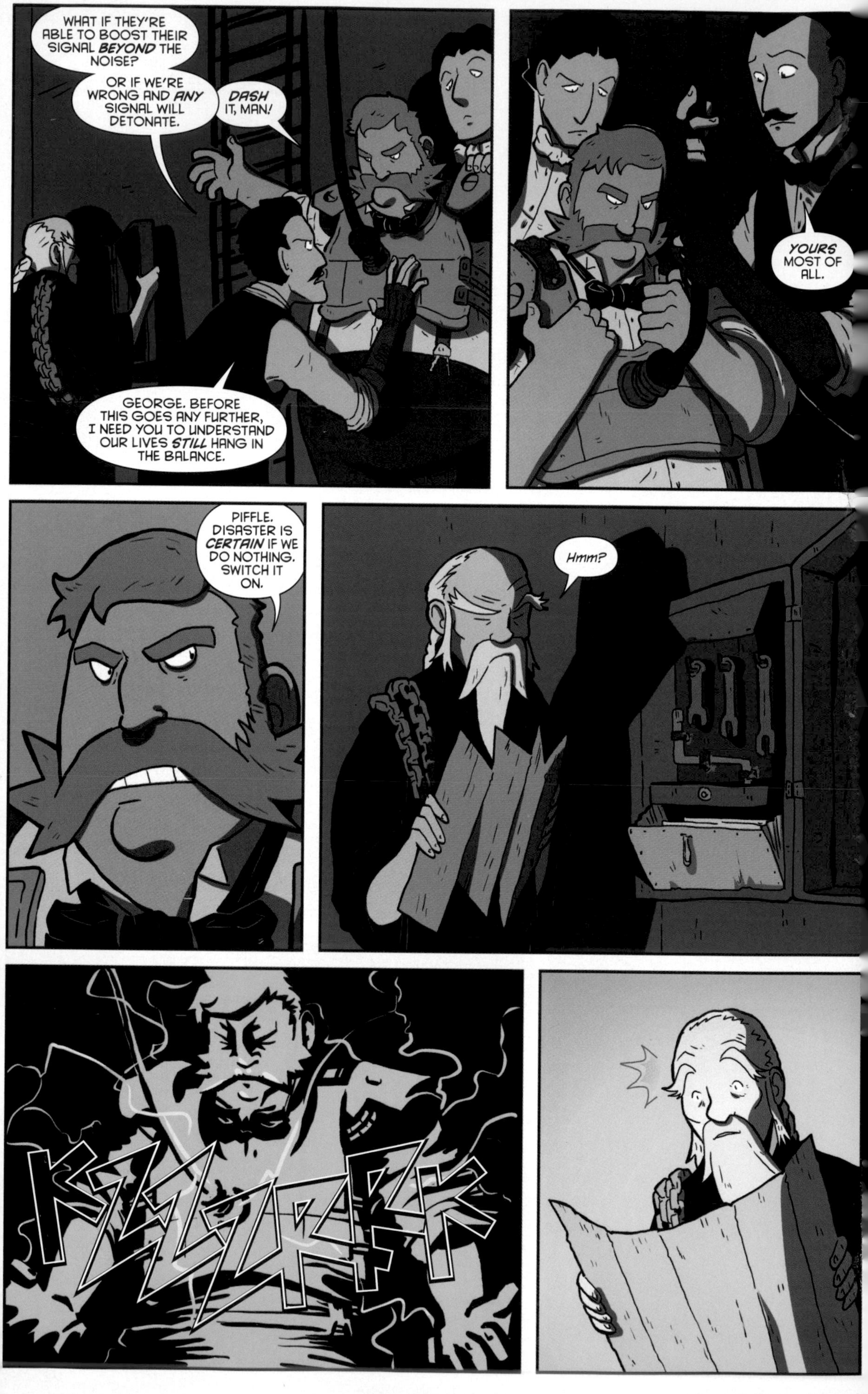
WHAT IF THEY'RE ABLE TO BOOST THEIR SIGNAL BEYOND THE NOISE?
OR IF WE'RE WRONG AND ANY SIGNAL WILL DETONATE.
DASH IT, MAN!
GEORGE. BEFORE THIS GOES ANY FURTHER, I NEED YOU TO UNDERSTAND OUR LIVES STILL HANG IN THE BALANCE.
YOURS MOST OF ALL.
PIFFLE. DISASTER IS CERTAIN IF WE DO NOTHING. SWITCH IT ON.
Hmm?
KZZZZAPPK

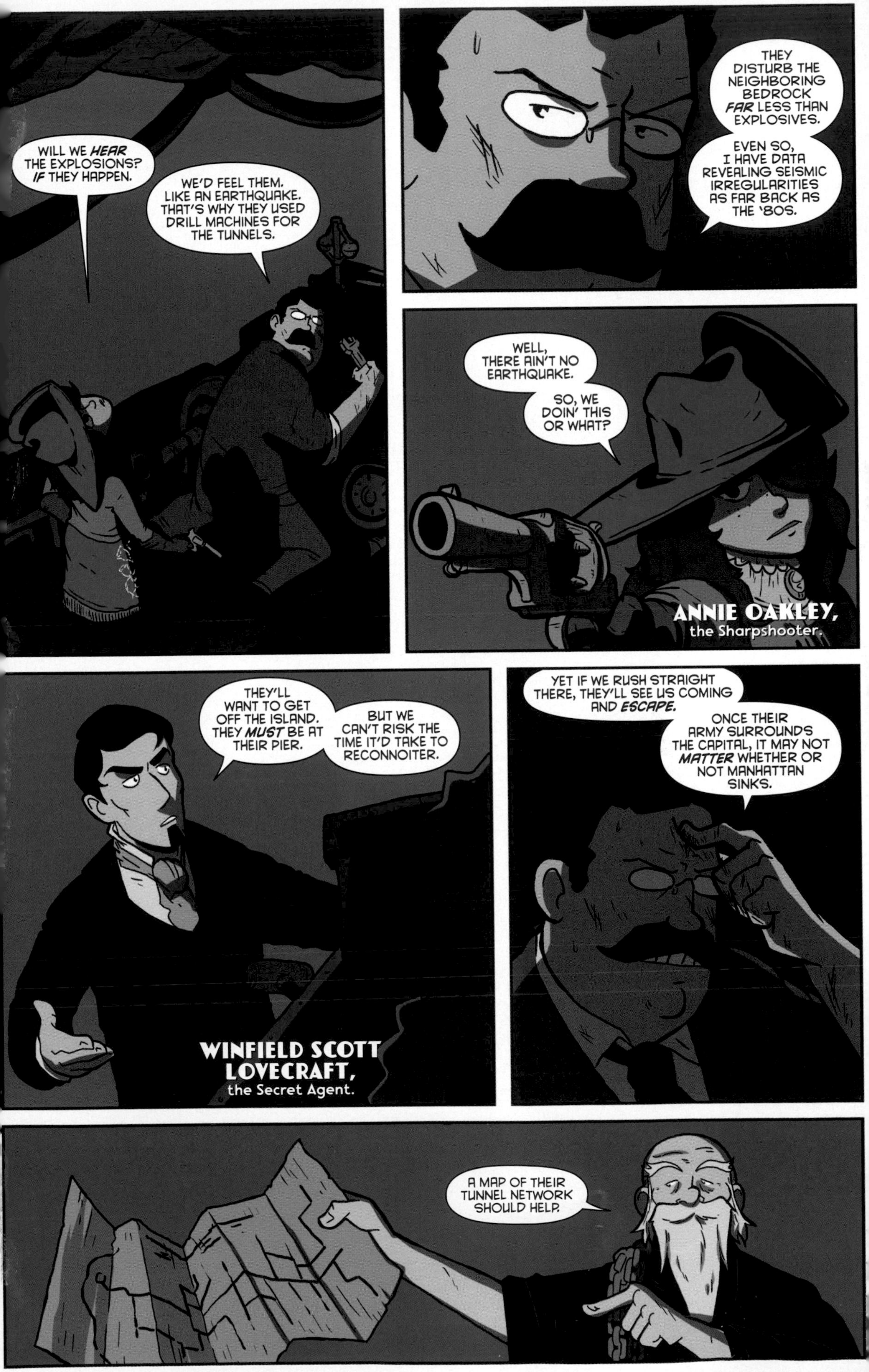
WILL WE HEAR THE EXPLOSIONS? IF THEY HAPPEN.
WE'D FEEL THEM. LIKE AN EARTHQUAKE. THAT'S WHY THEY USED DRILL MACHINES FOR THE TUNNELS.
THEY DISTURB THE NEIGHBORING BEDROCK FAR LESS THAN EXPLOSIVES.
EVEN SO, I HAVE DATA REVEALING SEISMIC IRREGULARITIES AS FAR BACK AS THE '80S.
WELL, THERE AIN'T NO EARTHQUAKE.
SO, WE DOIN' THIS OR WHAT?
ANNIE OAKLEY, the Sharpshooter.
THEY'LL WANT TO GET OFF THE ISLAND. THEY MUST BE AT THEIR PIER.
BUT WE CAN'T RISK THE TIME IT'D TAKE TO RECONNOITER.
WINFIELD SCOTT LOVECRAFT, the Secret Agent.
YET IF WE RUSH STRAIGHT THERE, THEY'LL SEE US COMING AND ESCAPE.
ONCE THEIR ARMY SURROUNDS THE CAPITAL, IT MAY NOT MATTER WHETHER OR NOT MANHATTAN SINKS.
A MAP OF THEIR TUNNEL NETWORK SHOULD HELP.

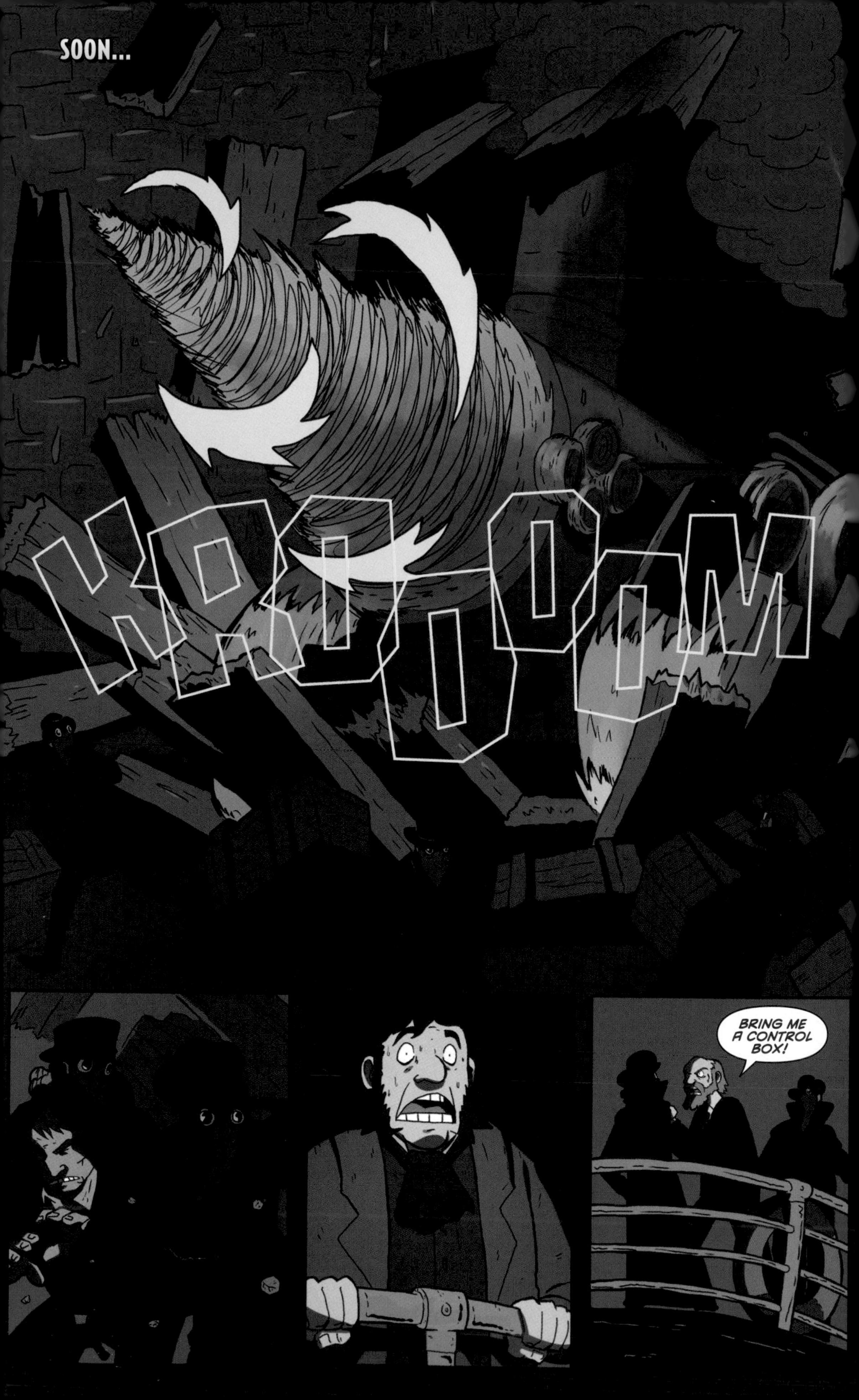
SOON...
KRRUDOOM
BRING ME A CONTROL BOX!

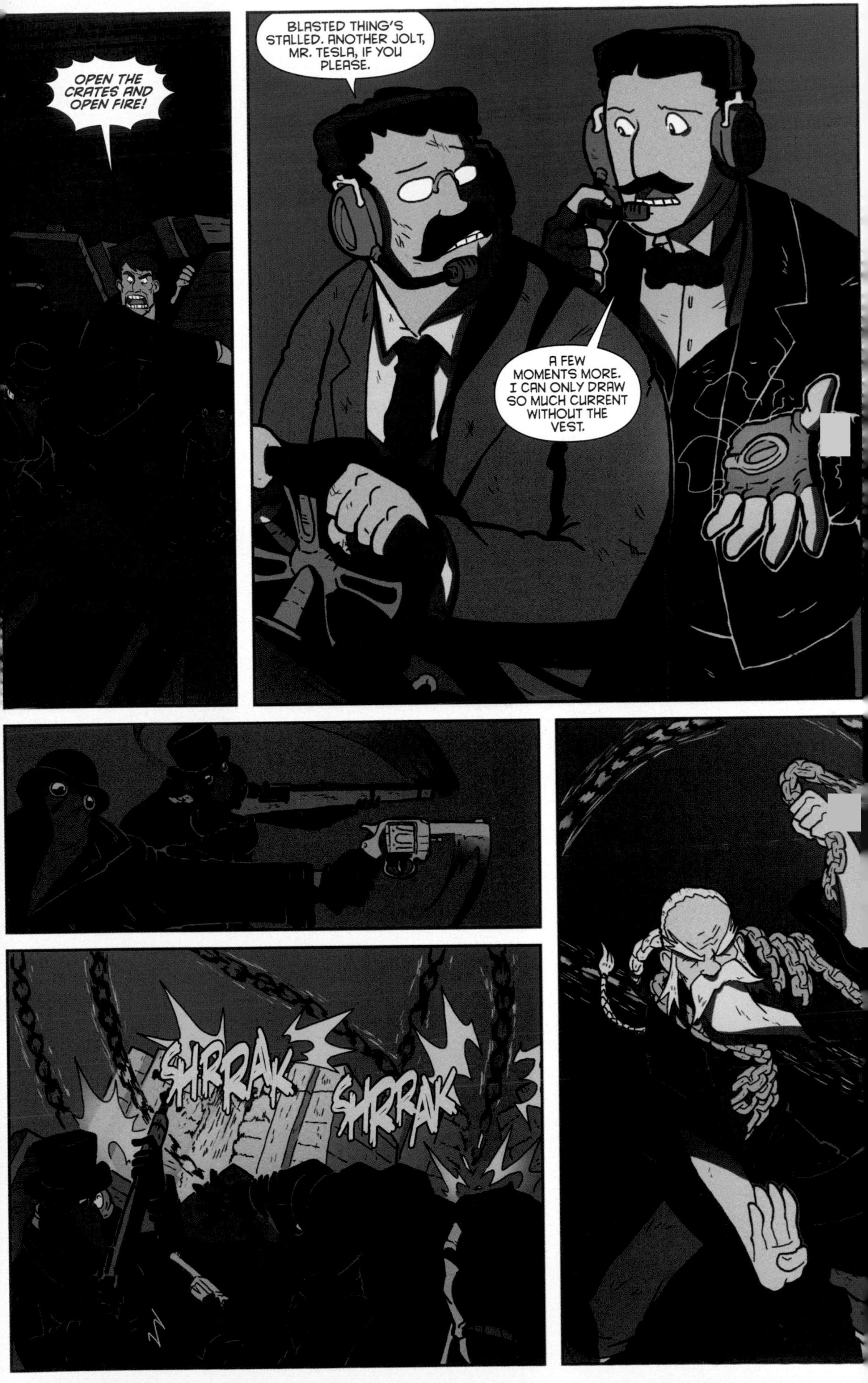
OPEN THE CRATES AND OPEN FIRE!
BLASTED THING'S STALLED. ANOTHER JOLT, MR. TESLA, IF YOU PLEASE.
A FEW MOMENTS MORE. I CAN ONLY DRAW SO MUCH CURRENT WITHOUT THE VEST.
SHRRAK
SHRRAK

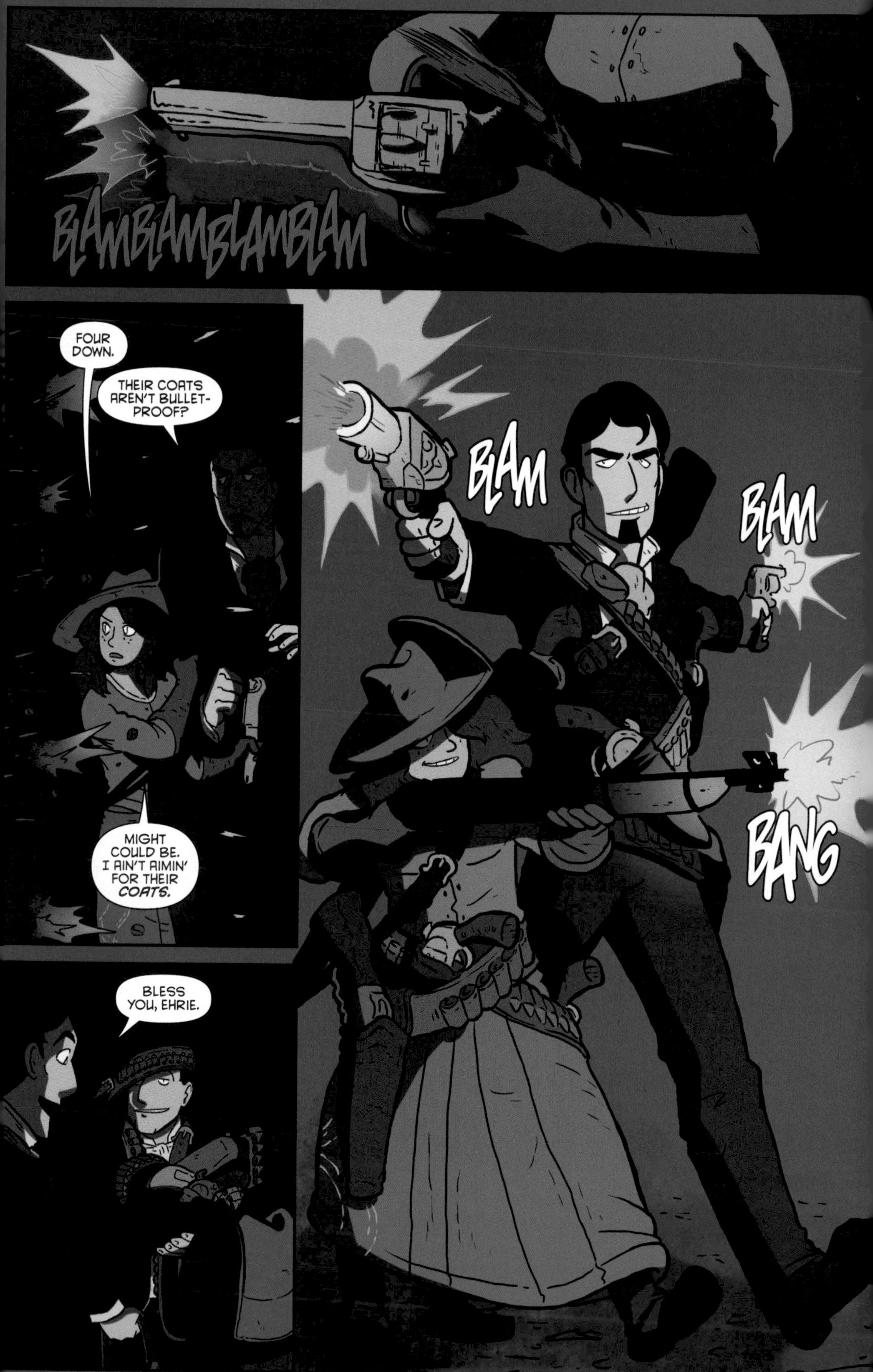
BLAMBLAMBLAMBLAM
FOUR DOWN.
THEIR COATS AREN'T BULLET-PROOF?
MIGHT COULD BE. I AIN'T AIMIN' FOR THEIR *COATS.*
BLAM
BLAM
BANG
BLESS YOU, EHRIE.

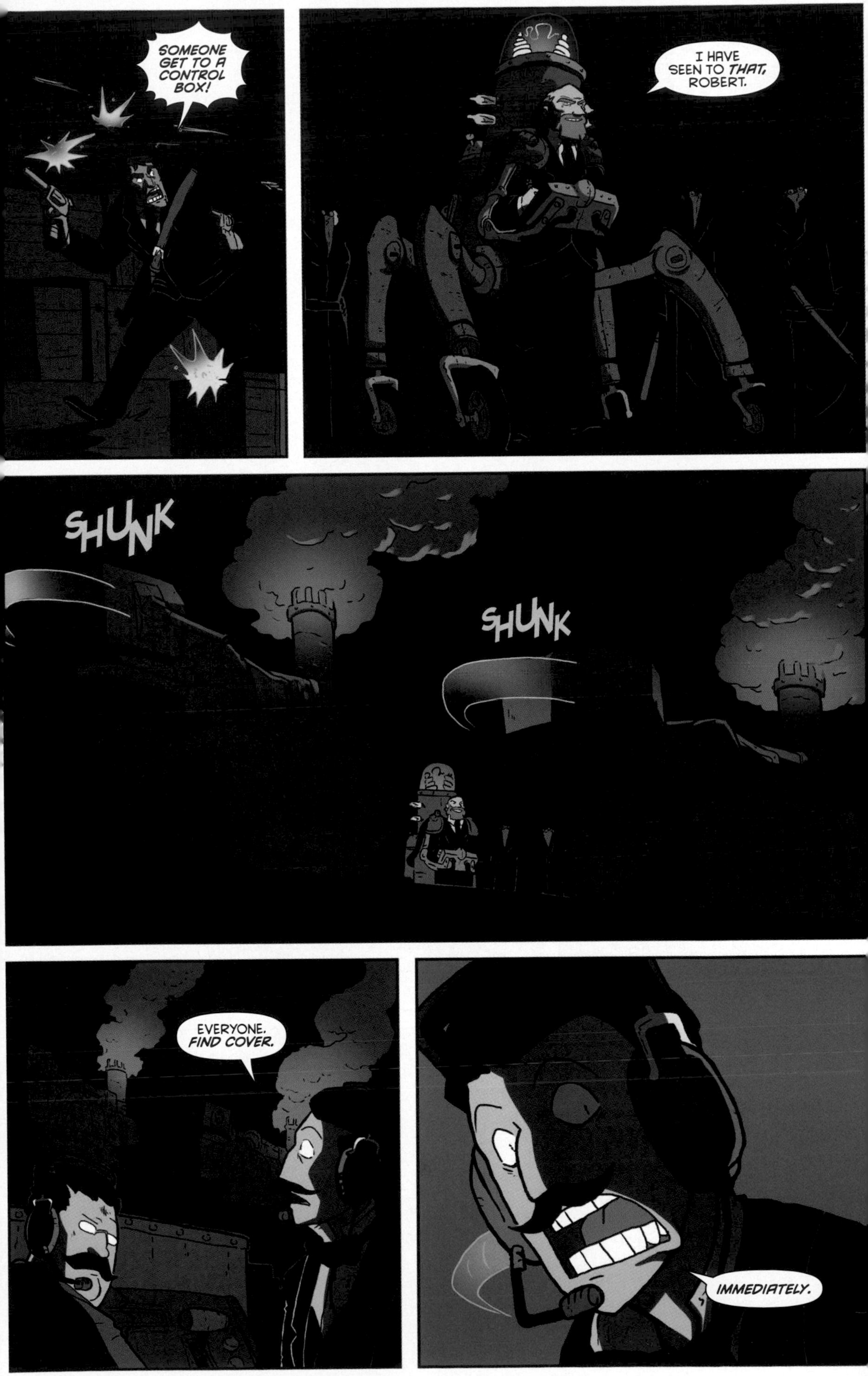
SOMEONE GET TO A CONTROL BOX!
I HAVE SEEN TO *THAT,* ROBERT.
SHUNK
SHUNK
EVERYONE. *FIND COVER.*
IMMEDIATELY.

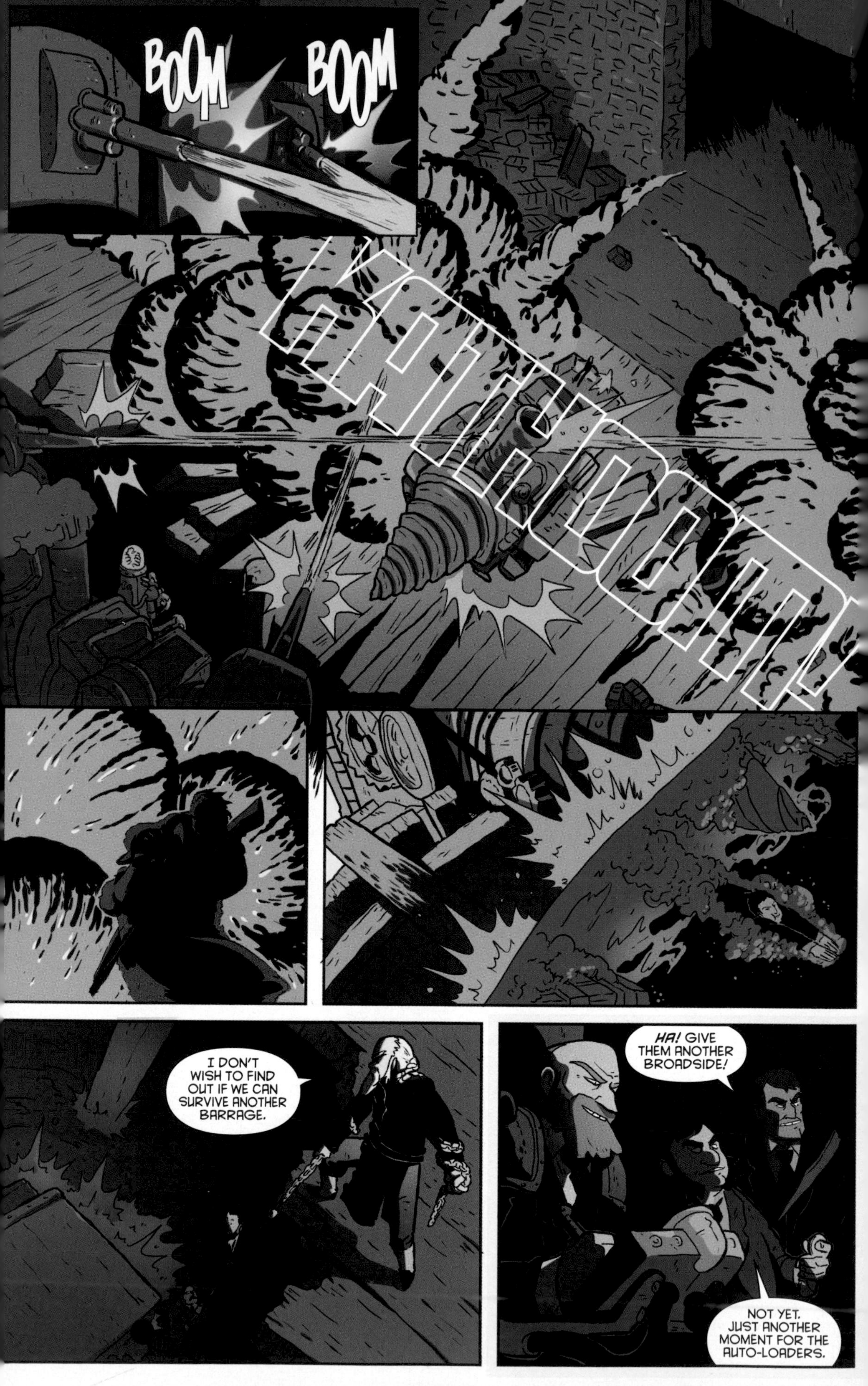
BOOM
BOOM
I DON'T WISH TO FIND OUT IF WE CAN SURVIVE ANOTHER BARRAGE.
HA! GIVE THEM ANOTHER BROADSIDE!
NOT YET. JUST ANOTHER MOMENT FOR THE AUTO-LOADERS.

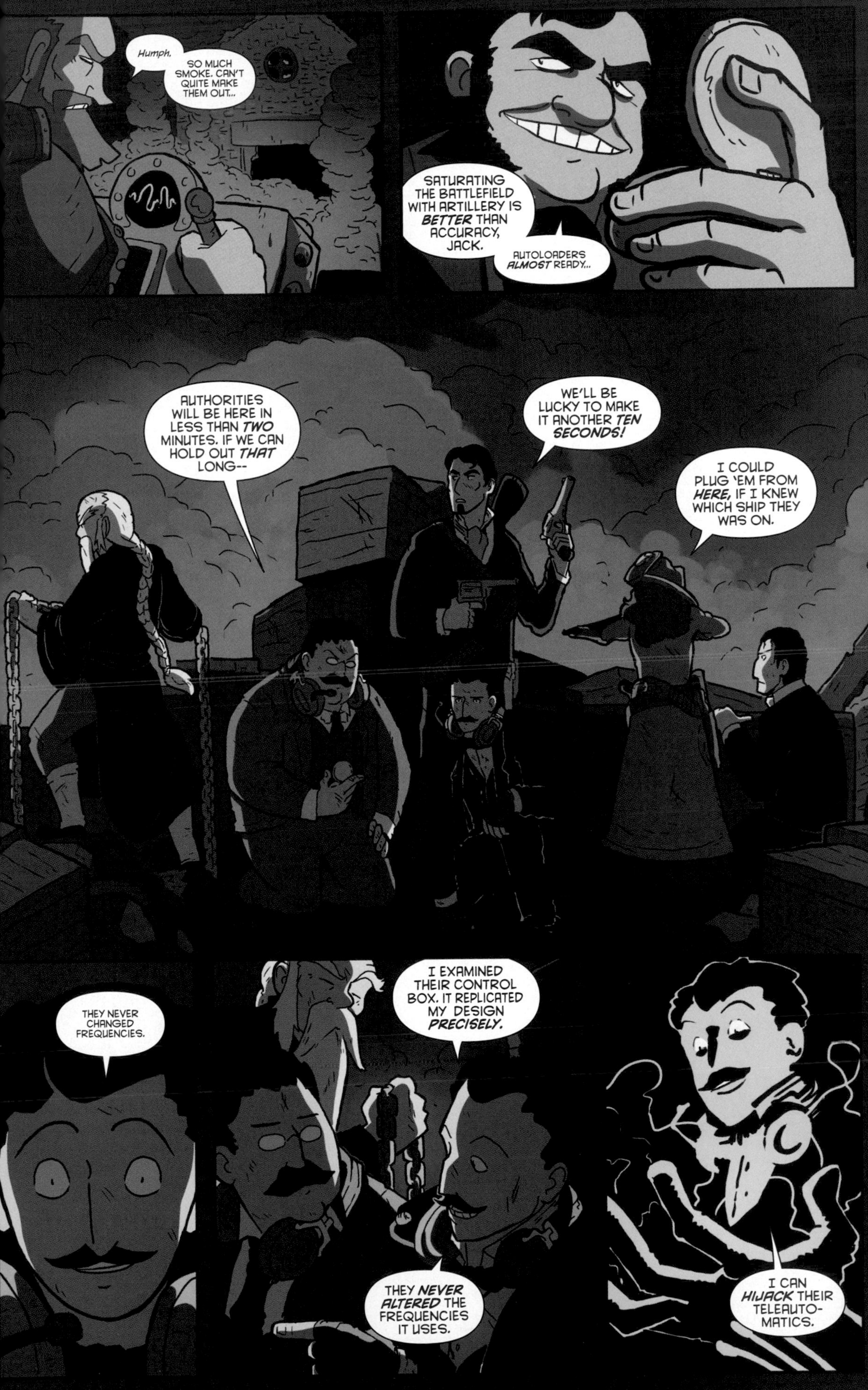

Humph.
SO MUCH SMOKE. CAN'T QUITE MAKE THEM OUT...
SATURATING THE BATTLEFIELD WITH ARTILLERY IS *BETTER* THAN ACCURACY, JACK.
AUTOLOADERS *ALMOST* READY...
AUTHORITIES WILL BE HERE IN LESS THAN *TWO* MINUTES. IF WE CAN HOLD OUT *THAT* LONG--
WE'LL BE LUCKY TO MAKE IT ANOTHER *TEN SECONDS!*
I COULD PLUG 'EM FROM *HERE,* IF I KNEW WHICH SHIP THEY WAS ON.
THEY NEVER CHANGED FREQUENCIES.
I EXAMINED THEIR CONTROL BOX. IT REPLICATED MY DESIGN *PRECISELY.*
THEY *NEVER ALTERED* THE FREQUENCIES IT USES.
I CAN *HIJACK* THEIR TELEAUTO-MATICS.

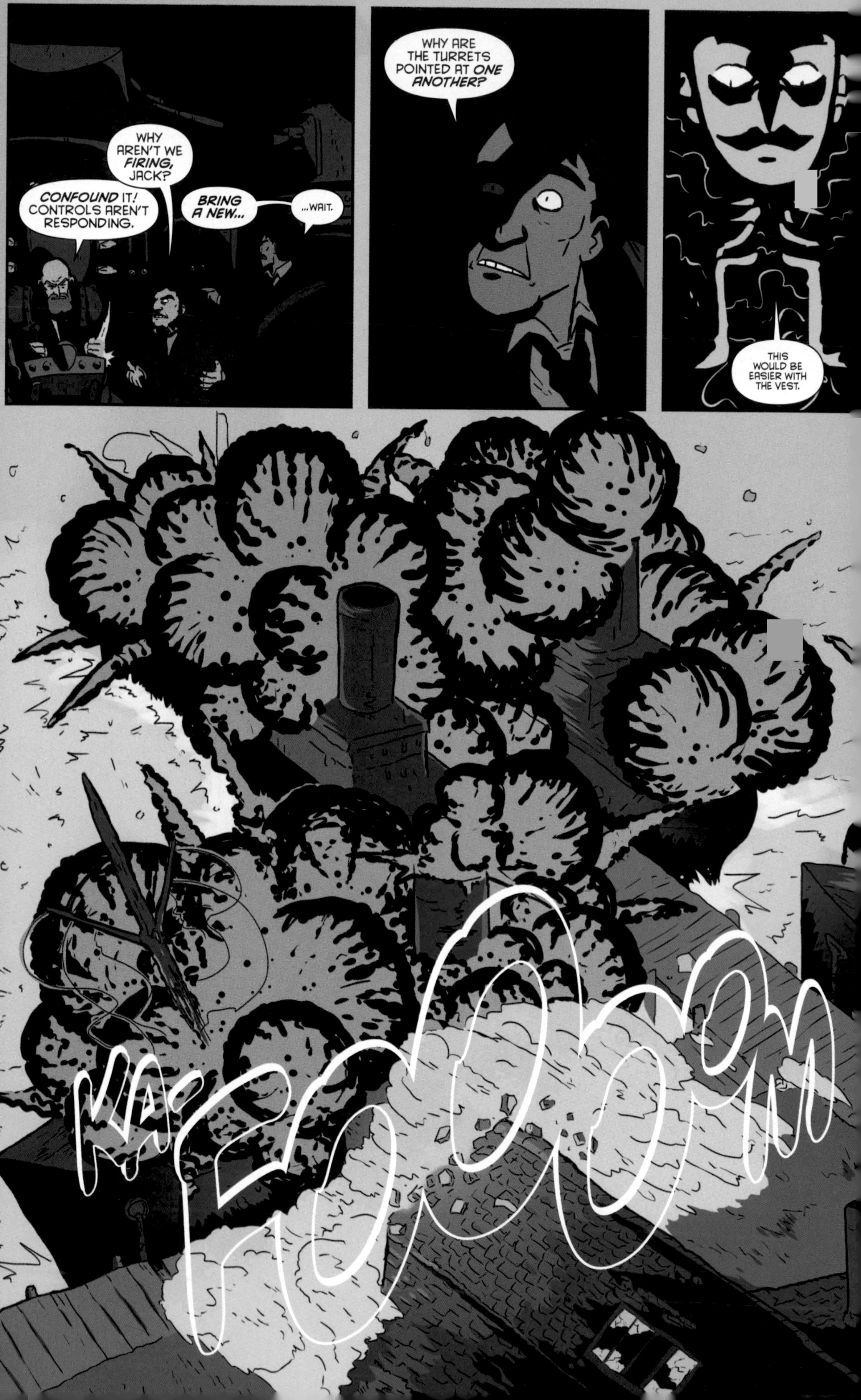
WHY AREN'T WE FIRING, JACK?
CONFOUND IT! CONTROLS AREN'T RESPONDING.
BRING A NEW...
...WAIT.
WHY ARE THE TURRETS POINTED AT ONE ANOTHER?
THIS WOULD BE EASIER WITH THE VEST.
KA-FOOOOM

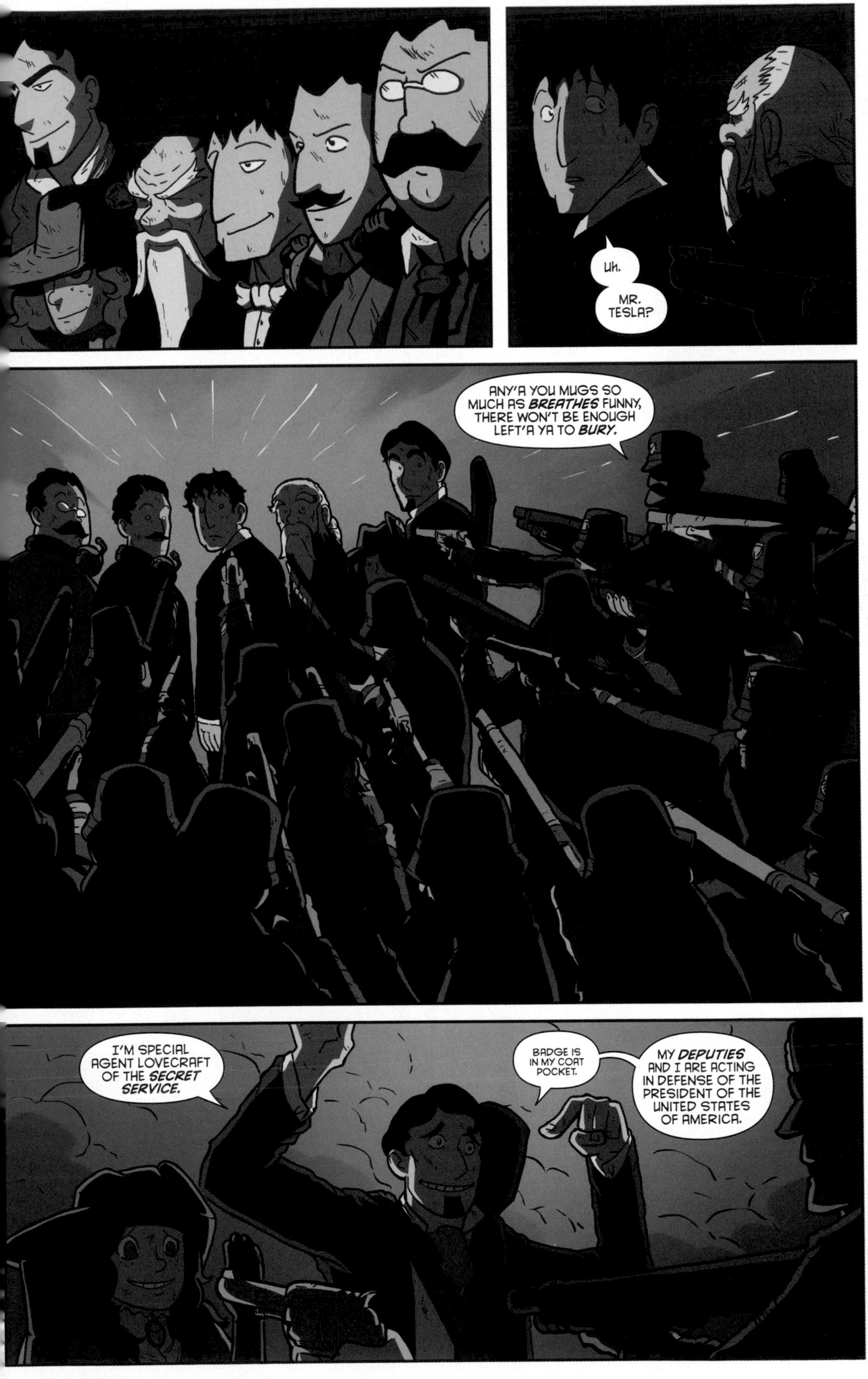
Uh.
MR. TESLA?
ANY'A YOU MUGS SO MUCH AS BREATHES FUNNY, THERE WON'T BE ENOUGH LEFT'A YA TO BURY.
I'M SPECIAL AGENT LOVECRAFT OF THE SECRET SERVICE.
BADGE IS IN MY COAT POCKET.
MY DEPUTIES AND I ARE ACTING IN DEFENSE OF THE PRESIDENT OF THE UNITED STATES OF AMERICA.

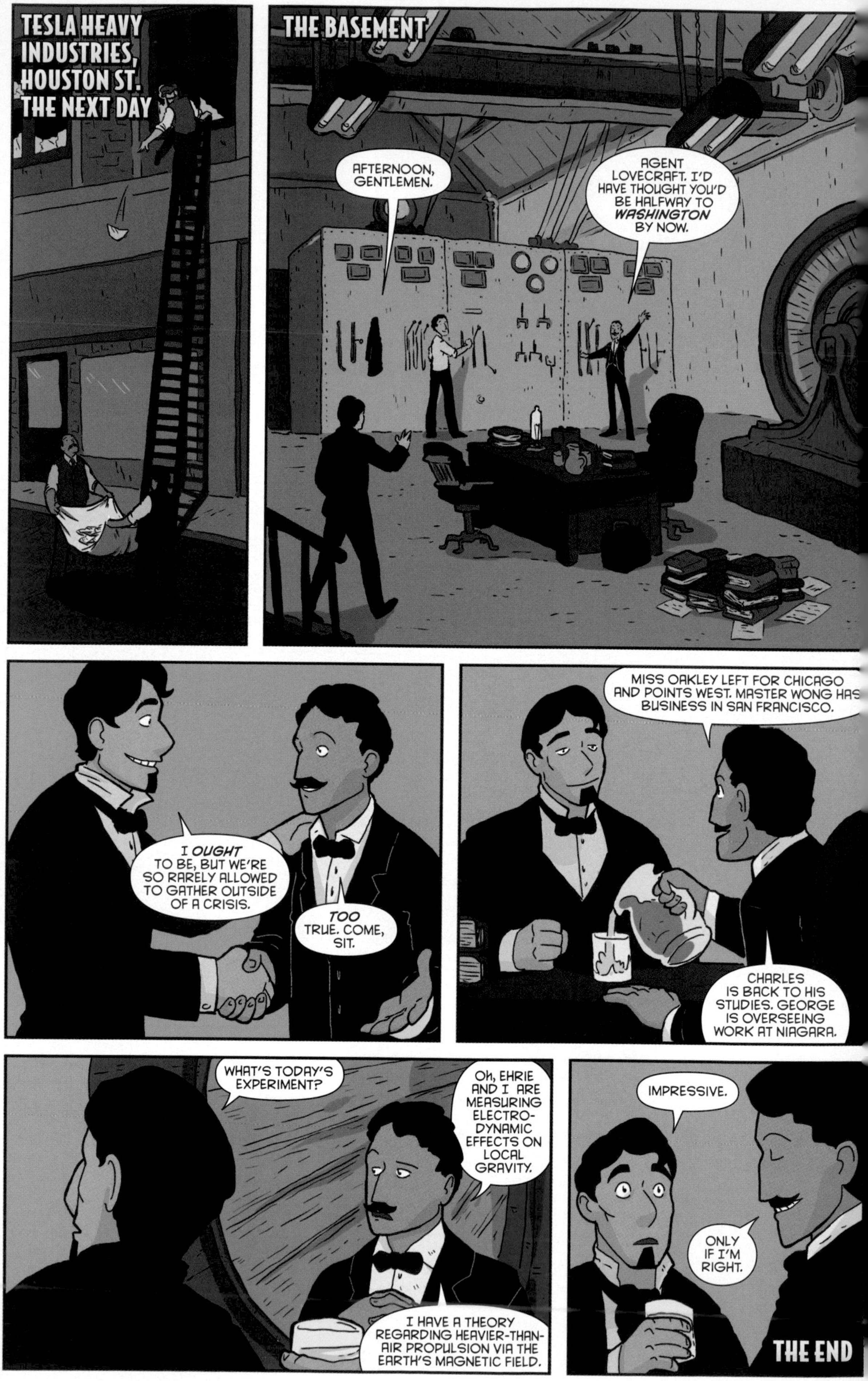
TESLA HEAVY INDUSTRIES, HOUSTON ST. THE NEXT DAY
THE BASEMENT
AFTERNOON, GENTLEMEN.
AGENT LOVECRAFT. I'D HAVE THOUGHT YOU'D BE HALFWAY TO WASHINGTON BY NOW.
I OUGHT TO BE, BUT WE'RE SO RARELY ALLOWED TO GATHER OUTSIDE OF A CRISIS.
TOO TRUE. COME, SIT.
MISS OAKLEY LEFT FOR CHICAGO AND POINTS WEST. MASTER WONG HAS BUSINESS IN SAN FRANCISCO.
CHARLES IS BACK TO HIS STUDIES. GEORGE IS OVERSEEING WORK AT NIAGARA.
WHAT'S TODAY'S EXPERIMENT?
Oh, EHRIE AND I ARE MEASURING ELECTRO-DYNAMIC EFFECTS ON LOCAL GRAVITY.
I HAVE A THEORY REGARDING HEAVIER-THAN-AIR PROPULSION VIA THE EARTH'S MAGNETIC FIELD.
IMPRESSIVE.
ONLY IF I'M RIGHT.
THE END

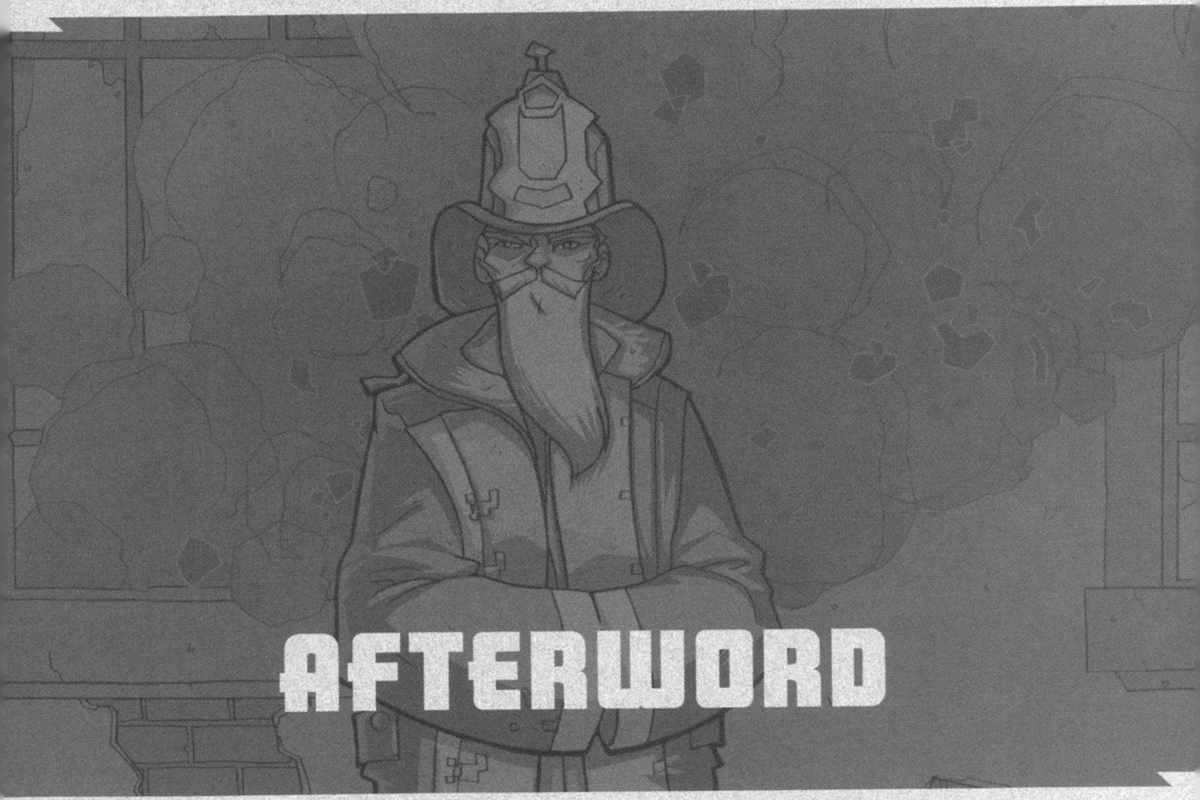

AFTERWORD

"WHAT IF NIKOLA TESLA HAD HIS OWN OCEAN'S 11?"

That was where it all started. Then it turned into Tesla's 7, and thank God it did, because it was hard enough to juggle a cast of even that size. Especially when that cast is made up of the kind of historical figures who could carry individual titles alone and still only cover half of what made each one such an amazing person.

We make extensive use of historical figures in the pages of Atomic Robo. Often this happens by accident. We'll research an event or an era to build up a plausible fictional character to fit a specific role for a story, and end up finding a real person too implausible to make up. That's how Nikola Tesla became Robo's creator, for one. Why create a character for that role when real life already provided the perfect actor?

Historical figures impart tremendous narrative power. If you don't see a hundred adventures spooling out of the phrase "Annie Oakley and her Fifty Lady Sharpshooters*," then I don't know what's wrong with you. But that doesn't mean these people are action figures for us to mash together. Well, I guess we can. But shouldn't. They were real people with real desires and goals and tragedies. They deserve our respect.

We use them to fuel our stories and we do it without their permission. The way we see it, the least we can do in return is to respect the truth of those lives when we invoke their names to elevate our fiction.

INTRODUCING THE CENTURIONS OF SCIENCE

I'm not entirely certain of the club's origins, but it almost certainly begins with Tesla and Westinghouse realizing that their talents and resources alone would not be enough to meet the late 19th century's growing tide of scientific mischief.

For purely narrative purposes, the Centurions would have to be loosely associated; an informal society that would not unnecessarily restrain the gifts, brilliance, and derring-do of its members. That way their association wouldn't overly impact the course of their lives and we'd be free to draw upon their individual exploits for future adventures.

NIKOLA TESLA
The Mastermind

Tesla is the center around which the rest of the group orbits. Born in what is now Croatia in 1856, he was a genius able to perform complex calculus in his head. Even at an early age he possessed an aptitude for experimentation and invention with a particular interest in all things electrical.

In 1884 he emigrated to the United States of America to work for Edison Machine Works in New York City. He would quit less than a year later over a pay dispute with Thomas Edison himself over $50,000 (around $1 million today). One wonders what the 20th century might have been if they'd formed a collaborative rather than combative relationship.

The next four years he worked as a ditch-digger to make ends meet while searching for funding to create and popularize his inventions. His efforts finally paid off in 1888 when his engineering work was brought to the attention of George Westinghouse's Electric & Manufacturing Company.

Tesla quickly rose through the ranks of Westinghouse's organization and the two men became good friends. Although Tesla never stopped inventing and theorizing, some of his most influential and revolutionary work was accomplished during this partnership. Together, they won the so-called "War of the Currents" against Edison, but it was a Pyrrhic victory. Edison lost control of his electrical company, but Westinghouse was forced to sever his financial obligations to Tesla in order to save his own company.

The last half of Tesla's life would mirror all too closely the hardships he faced before meeting Westinghouse. He would never again find a reliable source of capital for his experiments. Projects like his dream of providing free energy to all points on the globe were too impractical for investors more concerned with rate of return than philanthropy.

Tesla died alone and penniless at the age of 86 on January 7, 1943.

GEORGE WESTINGHOUSE
The Industrialist

Westinghouse was world famous years before his association with Nikola Tesla. Already inventing steam engines by the age of 19, he would revolutionize rail travel just three years later with his invention of the air brake – a technology still in use today.

Westinghouse developed an early interest in electrification through Edison's work with Direct Current generators and transmission. However, Westinghouse recognized the technological limits of DC electricity meant that it would be prohibitively expensive to scale the technology to an entire city, much less a nation. He immediately shifted his attention toward alternating current technologies. There was just one problem: no one could figure out how to make efficient AC generators!

Enter Nikola Tesla. Though their business relationship would only last a handful of years, Tesla and Westinghouse eventually won the War of the Currents with their alternating current innovations that made widespread electrification possible and shaped the course of the 20th century.

CHARLES FORT
The Investigator

Fort was a writer and researcher interested in the anomalous, with a wide anti-authoritarian streak present in all of his surviving works. Fort spent decades researching scientific journals, newspapers, and magazines in search of unexplainable phenomena.

Fort's work makes repeated demonstrations of the myriad failures of scientific consensus to explain unusual events; this is sometimes mischaracterized as a mockery of scientific pursuit itself. His work is, if anything, a warning against complacency with conclusions as they stand. It's a reminder for more rigorous investigation into all the gaps in our collected knowledge.

His zeal for this work kicked off an entire subculture of independent investigators of the unusual: the Forteans, an army of early 20th century Fox Mulders diligently researching occurrences that could not be explained through conventional theories.

WINFIELD SCOTT LOVECRAFT
The Secret Agent

Winfield is one of two Centurions known more for their famous sons -- in his case, the author Howard Phillips Lovecraft.

Little is known of Winfield's life. He was a traveling jewelry salesman until 1893, when he became "acutely psychotic" and was admitted to Butler Hospital, a psychiatric institution in Providence, Rhode Island. He died there in 1898. Howard was eight years old.

We take a lot of liberties with the Centurions as historical persons, and Winfield comes in for his share and then some (but then, it's nothing we haven't already done with his son in Volume 3: *Atomic Robo and the Shadow From Beyond Time*).

EHRICH WEISS
The Escapist

Ehrich "Ehrie" Weiss was the most famous stage magician and escape artist in history -- he's better known by his stage name, Harry Houdini.

Weiss became enchanted by stage magic so early in life that he conducted his first performances at the age of nine. As a young man he was already a gifted and well-rounded athlete, almost certainly due to his zealous pursuit of the methods behind stage magic which, he maintained, required a great deal of mental and physical dedication.

Weiss began performing under the name Harry Houdini in 1891, but he would work in almost total obscurity until joining the Orpheum circuit in 1899, where he quickly gained a reputation for his amazing handcuff escapes. As his fame grew, so did the complexity of his escapes.

His efforts to debunk spiritualists, while lesser known today, are nonetheless significant as he exposed an industry of deception by demonstrating the entirely mundane tricks behind fraudulent mediums' "miracles".

Houdini would be an international star until his untimely death in 1926. He'd been in pain for days, and was urged by his doctor to undergo an appendectomy right away. Houdini refused. He died of peritonitis just days later.

ANNIE OAKLEY
The Sharpshooter

America's first female superstar and the most well-known lady sharpshooter in history, by the age of 15 Annie Oakley was already legendary for her marksmanship. Her fate was sealed when a traveling showman named Francis Butler lost a shooting match against her in Cincinnati. They eventually married. Butler gave up his career in order to support his more talented wife. He helped Oakley get a place in Buffalo Bill's world-famous Wild West Show, and before long she was giving VIP performances for the royal families of Europe.

Later in life Oakley suffered spinal injuries during a train wreck and was paralyzed for a time afterward. Although she eventually recovered, she focused her career to stage acts which would incur less strain on her person. Even so, she continued to set marksmanship records well into her sixties.

WONG KEI-YING
The Physician

Wong is the other Centurion mostly remembered due to his son, the folk hero, revolutionary, and early wuxia film industry enthusiast Wong Fei-hung. Even without his son's fame, Wong was among the most well known martial artists of the late Qing period as well as an accomplished doctor.

The historic Wong died in 1886, but we decided it'd be more interesting for him to live a little longer. One day we'll tell the story of what brought the elder Wong to the West while his son stayed behind to fight injustices at home.

THE TRIUMVERATE

The original concept for this volume was Real 19th Century Historical Figures vs. the Last of the 19th Century's Science Fiction Characters. It was to be a turning point in the history of Robo's world: the moment scientific adventure leapt away from lone mad scientists and their freaks and began, for good or ill, lurching toward the corporatization and industrialization of the 20th century.

We needed a solid line up of easily recognized 19th century sci-fi characters for the theme to connect to the average reader. Enter our first problem: all the "good" ones were already taken. Worse, they were largely taken by Alan Moore and Kevin O'Neill for *League of Extraordinary Gentlemen*, the series which made those forgotten characters instantly recognizable to today's readers. The last thing we wanted was to produce a story where it looked like we were planting our flag on lands already explored by a critically-acclaimed creative team.

So we widened our net using Jess Nevins' incredible resource, *The Encyclopedia of Fantastic Victoriana*. You don't need the most recognizable characters if you can find also-rans and knock-offs that share enough of what made the better-known character so iconic. If Captain Nemo is taken, we'll just use the very similarly-constructed Captain Kiang Ho. Problem solved, right? Well, maybe. It still ran the risk of sending the wrong message.

And that's when the solution hit us. A popular subgenre of adventure fiction in the late 19th century starred boy genius characters inspired by the industrial giants of the age, most prominently Thomas Edison, for whom the genre is named: The Edisonade. These characters conjured up incredibly advanced technologies, usually electricity-themed, and gallivanted around the globe, perpetrating violence against, well, foreigners basically. What a bunch of jerks!

So, we took the three most popular ones and let them grow up to amass their own industrial empires and then use their vast riches and advanced technologies to overthrow the U.S. government!

FRANKLIN READE JR.

Frank Reade, Jr., was created by Luis Senarens and debuted in "Frank Reade Jr. and His Steam Wonder" in 1879. Senarens was one of the most prolific of all dime novel writers as well as the creator of Jack Wright.

The Frank Reade stories were the most famous and successful of the Edisonade genre of dime novels lasting for 184 stories over twenty-three years.

Our Frank Reade arms the forces of the Triumvirate with the most advanced portable weapons of the 19th century thanks to Reade Industries, his conglomerate of mining operations, freight companies, processing plants, and factories.

JACK WRIGHT

Jack Wright was also created by Senarens and debuted in 1891's "Jack Wright, the Boy Inventor; or, Hunting for a Sunken Treasure". Wright went on to appear in 120 more stories.

Our Jack Wright is the most senior of our dastardly industrialists. Through his Wright Ironworks, he provides the Triumvirate's forces with the advanced war machines they need to successfully siege Washington D.C.

ELECTRIC BOB a.k.a. ROBERT TRYDAN

Electric Bob was created by "Robert T. Toombs" and appeared in five stories, beginning with "Electric Bob and His White Alligator; or, Hunting for Confederate Treasure in the Mississippi River" in 1893. Nothing is known about "Robert T. Toombs," and the name may be a pseudonym.

Like later Edisonade heroes, Electric Bob creates a variety of electric weaponry and equipment, but his specialty is vehicles in the form of animals.

We couldn't let one of our characters run around with the name "Electric Bob," so we took to Google Translate to find a word from anywhere in Europe for "electric" to use as a last name. Should be simple, right?

Let me tell you something. "Electric" does not change a whole lot from one Romance language to another. "Eléctrico" is about par for the course. Eventually we found "trydan" -- God bless the Welsh!

Since we already had vehicle and arms manufacturers, we needed someone to supply the morally questionable men to employ those devices for evil. Enter the Trydan Detective Agency, a vast criminal empire operating under the guise of a legitimate investigative body. Some would say the difference between this and the historical Pinkerton Detective Agency is a matter of spelling.

Also available from Red 5 Comics...

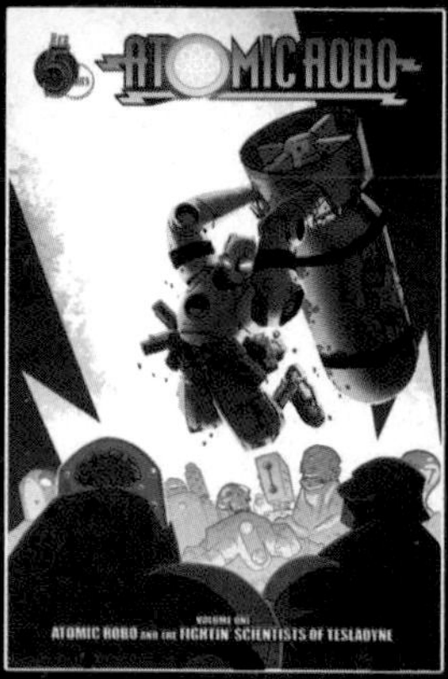
ATOMIC ROBO
VOLUME ONE
ATOMIC ROBO AND THE FIGHTIN' SCIENTISTS OF TESLADYNE

Atomic Robo and the Fightin' Scientists of Tesladyne
ISBN: 978-0-9809302-0-7

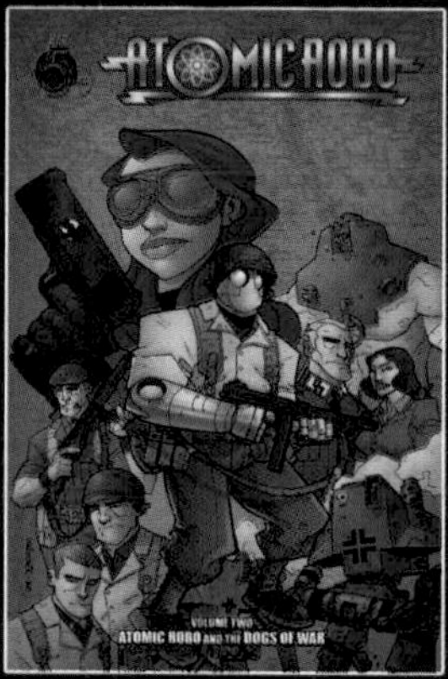
ATOMIC ROBO
VOLUME TWO
ATOMIC ROBO AND THE DOGS OF WAR

Atomic Robo and the Dogs of War
ISBN: 978-0-9809302-2-1

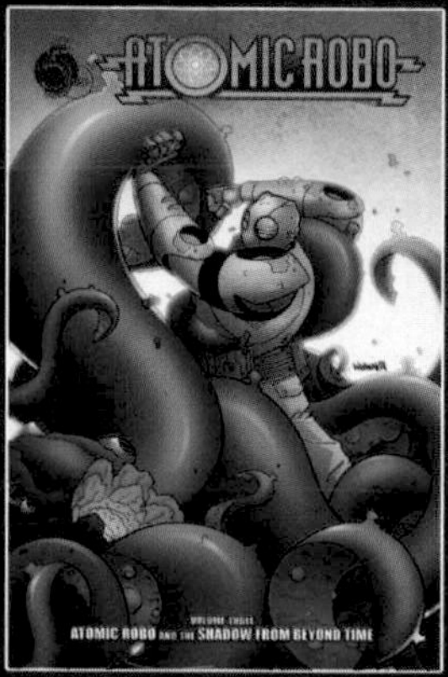
ATOMIC ROBO
VOLUME THREE
ATOMIC ROBO AND THE SHADOW FROM BEYOND TIME

Atomic Robo and the Shadow from Beyond Time
ISBN: 978-0-9809302-5-2

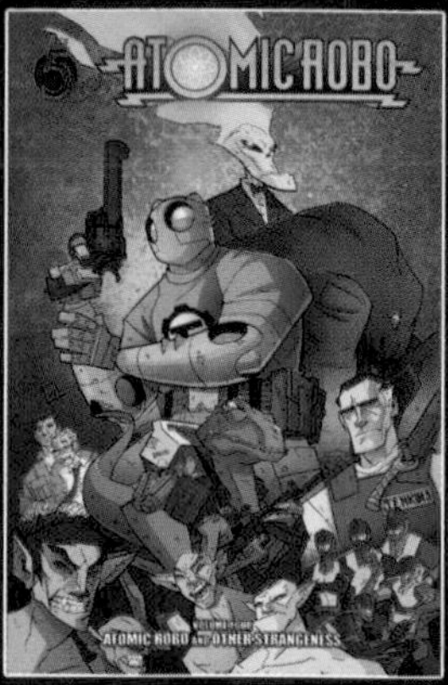
ATOMIC ROBO
ATOMIC ROBO AND OTHER STRANGENESS

Atomic Robo and Other Strangeness
ISBN: 978-0-9809302-8-3

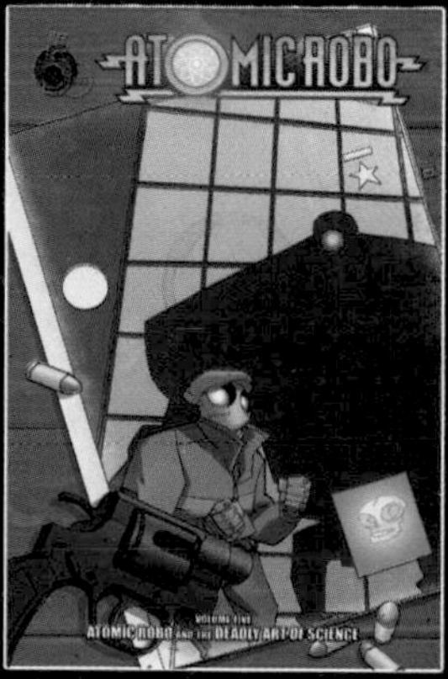
ATOMIC ROBO
VOLUME FIVE
ATOMIC ROBO AND THE DEADLY ART OF SCIENCE

Atomic Robo and the Deadly Art of Science
ISBN: 978 0 9809302-4 5

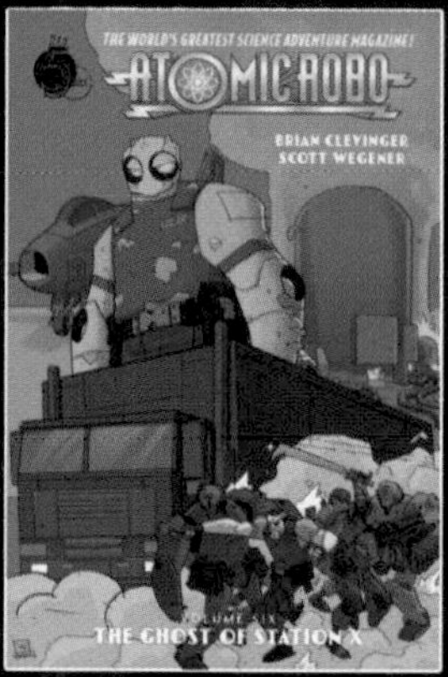
THE WORLD'S GREATEST SCIENCE ADVENTURE MAGAZINE!
ATOMIC ROBO
BRIAN CLEVINGER
SCOTT WEGENER
THE GHOST OF STATION X

Atomic Robo and the Ghost of Station X
ISBN: 978 0 9868985 0 1

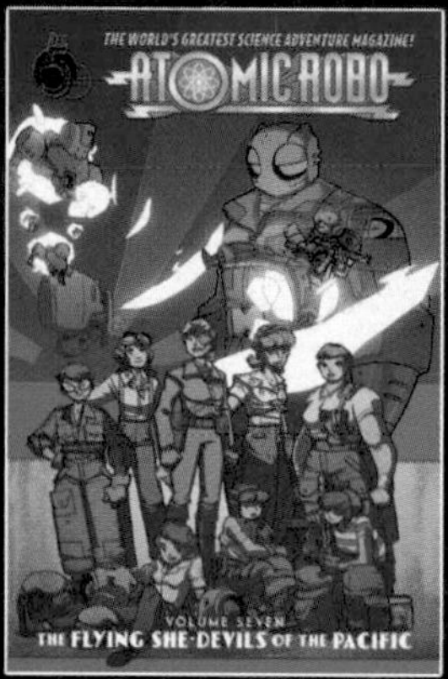
THE WORLD'S GREATEST SCIENCE ADVENTURE MAGAZINE!
ATOMIC ROBO
VOLUME SEVEN
THE FLYING SHE-DEVILS OF THE PACIFIC

Atomic Robo and the Flying She-Devils of the Pacific
ISBN: 978-0-9868985-2-5

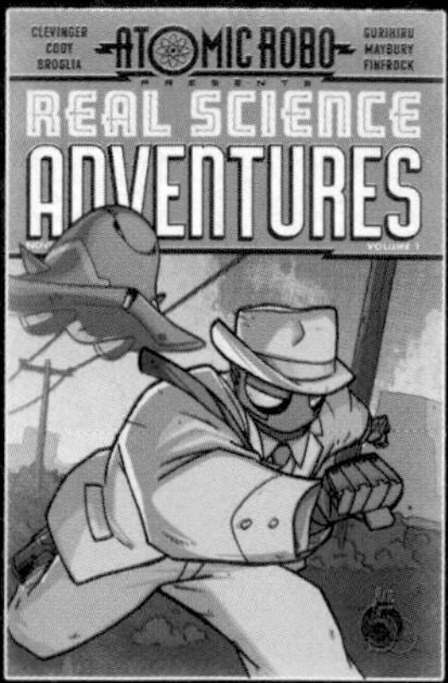
ATOMIC ROBO
PRESENTS
REAL SCIENCE ADVENTURES

Atomic Robo presents Real Science Adventures
ISBN: 978 0-9868985 1 8

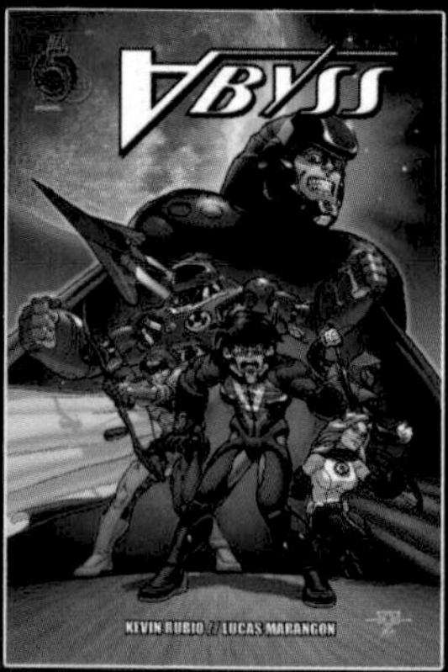
ABYSS
KEVIN RUBIO // LUCAS MARANGON

Abyss: Volume One
Surprise! Your dad's a super villain.
ISBN: 978-0-9809302-1-4

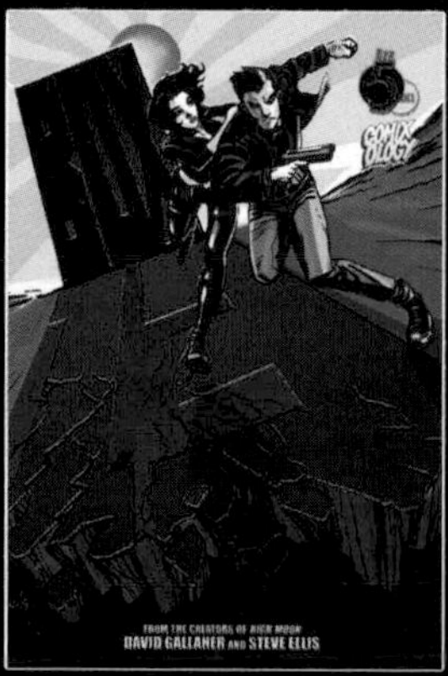
DAVID GALLAHER AND STEVE ELLIS

Box 13
Deadly noir delivered.
ISBN: 978-0-9809302-6-9

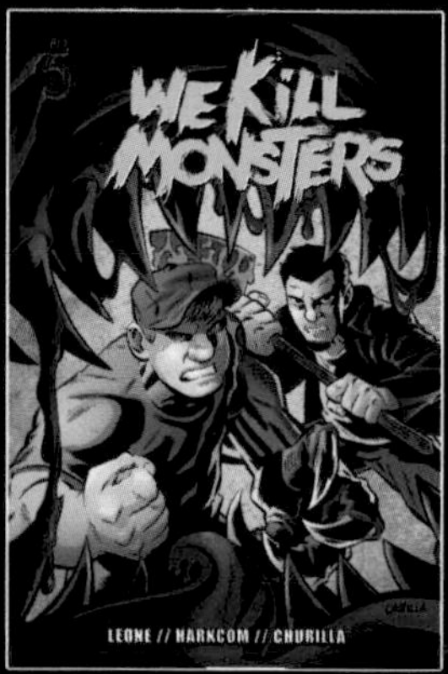
WE KILL MONSTERS
LEONE // HARKCOM // CHURILLA

We Kill Monsters
Rednecks out for blue blood.
ISBN: 978-0-9809302-7-6

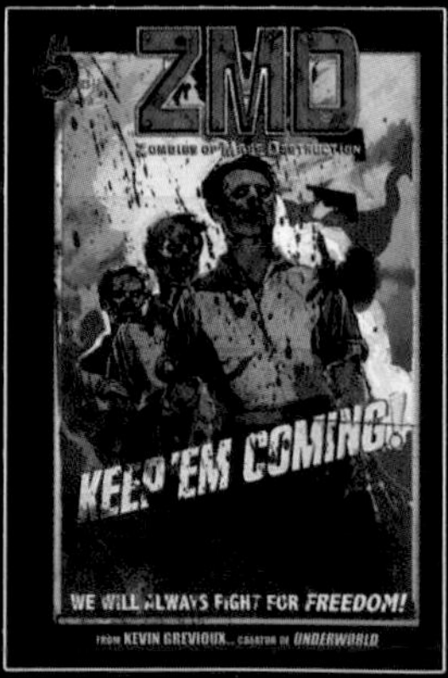
ZMD
KEEP 'EM COMING!
WE WILL ALWAYS FIGHT FOR FREEDOM!

Zombies of Mass Destruction
Let the dead handle the Middle East.
ISBN: 978-0-9809302-9-0